Translation and Conflict

'A compelling account and an intellectually honest enquiry into the issues involved in handling competing narratives, of vital interest not only to translators and translation theorists but also to users of translation products.'

Ian Mason, *Heriot-Watt University, Scotland*

'Scientific and critical, never gratuitously polemic…this groundbreaking volume rigorously examines the relation between translation, power and conflict. In this courageous volume, Mona Baker shows the importance in today's global world of translation and interpreting for life over the planet, and succeeds in calling our attention to the responsibilities that the translator and interpreter must never evade.'

Susan Petrilli, *University of Bari, Italy*

Translation and Conflict: A Narrative Account demonstrates that translation is part of the institution of war and that translators and interpreters participate in circulating as well as resisting the narratives that create the intellectual and moral environment for violent conflict. Drawing on narrative theory and using numerous examples from historical as well as contemporary conflicts, the author provides an original and coherent model of analysis that pays equal attention to micro- and macro-aspects of the circulation of narratives in translation, to translation and interpreting, and to questions of dominance and resistance. The study is particularly significant at this juncture of history, with the increased interest in the positioning of translators in politically sensitive contexts, the growing concern with translators' and interpreters' divided loyalties in settings such as Guantanamo Bay, Iraq, Afghanistan, Kosovo, and a host of other arenas of conflict, and the emergence of several activist communities of translators and interpreters with highly politicized agendas of their own, including Babels, Translators for Peace, ECOS and Translators and Interpreters Peace Network.

Including further reading suggestions at the end of each chapter, *Translation and Conflict: A Narrative Account* will be of interest to students on courses in translation, intercultural studies and sociology as well as the reader interested in the study of social and political movements.

Mona Baker is Professor of Translation Studies and Director of the Centre for Translation and Intercultural Studies, University of Manchester. She is author of *In Other Words: A Coursebook on Translation*, editor of *The Routledge Encyclopedia of Translation Studies*, Founding Editor of *The Translator*, and Vice President of the International Association for Translation and Intercultural Studies.

BRIGITTE REGNIER
703-548-8994
613 TENNESSEE AVE
ALEXANDRIA, VA 22305

Make Checks Payable To:
Fidelity Brokerage Services LLC

Mail To:

Fidelity Investments®
P.O. BOX 770001
CINCINNATI, OH 45277-0003

DATE

FROM	DOLLARS	CENTS
1 MD 6	554.	16
2 G. Curtis	378.	ᴐᴐ
3		
4		
TOTAL	932	16

Minimum Investment $50.00. If multiple
checks, each must be at least $50.00

002 0537226017   20   000

Translation and Conflict

A Narrative Account

Mona Baker

Routledge
Taylor & Francis Group

LONDON AND NEW YORK

First published 2006
by Routledge
2 Park Square, Milton Park Abingdon, Oxon, OX14 4RN

Simultaneously published in the USA and Canada
by Routledge
270 Madison Ave, New York, NY 10016

Routledge is an imprint of the Taylor & Francis Group

Typeset in by Bembo by Bookcraft Ltd, Stroud, Gloucestershire

Printed and bound in Great Britain by
The Cromwell Press, Trowbridge, Wiltshire

British Library Cataloguing in Publication Data
A catalogue record for this book is available
from the British Library

Library of Congress Cataloging in Publication Data
Baker, Mona.
   Translation and conflict : a narrative account / Mona Baker.
      p. cm.
   Includes bibliographical references and index.
   1. Translating and interpreting. 2. Narration (Rhetoric) 3. Discourse analysis,
   Narrative. I. Title.
   p306.2.B356 2005
   418'.02--dc22

                                                              2005024063

ISBN10: 0-415-38396-X (pbk)
ISBN10: 0-415-38395-1 (hbk)
ISBN10: 0-203-09991-5 (ebk)

ISBN13: 978-0-415-38396-7 (pbk)
ISBN13: 978-0-415-38395-0 (hbk)
ISBN13: 978-0-203-09991-9 (ebk)

For Sanaa and Zeinab

A ship in the harbour is safe, but that's not what ships are made for.

... one would want to avoid ... a utopian impulse to joyfully display all humanity in tolerant and harmonious contact across all lines of difference, or a dystopian impulse to bemoan a world homogenised by western media or run only by misunderstanding and bad intentions.

(Pratt 1987: 61)

Contents

Figures

Acknowledgements

The research conducted for this book was made possible by a grant from the Arts and Humanities Research Council (AHRC; formerly Arts and Humanities Research Board) in Britain. I am grateful to the AHRC and the School of Languages, Linguistics and Cultures, University of Manchester, for the unusual luxury of being able to work intensively on a research project of my choice for an entire year.

Some of the detailed research undertaken for this book was done during a particularly productive period I spent as Visiting Professor with City University of Hong Kong, in January/February 2005. The Department of Chinese, Translation and Linguistics offered a superb environment for research: excellent facilities, friendly atmosphere, and intelligent debates. I am grateful to Maggie Cheung and Mr Lam for friendly and efficient administrative assistance, and especially to Zhu Chunshen and other colleagues in the department for their collegial support and friendship. The warm hospitality and companionship of Martha Cheung and Jane Lai from the Baptist University ensured that my stay in Hong Kong was even more enjoyable and productive.

Several colleagues have been kind enough to read through sections of the manuscript and make suggestions for improving it. Dorothy Kenny gave valuable advice on rival place names in Northern Ireland, Ibrahim Muhawi on folklore studies, Luis Peréz-González on Spanish, Dimitris Asimakoulas on Greek examples, and Wenjing Zhao on Chinese references. I am particularly grateful to Sameh Fekry Hanna and Francesca Billiani, who read large sections of the manuscript and commented on them in detail. I have also enjoyed working with Louisa Semlyen and Elizabeth Johnston, my editors at Routledge, whose support made life much easier throughout the past year.

The author and the publisher are grateful to the copyright holders of the following material for permission to reprint images and text: Associated Press for the photographs by Jean-Marc Bouju of an Iraqi man comforting his four-year-old son at a regroupment centre for prisoners of war of the 101st Airborne Division near An Najaf, 31 March 2003 (Figure 2) and by John Moore of a detainee in an outdoor solitary confinement cell at the Abu Ghraib prison, 22 June 2004 (Figure 3). Paul Fitzgerald and the *New Internationalist* magazine (www.newint.org) for the 'Big

Bad World' cartoon (Figure 5). The Anti-Apartheid Wall Campaign (http://stopthewall.org) for the photo of Palestinian activists posing as indigenous Americans, Ramallah, 8 April 2005 (Figure 6), and photos of graffiti and slogans on Israel's Wall (Figures 12 and 13). Mohammad Bakri for screen shots from *Jenin Jenin* (Figures 7 and 14). Marc Abrahams and the *Annals of Improbable Research* (www.improbable.com) for front covers of the January/February 2002 and September/October 2004 issues of *AIR* (Figures 8 and 9). Thomas Scott for permission to reproduce graphics and text from the (alternative) Preparing for Emergencies website (Figure 10). Hart Seely for permission to reproduce the cover of *Pieces of Intelligence: The Existential Poetry of Donald H. Rumsfeld* (Figure 11) and the 'poems' *The Unknown, Clarity* and *A Confession* (Chapter 5). Andrew Rubin, Georgetown University, for permission to reproduce his letter to the Executive Council of the Modern Languages Association (Chapter 7).

Mona Baker
October 2005

1   Introduction

Wherever we happen to be in the world and whatever type of activity or profession we may be involved in, we now live and function in a climate of conflict that cuts across national boundaries and constantly forces itself on our consciousness. In this conflict-ridden and globalized world, translation is central to the ability of all parties to legitimize their version of events, especially in view of the fact that political and other types of conflict today are played out in the international arena and can no longer be resolved by appealing to local constituencies alone. This book draws on narrative theory to examine the ways in which translation and interpreting function in this context and to explore how the discursive negotiation of conflictual and competing narratives is realized in and through acts of translation and interpreting.

1.1 Translation, power, conflict

Definitions of conflict inevitably draw on notions of power, and vice versa. Traditional scholarship assumed that power is something that some people have over others. Some theorists of power, such as Bachrach and Baratz (1962, 1970), further insisted that power is only present in situations of observable conflict, where one party forces another to act against its will or what it perceives to be its own interest. More robust definitions of power, however, acknowledge that the supreme exercise of power involves shaping and influencing another party's desires and wants in such a way as to avert observable conflict, that 'the most effective and insidious use of power is to prevent ... conflict from arising in the first place' (Lukes 1974: 23).[1] Good (1989), Clegg (1993), Ehrenhaus (1993) and Philips (2001) provide excellent overviews of the relevant issues. The standard reference on power is Lukes (1974).

In its broadest meaning, conflict refers to a situation in which two or more parties seek to undermine each other because they have incompatible goals, competing interests, or fundamentally different values. In this sense, conflict is a natural part of everyday life rather than an exceptional circumstance. However, most people understand conflict in its political sense, as a state of hostility between groups of people, usually belonging to different races, religions or nation states. This book adopts the broader definition of conflict but draws extensively – though not exclusively – on examples of political, armed conflict in elaborating its theoretical premises. It also assumes that translation and interpreting are part of the *institution of war* and hence play a major role in the management of conflict – by all parties, from warmongers to peace activists.

Translation and interpreting participate in shaping the way in which conflict unfolds in a number of ways. First, as Chilton (1997: 175) reminds us, a declaration of war is, after all, 'a linguistic act'. Clearly, this verbal declaration has to be communicated to other parties in their own languages; there is no point in the USA declaring war on Iraq without ensuring that the Iraqis and the rest of the world 'hear' that declaration. Second, once war is declared, the relevant military operations can only begin and continue through verbal activity (1997: 175). Much of modern warfare is based on coordinating several armies from different countries and linguistic communities; recent examples include the UN in Bosnia and the US command in Iraq. The very process of mobilizing military power then is heavily dependent on continuous acts of translation and interpreting, including – crucially – acts of translation and interpreting that allow military personnel to communicate with civilians living in the region. Propaganda leaflets dropped by US forces over Iraq in March 2003 communicated a variety of messages to Iraqi civilians and soldiers, such as 'The Coalition does not wish to destroy your landmarks' and 'Coalition Air Power can strike at will. Any time. Any place' (Moss 2003: 12–13). The legend underneath photographs of these leaflets in *The Guardian* read: '*English translations* of some of the propaganda leaflets dropped in Iraq by US planes and targeted at soldiers and civilians' (1997: 175; emphasis added). More likely, the leaflets were first prepared in English and then translated and dropped in Iraq in Arabic, but the media often confuse these issues.

Third, it is not only the military but also ordinary people who have to be mobilized to initiate and support a war. Smith (1997: 200) reminds us that in the wake of the break-ups of the USSR and Yugoslavia successful political leaders were those who employed effective strategies for mobilizing ordinary people. Declaring and sustaining a war have to be discursively justified and legitimated; politicians have to pave the way for war to be accepted, for human sacrifice to be justified. Contemporary wars have to be sold to an international and not just domestic audiences, and translation is a major variable influencing the circulation and legitimation of the narratives that sustain these activities. And finally, once war is underway, attempts to broker and manage an end to the conflict typically take the form of meetings, conferences and public seminars, in addition to secret negotiations. All these require the mediation of translators and interpreters. Smith (1997: 210) recognizes that 'if the meeting is conducted through language interpreters, the problems of translation, especially of emotionally charged terms, adds a further layer to the uncertainty generated by the incompatible discursive interpretations of the two conflict parties and the third party'.

More important perhaps than all the above, translation and interpreting are essential for circulating *and* resisting the narratives that create the intellectual and moral environment for violent conflict in the first place, even though the narratives in question may not directly depict conflict or war. Indeed, some of these narratives, as we will see, may be packaged as disinterested, abstract scientific theories, others as literary texts, cartoons, or innocent entertainment.

1.2 Why narrative?

Narratives 'constitute crucial means of generating, sustaining, mediating, and representing conflict at all levels of social organization' (Briggs 1996: 3). This book draws on the notion of narrative as elaborated in social and communication theory, rather than in narratology or linguistics, to explore the way in which translation and interpreting participate in these processes. Narratives, in the sense used here, are the everyday stories we live by, and indeed I will be using 'narrative' and 'story' interchangeably throughout the book. One of the attractions of narrative is that it is a highly transparent and intuitively satisfying concept that can easily be understood by anyone.

The notion of narrative used in this book overlaps to some extent with Foucault's 'discourse' and Barthes' 'myths', especially in its emphasis on the normalizing effect of publicly disseminated representations (see Chapter 2, section 2.1.2). But the concept of narrative is much more concrete and accessible, compared with the abstract notion of discourse as a vehicle for social and political processes and myth as an element in a second-order semiological system. Also, unlike myth, and much more so than discourse, the notion of narrative is not restricted to public representations but applies equally to individual stories (see Chapter 3, section 3.1, on ontological narratives). Thus, as Whitebrook explains, one of the strengths of narrative theory is that it 'make[s] the political agent concrete':

> A turn to narratives allows for the de-personalized persons of theory, the bearers of a representative or typified identity, to be understood as separate persons – characters – with singular sets of characteristics, including but not confined to their political context and/or group identity.
>
> (2001: 15)

Narratives, as understood here, are dynamic entities; they change in subtle or radical ways as people experience and become exposed to new stories on a daily basis. This assumption has a number of consequences. First, narrative theory recognizes that people's behaviour is ultimately guided by the stories they come to believe about the events in which they are embedded, rather than by their gender, race, colour of skin, or any other attribute.[2] Second, because narratives are dynamic, they cannot be streamlined into a set of stable stories that people simply choose from. Narrative theory recognizes that at any moment in time we can be located within a variety of divergent, criss-crossing, often vacillating narratives, thus acknowledging the complexity and fluidity of our positioning in relation to other participants in interaction. Third, because narratives are continually open to change with our exposure to new experience and new stories, they have 'significant subversive or transformative potential' (Ewick and Silbey 1995: 199; see Chapter 2 on the political import of narrativity). Undermining regimes such as those of Nazi Germany or South Africa under apartheid, then, becomes – above all – a question of challenging the stories that sustain them (Hinchman and Hinchman 1997a: xxvii). This challenge, in turn, is articulated in the form of alternative stories.

Another strength of narrative theory is that unlike much of the existing scholarship in translation studies, it allows us to examine the way in which translation features in the elaboration of narratives that cut across time and texts. 'The value of the concept *narrative*', Ehrenhaus explains, is

> its convenience as a shorthand notation for the multiplicity of interesting fragments that the critic circumscribes in constituting a working text – a story grounded in the social formations through which individuals, as members of an interpretive community, understand the world they inhabit and reproduce that world through their discursive participation and actions.
>
> (1993: 80)

While narratology and linguistics tend to focus on one text at a time, the first mostly on literary text (and more recently cinema) and the second mostly on oral narratives, narrative theory as outlined here treats narratives – across all genres and modes – as diffuse, amorphous configurations rather than necessarily discrete, fully articulated local 'stories'. It is simultaneously able to deal with the individual text and the broader set of narratives in which it is embedded, and it encourages us to look beyond the immediate, local narrative as elaborated in a given text or utterance to assess its contribution to elaborating wider narratives in society. Narrative theory further allows us to piece together and analyse a narrative that is not fully traceable to any specific stretch of text but has to be constructed from a range of sources, including non-verbal material. In so doing, it acknowledges the constructedness of narratives and encourages us to reflect critically on our own embeddedness in them.[3]

1.3 Overview of chapters

Chapter 2, 'Introducting narrative', offers a broad overview of narrativity as understood and applied in this book. It starts with a discussion of the status and effects of narrativity, including its relationship to genres, science, categories, fact and fiction, as well as the normalizing function of narratives. It then offers a definition of narrative that provides the basis for the model of analysis elaborated in the rest of the book. The chapter concludes with a discussion of the political import of narratives and the interplay of resistance and dominance evident in the way narratives are elaborated and received, stressing that narrative both reproduces existing power structures *and* provides a means of contesting them.

Drawing on Somers (1992, 1997) and Somers and Gibson (1994), Chapter 3 discusses four types of narrative and the way in which translators and interpreters mediate their circulation in society. Ontological narratives are personal stories that we tell ourselves about our place in the world and our own personal history; they are interpersonal and social in nature but remain focused on the self and its immediate world. Public narratives are stories elaborated by and circulating among social and institutional formations larger than the individual, such as the family, religious or educational institution, the media, and the nation. Individuals in any society either buy into dominant public narratives or dissent from them. Translators and interpreters play a crucial role in both disseminating and contesting public narratives within and across national boundaries. Conceptual, or disciplinary, narratives are the stories and explanations that scholars in any field elaborate for themselves and others about their object of inquiry. And finally, meta-narratives are public narratives 'in which we are embedded as contemporary actors in history ... Progress, Decadence, Industrialization, Enlightenment, etc.' (Somers and Gibson 1994: 61), including 'the epic dramas of our time: Capitalism vs. Communism, the Individual vs. Society, Barbarism/Nature vs. Civility' (Somers 1992: 605).

Chapters 4 and 5 explain how narratives function in terms of how they construct the world for us. Chapter 4 focuses on the four core features of narrativity, namely temporality, relationality, causal emplotment and selective appropriation. Chapter 5 draws on Bruner (1991) to supplement these core features with another four: particularity, genericness, normativeness (including canonicity and breach), and narrative accrual. The eight features overlap and are highly interdependent. Temporal and spatial sequences participate in elaborating patterns of causal emplotment, and causal emplotment in turn is partly realized through selective appropriation, and so on. But discussing these features under separate headings allows me to clarify some of the complex ways in which narrativity mediates our experience of the world.

In Chapter 6, the notion of frame as elaborated in the work of Goffman and the literature on social movements is used to examine some of the many ways in which translators and interpreters – in collaboration with publishers, editors and other agents involved in the interaction – accentuate, undermine or modify aspects of the narrative(s) encoded in the source text or utterance, and in so doing participate in shaping social reality. Processes of (re)framing can draw on practically any linguistic or non-linguistic resource, from paralinguistic devices such as intonation and typography to visual resources such as colour and image, to numerous linguistic devices such as tense shifts, deixis, code switching, use of euphemisms, and many more. The chapter focuses on four key strategies for mediating the narrative(s) elaborated in a source text or utterance: temporal and spatial framing, framing through selective appropriation, framing by labelling (including rival place names and titles), and repositioning of participants.

Given that the version of narrative theory elaborated in this book stresses that narrative constitutes reality rather than merely representing it, and hence that none of us is in a position to stand outside any narrative in order to observe it 'objectively', we might conclude that there can be no criteria for assessing narratives and no sensible means for us to establish whether we should subscribe to or challenge any specific narrative. In Chapter 7, I argue that our embeddedness in narrative does not preclude our ability to reason about individual narratives. Walter Fisher's influential narrative paradigm (1984, 1985, 1987, 1997) allows us to assess a narrative elaborated in a single text as well as diffuse narratives that have to be pieced together from a variety of sources and media. It can also be used to assess any narrative: ontological, public or conceptual, whether elaborated by an individual or an institution. I draw on Fisher's work to assess two narratives that are of immediate interest to translators and interpreters. The first narrative contests the Modern Languages Association's practice of allowing the CIA to advertise for and recruit prospective language instructors at its annual convention. The second narrative is elaborated by a group of volunteer translators, Translators Without Borders, across different texts and media. The assessment touches on the relationship between humanitarian and commercial concerns and the involvement of translation companies in charity work. Needless to say, the assessment in both cases is not and cannot be objective; it is inevitably guided by the assessor's own values and narrative location. The value of Fisher's paradigm lies in enabling us to retrace our steps and articulate our reasons for supporting or opposing any given narrative, without dictating what we should or should not believe.

The various examples used to illustrate the theoretical framework elaborated in this book suggest that translation is not a by-product, nor simply a consequence, of social and political developments, nor is it a by-product of the physical movement of texts and people. It is part and parcel of the very process that makes these developments and movements possible in the first place. Moreover, narrative theory recognizes that undermining existing patterns of domination cannot be achieved by concrete forms of activism alone – demonstrations, sit-ins, civil disobedience – but must involve a direct challenge to the stories that sustain these patterns. As language mediators, translators and interpreters are uniquely placed to initiate this type of discursive intervention at a global level, as many of the examples discussed in the following chapters attest.

Finally, much of what I have to say in this book will be interpreted as a strong condemnation of US, UK and Israeli policies towards the so-called third world in general and the Arab World in particular. I make no apologies for this stance. However, the fact that I have chosen to focus on the narratives of the political elites in particular regions must not be taken to imply that I see these elites and their narratives as representative of the relevant societies as a whole. Indeed, much of the critique of US, UK and Israeli policies I draw on here comes from American, British and Israeli sources. I am also aware that Arab and Islamic societies generate their own highly questionable narratives, often fuelling the very conflicts that continue to tear these regions apart. I have chosen to prioritize the narratives of the Anglo-American and Israeli political elites because, in my own narrative of current conflicts, they deserve special attention given the enormous war and media machines they have at their disposal.

Core References

Chilton, Paul (1997) 'The Role of Language in Human Conflict: Prolegomena to the Investigation of Language as a Factor in Conflict Causation and Resolution', *Current Issues in Language & Society* 4(3): 174–89.

Clegg, Stewart R. (1993) 'Narrative, Power, and Social Theory', in Dennis K. Mumby (ed.) *Narrative and Social Control: Critical Perspectives*, Newbury Park CA: Sage, 15–45.

Good, Leslie (1989) 'Power, Hegemony, and Communication Theory', in Ian Angus and Sut Jhally (eds) *Cultural Politics in Contemporary America*, New York and London: Routledge, 51–64.

Lukes, Steven (1974) *Power: A Radical View*, Basingstoke and London: Macmillan Education.

Philips, Susan U. (2001) 'Power', in Alessandro Duranti (ed.) *Key Terms in Language and Culture*, Oxford: Blackwell, 190–6.

Smith, Dan (1997) 'Language and Discourse in Conflict and Conflict Resolution', *Current Issues in Language & Society* 4(3): 190–214.

Further reading

Damrosch, David (2005) 'Death in Translation', in Sandra Bermann and Michael Wood (eds) *Nation, Language, and the Ethics of Translation*, Princeton NJ and Oxford: Princeton University Press, 380–98.

Draper, Jack (2002) 'Breaking the Imperial Mold: Fragmented Translations'. Paper presented at the Colloquium *Problems of Translation: Violence as Language Within Global Capital*, 26 January 2002. Available online at www.duke.edu/~jad2/draper.htm (accessed 28 June 2005).

Jones, Francis R. (2004) 'Ethics, Aesthetics and Décision: Literary Translating in the Wars of the Yugoslav Succession', *Meta* 49(4): 711–28.

Krog, Antje (1998) *Country of My Skull*, London: Vintage.

Nelson, Daniel (2002) 'Language, Identity and War', *Journal of Language and Politics* 1(1): 3–22.

Palmer, Jerry and Victoria Fontan (2006, in press) '"Our Ears and Our Eyes": Journalists and Fixers in Iraq', *Journalism*.

Saar, Erik and Viveka Novak (2005) *Inside the Wire: A Military Intelligence Soldier's Eyewitness Account of Life at Guantanamo*, New York: Penguin Press.

Schäffner, Christina (2004) 'Political Discourse Analysis from the Point of View of Translation Studies', *Journal of Language and Politics* 3(1): 117–50.

2 Introducing narrative theory

The notion of narrative has attracted much attention in a wide range of disciplines, and has accordingly been defined in a variety of ways. This chapter will draw primarily on social and communication theory to elaborate a definition of narrative that is particularly suited to investigating the way in which translators and interpreters function in situations of conflict. I start with an overview of the status and effects of narrativity, including its relationship to genres, science, categories, fact and fiction, and conclude with a discussion of the political import of narratives and the way in which narrative both reproduces existing power structures and provides a means of contesting them.

2.1 The status and effects of narrativity

Many scholars, especially in literary studies and linguistics, tend to treat narrative as an optional mode of communication, often contrasting it with argumentation or exposition. Approaches that treat narrative as an optional mode tend to focus on the internal structure of orally delivered or literary narratives – in terms of phases, episodes and plots, for instance – and to stress the advantages of using narrative, rather than other modes of communication, to secure the audience's commitment and involvement. The best and most influential example of this tradition is Labov. A very brief summary of his approach might help clarify important differences between literary and linguistic approaches to narrative and the broadly sociological approach adopted in this book.

Labov defines narrative as '*one method* of recapitulating past experience by matching a verbal sequence of clauses to the sequence of events which (it is inferred) actually occurred' (1972: 359–60; emphasis added), and what he calls a '*minimal narrative*' as 'a sequence of two clauses which are *temporally ordered*' (1972: 360; emphasis in original). Like most scholars in linguistics and pragmatics, having defined narrative as only one way of recapitulating experience, Labov goes on to focus on oral narratives and on their structural make-up. He elaborates a structural framework that divides these orally delivered stories into six components: abstract, orientation, complicating action, evaluation, result or resolution, and coda (1972: 362ff.). The components are all assumed to be realized in the form of clauses. For example, the abstract occurs at the beginning of the narration and consists of 'one or two clauses summarizing the whole story' (1972: 363); the orientation can occur 'in the course of the first several narrative clauses, but more commonly there is an orientation section composed of free clauses' (1972: 364); and so on. In its exclusive attention to oral narratives, its treatment of narrative as an optional mode of communication, and its preoccupation with the structural make-up of stories, this approach is very different from the one I intend to adopt in this book and which I attempt to elaborate in some detail in this chapter.

> Narration is the context for interpreting and assessing all communication – not a mode of discourse laid on by a creator's deliberate choice but the shape of knowledge as we first apprehend it.
>
> (Fisher 1987: 193)

In social and communication theory, as well as in the work of some historians such as Hayden White, narrative tends on the whole to be treated as *the* principal and inescapable mode by which we experience the world. Thus, Somers argues that 'it is through narrativity that we come to know, understand, and make sense of the social world, and it is through narratives and narrativity that we constitute our social identities' (1992: 600). Hayden White similarly stresses that

> far from being one code among many that a culture may utilize for endowing experience with meaning, narrative is a meta-code, a human universal on the basis of which transcultural messages about the nature of a shared reality can be transmitted.
>
> (White 1987a: 1)

An important difference between literary and linguistic approaches and the approach adopted in this book then concerns the status of narrative as an optional mode of communication or as a meta-code that cuts across and underpins all modes of communication. Narrative theory, as elaborated here, adopts the latter view.

Another important difference concerns the issue of genres more specifically. Whereas most literary and linguistic approaches tend to treat narrative itself as a genre, the view of narrative adopted in this book assumes that 'there is no genre, including even technical discourse, that is not an episode in the story of life' (Fisher 1987: 85). The issue of genre is important to address at the outset, since many readers might assume that a narrative framework can only be helpful if we wish to study the translation of literature, folktales, possibly political discourse, but certainly not scientific or technical text.

Landau stresses the power of narrative as a mode of being that is independent of genre in the following terms:[1]

> The growth of a plant, the progress of a disease, the formation of a beach, the evolution of an organism – any set of events that can be arranged in a sequence

and related can also be narrated. This is true even of a scientific experiment. Indeed, many laboratory reports, with their sections labelled 'methods,' 'results,' and 'conclusions,' bear at least a superficial resemblance to a typical narrative, that is, an organized sequence of events with a beginning, a middle, and an end. Whether or not scientists follow such a narrative structure in their work, they do not often recognize the extent to which they use narrative in their thinking and in communicating their ideas. Consequently, they may be unaware of the narrative presuppositions which inform their science.

(1997: 104)

Scientific theories and reports are narratives in the sense that they are ultimately 'stories' that have a beginning, middle and end. More specifically, narrative does much of the work that we identify with 'objective' scientific discourse. It is narrativity that turns the continuous flow of experience into a set of delineated categories that can be processed in various ways, and this – as I will attempt to demonstrate shortly (section 2.1.3 on p. 15) – includes scientific categories. Categories, whether scientific or otherwise, do not exist outside the narrative within which they are constituted. Moreover, the process of (narrative) categorization is far from disinterested, even in the most abstract and apparently 'objective' of sciences, such as statistics. Zureik (2001) discusses several examples of the use of census counting in colonial and post-colonial societies to categorize identities in a manner that facilitates population control.[2] Needless to say, every set of statistical figures participates in elaborating a different, and often competing narrative. In the context of the Middle East, for example, both Palestinians and Israelis appeal to a different set of statistical/census data 'to garner legitimacy for their respective claims' (2001: 215). Each set is 'rigorously' derived from the data; but data, like the world, cannot be accessed without narrative mediation. Thus, even technical procedures and (numerical) data 'should be interpreted in a storied context' (Fisher 1987: 48).

2.1.1 Scientific narratives

Narrative, including scientific narrative, categorizes the world into types of character, types of event, bounded communities. It also systematizes experience by ordering events in relation to each other – temporally, spatially, socially. And it does more than that. Narrative allows us 'not only to relate events, but also stances and dispositions towards those events' (Baquedano-López 2001: 343), thus categorizing behaviour along a moral and socially sanctioned cline into valued vs. non-valued, normal vs. eccentric, rational vs. irrational, legitimate vs. non-legitimate, legal vs. criminal. Scientific narratives participate in this process of legitimation and justification that is ultimately political in import. For example, the nineteenth-century 'scientific' approach to the difference that was assumed to exist between blacks and whites consisted of explaining this difference in environmental terms: we are all born equal, the scientific narrative went, but the environment in which we are born determines our place in an established hierarchy – with whites at the top and blacks at the bottom. In some versions of the theory, a black person could occupy a superior position in the hierarchy alongside a white European if they were to be removed from Africa at an early age and live in a white environment. These scientific theories, which were then perceived and projected as objective, detached and disinterested, were used to justify slavery. Science, as Farrands (2003: 14) asserted following the death of the British government weapons inspector David Kelly in July 2003,[3] is 'just politics in a lab coat'.

Because scientific narratives – like all narratives – are ultimately concerned with legitimizing and justifying actions and positions in the real world, they can be highly threatening in a direct political sense. Witness the immense row that followed the publication in the journal *Human Immunology* of a keynote research paper showing that Middle Eastern Jews and Palestinians are genetically almost identical (McKie 2001). McKie, Science Editor of *The Observer*, explained that

> In common with earlier studies, the team found no data to support the idea that Jewish people were genetically distinct from other people in the region. In doing so, the team's research challenges claims that Jews are a special, chosen people and that Judaism can only be inherited.

Not only was the article subsequently removed from the journal website, but academics who had received the hard copy were urged to 'rip out the *offending* pages' (McKie 2001; emphasis added), letters were sent to libraries all over the world asking them to physically remove the article from their copies, and the editor 'was threatened with mass resignations from members if she did not retract the article'! This near hysterical response testifies to the political import of scientific narratives and their potential for both supporting and unsettling existing relations of dominance. And yet, translators of scientific texts are rarely aware that what they translate are ultimately narrative accounts of the world that may have significant political consequences.

2.1.2 The normalizing function of narratives

One of the effects of narrativity is that it normalizes the accounts it projects over a period of time, so that they come to be perceived as self-evident, benign, uncontestable and non-controversial. This explains why the leading nineteenth-century scientist Georges Cuvier (1769–1832) could write as follows in his *Elementary Survey of the Natural History of Animals* in 1798 without raising an eyebrow:[4]

> The white race, with oval face, straight hair and nose, to which the civilized peoples of Europe belong and which appear to us the most beautiful of all, is also superior to others by its genius, courage and activity. ... [There is a] cruel law which seems to have condemned to an eternal inferiority the races of depressed and compressed skulls. ... and experience seems to confirm the theory that there is a relationship between the perfection of the spirit and the beauty of the face.

By 1815, Cuvier's narrative had come to seem so natural and self-evident that he was able to perform, without censure, his infamous 'scientific' dissection of the

Figure 1 'La Belle Hottentot' – early nineteenth-century French print depicting Saartjie Baartman on display in London

South African woman Saartjie Baartman, known as the 'Hottentot Venus', to solve the mysteries of her genitalia.

Before she died, and before Cuvier performed his 'scientific' dissection, this African woman had been taken to London in 1810 by Dr Alexander William Dunlop and put on public display as an anthropological curiosity. Members of the public queued up to inspect her large buttocks and marvel at her enlarged external genitalia (Figure 1). Many may have felt pity, even disgust at the spectacle, but they still queued up to inspect her and then went on merrily with their lives.[5] Their senses had been numbed by the narratives of their time, much as ours are by the narratives of today. When the Abu Ghraib scandal broke out in 2004, Ahdaf Soueif reminded us that we had all already been willing accomplices in this developing narrative, just as Cuvier's contemporaries had been accomplices in his degrading narrative of race:

> It was only a matter of time. In the past year the world has seen photos of many Iraqis stripped with their wrists tied behind their backs with plastic cord. At first we could look into their eyes and bear witness to what was happening. Then they were bagged. *At no point was there an outcry.*
>
> (Soueif 2004; emphasis added)[6]

Arguably, depending on one's narrative location, we are constantly being socialized into barbarous narratives even today, from the various narratives associated with 'security' and 'terrorism' to those of 'Islamic fundamentalism' and the

Figure 2 An Iraqi man comforts his four-year-old son at a regroupment centre for prisoners of war of the 101st Airborne Division near An Najaf. Associated Press Photo by Jean-Marc Bouju, 31 March 2003

Figure 3 A detainee in an outdoor solitary confinement cell talks with a military policeman at the Abu Ghraib prison on the outskirts of Baghdad. Associated Press Photo by John Moore, 22 June 2004

so-called 'Clash of Civilizations'. These and numerous other narratives that 'embody the truths of social elites and their publics', as Bennett and Edelman (1985: 158) argue, 'seem objective because they are confirmed time and again by self-fulfilling selection of documentary detail'. Moreover, many of these narratives start out as scientific theories before they gradually seep into our consciousness and become part of the everyday fabric of life. Consider, for instance, a comment made by the President of Columbia University, Lee Bollinger, in 2005 in the context of a major controversy over alleged bias against Israel in the Middle East and Asian Language and Culture Department of Columbia, where the late Edward Said taught: 'We could have a department that is double in size and still ... not be doing service or justice to the importance of those questions to the modern world,' he said.

> So that's the first thing: We have to expand the size of programs like MEALAC. The second thing is that we need to integrate better than we have other fields that have knowledge relevant to the work being done in MEALAC. *What is the relationship, for example, between the environmental facts of life in the Middle East and Asia, or its diseases, and the culture there?* We need to better bring together what we have. We need to add more people to do that, people in law, in journalism, and elsewhere.
>
> (Liebovitz 2005; emphasis added)

As a member of MEALAC faculty later commented in his statement to an ad hoc committee set up to investigate allegations against the department, clearly alluding to nineteenth-century scientific theories of race such as Cuvier's,

This retreat to 19th century climatology and medical anthropology is disturbing. Would President Bollinger also think that there is a relationship between 'environmental facts, its diseases and the culture' of African Americans or of American Jews?[7]

What is particularly interesting at this juncture in history, and what no theorist of narrative seems to appreciate so far, is that translation – including translation of scientific texts – plays a key role in naturalizing and promoting such narratives across linguistic boundaries. In our war-ridden contemporary societies, we must continually remind ourselves that all conflict starts and ends with constructing or deconstructing an enemy, 'an *other* who is so foreign and distant that *who* becomes *it*. *It* can be tortured, maimed, slaughtered; *who* cannot' (Nelson 2002: 8). One of the main aims of this book is to highlight and interrogate the many ways in which translators and interpreters participate in both circulating and resisting the narratives that turn the *who*s of our time into the *it*s whose suffering is either justifiable or at best simply 'regrettable' – a question of 'collateral damage', perhaps, as Gabe Bokor, editor of the *Translation Journal*, seems to suggest:

> We may differ in our views on many things, but I'm sure no translator condones mass murder. During the inevitable response of the U.S. government to the attacks which resulted in the death of thousands of innocent people, certainly including Muslims and other sympathizers of Arab causes, more civilian casualties will occur, including in countries where some of the contributors of the *Translation Journal* reside. I personally regret such casualties, and I'm keenly aware that the suffering of innocent civilian victims makes no distinction between the two sides of a conflict. However, I believe it is important to keep in mind the moral distinction between unintended 'collateral damage' in the course of military operations and deliberate slaughter of civilians.
>
> (Bokor 2001)

Published in October 2001, shortly after the attacks on the Twin Towers, this extract from an extended editorial by Gabe Bokor makes it clear that 'collateral damage' is acceptable when inflicted on the *its* of our world, and that state terrorism is not to be equated with the terrorism of individuals and groups who do not happen to be running the governments of *our* 'civilized' world. Indeed, Bokor seems willing to trust unquestioningly any narratives offered by those in power, whatever the consequences for the *its* that inhabit distant countries such as Iraq, as the editorial for the April 2003 issue makes clear:

> As of this writing, it seems likely that by the time you read these lines the United States will be at war with Iraq. Judging by the discussions in the different translators' electronic forums, the translator community is deeply divided on the merits of this war. It is not the policy of this publication to take sides in political disputes, and this applies especially to this issue, since our

decision to be for or against the war is made difficult by the fact that we, ordinary citizens, do not have all the information available to our leaders.

(Bokor 2003)

Bennett and Edelman (1985: 159) remind us that 'stock political narratives disguise and digest ideology for people who prefer to represent themselves as passive or objective reporters of the world around them'. It is also stock political narratives that we often digest, translate and circulate 'passively', without stopping to consider their implications for those we readily relegate to the category of *it*, the 'regrettable' victims of collateral damage.

2.1.3 Categories and stories

Nearly two centuries after Cuvier's death, he and other scientists of his era are parodied in Matthew Kneale's award-winning *English Passengers*, a historical novel which takes place in 1857 and depicts the colonization of Tasmania. One of the main characters, Dr Thomas Potter, is an amateur botanist who joins a ship bound for Tasmania in order to collect material for his scientific study, entitled *The Destiny of Nations: being a consideration upon the different strengths and characteristics of the many races and types of man, and the likely consequences of their future struggles*. When the ship docks in the Cape in October, Dr Thomas Potter – this parody of nineteenth-century science – writes the following notes in his diary:

1. British: Type = Saxon. Status = <u>natural rulers of Colony</u>.
2. Boers: Type = Belgic Celtic. Status = <u>assistants</u> to British.
3. Malays: Type = Oriental. Status = farm labourers + <u>servants</u>.
4. Hindoos: Type = Indian Asiatic. Status = as Malays but <u>lower</u>.
5. Native Africans: Type = Negro. Status = <u>low</u>.
6. Hottentots: Type = lower Negro. Status = low and <u>brutal</u>.

(Kneale 2000: 168–9; underlining in original)

By December of the same year, as his diary entry reveals, this scientific list of categories and taxonomies begins to take a more overtly narrative form as an excerpt from his forthcoming book. This is worth quoting at length:

This robust and ever-growing empire that is called British, is, as we are told by so-called political theorists, nothing more than the consequence of chance. ...

Such a view could be hardly more misleading. There is, in truth, no finer manifestation of the destiny of men than this mighty institution of imperial conquest. Here we see the stolid and fearless Saxon Type, his nature revealed as never before as he strides forth in his great quest, subduing and scattering inferior nations – the Hindoo, the American Indian, the Aboriginal race of Australia – and replacing these with his own stalwart sons. Brave yet unseeing, he little comprehends the unalterable destiny that leads him on: the all-powerful laws of the races of men. Beside him march others, though their step tells of a purpose less resolute. The Roman Type of France petulantly struts southwards across desert wastes, quelling once-proud Arab chieftains. The Slav Type of Russia dismally saunters through the icy east, overcoming Asiatics with his every step. The Iberian Type of South America rides across his Pampas, lazily extinguishing the savage Indian. The Belgic-Celtic Type plods onwards against island orientals, stolidly adding to his frail domain. All shall find themselves the unwitting destroyers of their conquered foes, until hardly a subject race, whether African, Australian or Asiatic, remains.

It is when this work is done, and only the strongest Types remain, that another stage in the unfolding of history shall begin. Thus will a new and terrible great conflagration draw near: a final battle of nations, when the trusty Saxon will be required to struggle anew; a conflict of Titans; a battle of the Supreme Types ...

(Kneale 2000: 280–1)

It is not always possible to trace the elaboration of categories into full-blown narratives directly in this way, nor to pinpoint the specific set of narratives that inform a given process of categorization with any certainty. Neverthless, our choice of what to categorize and how to categorize it is always dependent on our narrative location; this is why different people purportedly looking at the same phenomenon will always devise different sets of categories to account for it. Categories are never suspended in space; they are always dependent on, and in turn feed into, the narratives – including scientific narratives – of the time.

Accepting that the boundary between literary and scientific genres is highly porous, and that both rely on narrativity to elaborate what is ultimately an interested vision of the world, is a *sine qua non* of the narrative approach adopted in this book. Translators of both science and fiction must be alert to their own role in elaborating and promoting these narrative visions of society, with all the real world consequences that these visions entail. They might also consider that scientific narratives are no more truthful or robust than other narratives that provide our interface with the world. Like other narratives, they are always open to contestation, as this extract from a *Financial Times* editorial demonstrates (13 April 2005):[8]

Creationism's assault on science

As the religious right strengthens its hold on U.S. politics, the threat to teaching about evolution grows. The revival of creationism is a serious concern for the National Science Teachers Association. In a recent survey of 1,050 teachers, 30 per cent said they felt pressure to include creationism — sometimes disguised as 'intelligent design' — in their lessons.

Further, in a disturbing sign that the assault on science is moving from schools to public education in a wider sense, some science centres and museums in southern states have refused to show big-screen Imax films that refer to evolution. They are boycotting titles such as *Volcanoes of the Deep Sea*, which suggests that life might have begun more than 3 billion years ago.

2.1.4 Narrative and the world: fact and fiction

A related issue that has attracted much debate in the literature is the relationship between narrative and 'reality'. Bruner (1991: 5) explains that '[i]t was perhaps a decade ago that psychologists became alive to the possibility of narrative as a form not only of representing but of constituting reality' and dates this paradigm shift to the publication of *On Narrative*, a special issue of *Critical Inquiry*, Volume 7/1, 1980.[9] This view, or paradigm shift as Bruner describes it, has important theoretical and practical consequences. For one thing, and further distinguishing the view of narrative elaborated here from that adopted by most linguistic and literary scholars, it means that it makes little sense to follow a scholar such as Rimmon-Kenan in proposing a distinction between 'story' (or underlying plot) and 'text', where '[s]tory designates the narrated events, abstracted from their description in the text and reconstructed in their chronological order' and text is 'what we read. In it, events do not necessarily appear in chronological order, the characteristics of participants are dispersed throughout, and all the items of the narrative content are filtered through some prism or perspective' (1983: 3). Distinctions of this type are at odds with the basic definition of narrative adopted by scholars such as Bruner and Fisher, among many others, since there is an assumption here that the 'story' and the 'perspective' from which it is told can be separated, because there is a natural or objective order and sequence of events. But, as Bruner explains, 'knowledge is never "point-of-viewless" (1991: 3). Goodwin (1994: 606) similarly argues that '[a]ll vision is perspectival'; this includes scientific vision, or 'professional' vision as Goodwin refers to it. Within a theory that recognizes the role of narrative in constituting rather than merely representing reality, there can be no fully 'independent' story as such. Every story is a narrative and every experience is a narrative experience. Even history, as Kellner explains,

> is not 'about' the past as such, but rather about our ways of creating meanings from the scattered and profoundly meaningless debris we find around us ... There is no story *there* to be gotten straight; any story must arise from the act of contemplation.
>
> (Kellner 1989: 10; in Mishler 1995: 103)

The assumption of the constructedness of narratives means that in practice we can neither isolate and independently assess individual elements in a narrative nor assume that a default, chronological or logical storyline can be fully separated from the perspective of a given narrator. At the same time, because we have to take a position in relation to a variety of public, historical and personal narratives in order to act in the real world, we have to make judgements about the veracity and credibility of narratives that touch our lives. In other words, the constructedness of narratives and our embeddedness in them do not preclude us from reasoning about them (see Chapter 7). One aspect of this reasoning clearly concerns the believability of the narrative, which naturally assumes that events and happenings are verifiable by reference to some 'reality'. This brings in the whole question of the relationship between narrative and truth, an issue which has received much attention from historians in particular. Zhang Longxi offers an insightful overview and analysis of the different positions within this debate and ultimately argues that

> As human narratives, history may be prone to errors and lapses, not to mention ideological biases and spots of blindness, but, underneath all the layers of relations, descriptions and imagined dialogues or motivations, there is a core of verifiable facts as the basis of all the narration. This core of facts together with non-linguistic artefacts, relics and archaelogical findings would form a firm ground for judging the veracity of historical narratives. ... When we admit that whatever truth recovered from the past in historical writing is not final and absolute, but forms an approximation of truth and also part of the history to be studied, we may find it possible both to accept the truth-claim of historiography and to subject that claim to further investigation.
>
> (Zhang 2004: 400)[10]

To reframe this argument more broadly, we might say that while admitting that no narrative can represent the ultimate, absolute, uncontestable truth of any event or set of events, we have to accept that events do take place in real time and space and hence are verifiable by a range of means that are always extendable and open to refinement and reassessment. In some research traditions, for instance, verification is sought through the use of triangulation methods whereby several independent reports of an event are required in order to establish that the event really happened (see Polkinghorne 1995). In other contexts, we take our concerns about truth claims to a recognized adjudicating body that is assumed to be in a position to check the accuracy of these claims. For instance, Reynolds (2004: 333) reports how organizations such as the Green Party and Soil Association took their concerns about truth claims in a Monsanto advertising campaign to the British Advertising Standards Authority. In August 1999, the Authority declared as untruthful the claims in one of the advertising campaigns that 'Rigorous tests have been undertaken throughout Monsanto's 20 year biotech history to ensure ... food crops are safe and nutritious' and that 'government regulatory agencies in 20 countries ... have approved them' (advertisement reproduced in Reynolds 2004: 349). Thus, to the extent that we can verify the 'truth' of an event or narrative at any given moment in time, by whatever means, we are obliged to assess the narrative accordingly, whether consciously or otherwise, and to act on the basis of this assessment. Drawing on Walter Fisher's influential narrative paradigm (1984, 1985, 1987, 1997), Chapter 7 deals with the issue of how we assess narratives in some detail. In the meantime, in terms of the relationship between narrative and 'facts', the version of narrative theory adopted here acknowledges that 'narratives do not contain within them a measure for their truth value. A narrative gets truth-value from being conscious of the conditions of its production, and being cognizant of, and able to learn something from, its own evolution' (Klein 2000: 163).

It is also worth stressing that the assumption of constructedness does not simply mean the rejection of *a* truth in relation to a given set of events or the assertion that no one has direct access to *a* reality. Rather, acknowledging the constructed nature of narratives means that we accept the potential existence and worth of multiple truths. This is a key issue in claiming that narratives have political import and that they can unsettle and contest hegemonic views of the world. As Ewick and Silbey explain,

> the *political* commitment to giving voice and bearing witness through narrative is underwritten by the epistemological conviction that there is no single, objectively apprehended truth. Conversely, the *epistemological* claim that there are mutliple truths is based on the recognition that knowledge is socially and politically produced.
>
> (1995: 199; emphasis in original)

2.2 Defining narrative

The definition of narrative I intend to draw on in this book[11] is very much in line with that adopted by Fisher, Landau, Bruner, and Somers and Gibson. Narratives in this view are public and personal 'stories' that we subscribe to and that guide our behaviour. They are the stories we tell ourselves, not just those we explicitly tell other people, about the world(s) in which we live. The terms 'narrative' and 'story' are interchangeable in this context.

Ewick and Silbey (1995: 198) define narratives as 'sequences of statements connected by both a temporal and a moral ordering'. This is a useful definition, provided we do not interpret 'sequences of statements' too narrowly as a set of sentences within the confines of a single text or utterance. Because the emphasis within the framework adopted here is on the power and function of narratives rather than their structural make-up, it is 'the responsibility of critical analysis ... to construct texts from diverse fragments and then explain how interpretive communities are able to imbue those fragments with coherence' (Ehrenhaus 1993: 79). This is not to dismiss the obvious fact that very specific, detailed narratives are often fully articulated within the confines of a single text or group of texts (such as an advertising campaign), but even these will ultimately be embedded in and informed by broader narratives that cannot be located within individual stretches of language. Moreover, within the framework adopted here, the articulation of narratives is by no means restricted to textual material, but can also be realized through a range of other media. Polkinghorne uses the term 'storied narratives' to distinguish between an underlying narrative plot and the expressive form it may take, arguing that any given plot and the set of events it weaves into a narrative 'can be presented through various media, for example, through an oral telling, a ballet, a motion picture, or written document' (1995: 8). Kennedy (2003) offers a very good example of the articulation of the narrative of 11 September through an exhibition of photography.

In the final analysis, the emphasis in the strand of narrative theory which provides the starting point for our discussions in this book is not on the structural make-up or textual realization of narratives, but rather on the crucial fact that 'narrative shapes people's views of rationality, of objectivity, of morality, and of their conceptions of themselves and others' (Bennett and Edelman 1985: 159). In the following chapters,

I will attempt to complement this essentially social and political focus with attention to micro- and macro-analysis of text, especially translated texts and interpreted utterances. This is not an issue that is explicitly tackled in any detail in the social and communication theory literature, because ultimately, as Bruner (1991: 5–6) puts it, '[t]he central concern [in these theories] is not how narrative as text is constructed, but rather how it operates as an instrument of mind in the construction of reality'. From the point of view of scholars of translation and of language in general, this is a serious limitation that invites us to supplement the social theory approach to narrative with textual methods of analysis in order to offer a productive application of narrativity within translation studies. And although the discussions of narrative within linguistics and literary studies do focus very much on textual analyses, the definition of narrative within these studies, as I have explained above, is far too restricted for our current purposes, and the emphasis is very much on narrow linguistic and structural categories of analysis (plots, characters, episodes, etc.) in individual, mostly oral or literary narratives. As we proceed with our detailed examination of narrativity, I will attempt to draw together a number of disparate threads that might allow us to trace the elaboration of narratives across time and texts as well as in individual texts, using examples from a variety of genres and from translated texts and interpreted utterances specifically.

First, a brief word about the political import of narratives – how they are used to control as well as contest, to elaborate both hegemonic and subversive accounts of the world.

2.3 The political import of narratives

> The awareness that every acceptance of a narrative involves a rejection of others makes the issue politically and personally vital. In a critical sense the differences among competing narratives give all of them their meanings.
>
> Bennett and Edelman (1985: 160)

Any narrative, from the story of the invasion of Iraq to the story of human evolution, circulates in many different versions. Some of these versions may be completely at odds with each other; some may differ only in minor details or points of emphasis. Over time, different versions of a narrative may become more or less valued and may achieve more or less currency through various processes of reinforcement and contestation.

Because narratives of the past define and determine the narrative present, competition among different versions of a narrative may continue for centuries. To contest and challenge the present, both individuals and communities will draw on past narratives to highlight salient features of the current situation as elaborated in their narrative of the here and now. For example, Baquedano-López (2001) describes how the retelling of the narrative of *Nuestra Señora de Guadalupe* by Mexican immigrants at the Catholic parish of St Paul in Los Angeles allows them to create a sense of community with 'past experiences of oppression' (2001: 344). This is a story of a Mexican peasant by the name of Juan Diego. The events are supposed to have taken place in 1531 in Mexico City, then the centre of Spanish power in the Americas. The main storyline is that the Virgin Mary appeared to Juan Diego as an Aztec, addressing him in Nahuatl and insisting that a shrine be built in her honour, where she appeared 'among the conquered people' (2001: 344). She also sent him to 'evangelize' the Spanish clergy, who claimed to hold a monopoly on the 'truth'. The Virgin Mary is thus believed to have 'restored dignity and hope to native people who had been dehumanized by foreign oppression' (2001: 344). In the context of the present community of Mexican immigrants in the USA, the narrative 'becomes not only a story to live by, it affirms and contests the community's past, present, and possible stories' (2001: 344). African Americans similarly retell collective narratives from their past to underline and contest their continued oppression today, and Israelis, as Nossek (1994) explains, retell stories of the Holocaust over and over again to support their narratives of the present.

The retelling of past narratives is also a means of control. It socializes individuals into an established social and political order and encourages them to interpret present events in terms of sanctioned narratives of the past. This restricts the scope of their present personal narratives, their sense of who they are, if these are to be considered legitimate. In other words, it circumscribes the stock of identities from which individuals may choose a social role for themselves.

Where different versions of a narrative are completely at odds with each other, Liu (1999: 299) argues that 'there is no way a mutually-agreed upon decision can be reached on any issue of significance'. When people invest very heavily in specific versions of a narrative, giving up or adjusting those versions could result in major personal trauma for them. In this case, they simply cannot entertain other versions of the narrative nor agree a resolution to a conflict informed by a competing narrative. Eventually, they may end up isolating themselves within their own narrative communities, circles of people who subscribe to a similar version of the narrative(s) they regard as central to their lives.

In terms of protest groups, MacIntyre complains that 'the *utterance* of protest is characteristically addressed to those who already *share* the protestors' premises. The effects of incommensurability ensure that protestors rarely have anyone else to talk to but themselves' (1981: 69; emphasis in original). But while Fisher agrees that 'there will always be conceptual and/or logical incommensurability between or among people who are certain of their own version of truth' (1997: 312), he reminds us that there is always an audience around that is not yet invested in a particular version of the narrative, and this audience is worth appealing to:

> Fortunately, for the world to go on, they [the protestors] do not need to convince or to persuade one another. They must only gain the adherence of a relevant audience, others who are affected by the matter at hand and whose values are fundamental but not beyond discussion and debate.
>
> (Fisher 1997: 312)

Translation and interpreting play an extremely important role in this process, especially given the fact that most conflicts today are not restricted to specific monolingual communities but have to be negotiated in the international arena. Even local, domestic conflicts now typically have to be negotiated cross-culturally and cross-linguistically in view of the multicultural composition of most societies, especially in the Western world.

Take, for instance, the controversial decision by the French government in 2004 to ban all religious symbols and apparel in public schools. In some versions of this narrative, the ban specifically targeted Muslim school girls wearing headscarves or hijab. Competing versions of the narrative proliferated, some explaining the ban as an attack on individual freedom and a racist gesture towards an already embattled Muslim population, and others explaining it as a necessary measure to ensure unity and social cohesion, indeed even a goodwill gesture towards young Muslims, Sikhs and Jews, all of whom should be encouraged to integrate into French society. In one version of the narrative, translated from Urdu into English for wider circulation, the ban is described as

> a political statement by the French government. Because the French opposed the U.S. invasion of Iraq, it resulted in friction in the Franco-U.S. relations. In an effort to appease the Americans, the French targeted its [*sic*] own Muslim population.
>
> (Naseem 2004)

Newspapers across the planet carried stories about the ban, promoting some version of the narrative or another, through heavily mediated textual and visual representations. Demonstrations against the ban did not just take place in Paris; there were global demonstrations across Europe and North America, not to mention various parts of the Muslim world. The story also provided a focal point for drawing comparisons with numerous local events in various parts of the world: for example, a school deciding to expel a Muslim student for wearing the hijab in Canada or Britain because it was against the school's dress code immediately became embroiled in the French controversy. Even events that preceded the French ban could now be retold within this new narrative framework.

Every time a version of the narrative is retold or translated into another language, it is injected with elements from other, broader narratives circulating within the new setting or from the personal narratives of the retellers. The embellished version in turn may get retold in – and 'contaminate' – versions of the narrative in other languages and settings. Naseem's (2004) retelling of the narrative, 'To wear or not to wear the Hijab?', was translated from Urdu by Mohammed Jehangir and published in *Pakistan News*. It injects the story with Naseem's personal experience of lecturing at the Chicago Truman College, where a Pakistani student wearing a hijab questioned him aggressively on the attitude of liberal Muslims, and with his own positioning vis-à-vis religious members of his community:

> After finishing my lecture, I recited excerpts of poetry from my book. It was followed by a question-and-answer session. It was during this session that one of the Hijab-wearing Pakistani students surprised many of her class fellows by asking me questions very rudely.

For a moment I too was taken aback. Perhaps she was not willing to accept the reality that a Pakistani–American can also reach this level of success in literature and have his book included in the curriculum of an American college? Yet, it was not too surprising. Often I have to deal with people who have inverted inferiority complexes and suffer with a slave-like mentality. This girl student was no exception.

Naseem also re-sites the narrative in the context of several broader narratives relating to the position of Pakistani and Muslim women in the USA, their failure to engage with serious political issues, and their indifference to widespread illiteracy in the community. Thus, aspects of various versions of the narrative and elements from other narratives are added, emphasized, downplayed or simply suppressed through numerous processes of mediation, many of which will involve direct translation, as in the case of the article by Naseem.

2.3.1 The interplay of dominance and resistance

Much of the impetus for narrative research comes from a belief among theorists working in this area that unexamined assumptions encoded in narratives obscure patterns of domination and oppression that exclude the experiences of large sectors of society while legitimating and promoting those of the political, economic and cultural elite. There is also general agreement in the literature that narrative both reproduces the existing power structures *and* provides a means of contesting them. But the dynamics of this intricate interplay between dominance and resistance is difficult to capture.

> The ambiguity of the intercultural interpreter as embodied by la Malinche ... reminds us that power is not a straightforward game, based on evident, linear relationships between the dominant and the dominated, the powerful and the weak: hegemony and cultural strength are established through much subtler mechanisms, which also carry within themselves the possibility of resistance.
>
> (Polezzi 2001: 80)

For example, narrative dominance – which reflects and reinforces real world dominance – does not necessarily mean that marginalized or dissenting voices are completely silenced, except perhaps under the most autocratic regimes. Indeed, dominant institutions and individuals will often champion the causes of marginalized groups and publicly support their right to narrate the world in their terms. This can happen for various reasons. One reason may be that championing these causes – provided they are relatively 'safe', that is not too unsettling or risky – can improve a certain individual's or institution's appeal and enhance their own standing, whether social, political or financial. Bakan offers numerous examples in the context of business, where '[p]ious social responsibility themes now vie with sex for top billing in corporate advertising' (2004: 32). Another reason is that allowing dissenters and marginalized groups to speak freely diffuses the build up of tension in society. Mertz (1996: 154) cites Justice Brandeis' comments in *Whitney v. California* 274 U.S. 357, 375 (1927) to the effect that 'permitting dissenters free expression functions as a 'safety valve' protecting society from the disruption that might ensue were frustrated and stifled dissenters to turn their energies to action rather than speech'. Ehrenhaus' description of this process and the interplay of dominance and subversion is particularly insightful:

> Marginalized voices often can and will be heard. But these public expressions occur in ways that defuse those voices, often by integrating them into the broader system of social relations from which they have been excluded. ... This is not a matter of power relegating groups to the margins or of ignoring them once they are so marginalized. Rather, it is a matter of power adjusting to the disruptive potential of those who are marginalized. Through the communicative options it sanctions, power can defuse opposition before it crystallizes; it can create the illusion of opposition to demonstrate pluralism's openness and tolerance and inclusiveness: and power can dictate the conditions under which genuine opposition can and will be heard, thus rendering it ineffectual.
>
> (1993: 88)

This also means that opponents may project themselves as committed to a particular version of a competing narrative in a conscious attempt to 'co-opt the margins' and defuse opposition. Institutions and groups aligning themselves with existing power structures (for example the CIA) can thus hijack the agenda of a resistance group and replace it with a tamer, ineffectual form of opposition, as much of the literature on social movements has demonstrated (see, for example, Ehrenhaus 1993; Noakes 2000; Lambertus 2003; Cunningham and Browning 2004). All these strategies ultimately ensure that opposition is conducted within a prescribed space that does not spill over into or disrupt the mainstream.

Yameng Liu (1999) describes another interesting aspect of the dynamic interplay of dominance and subtle contestation of dominance by marginalized groups. He explains that the primary strategy of the Third World elite in advancing non-Western positions on issues such as human rights and democracy is to adopt the terms of debate set by the West, rather than the terms of debate current in their own native context. In arguing against unrestricted international trading in currency at the IMF-World Bank Hong Kong Convention in 1997, the Malaysian Prime Minister Mahathir Mohamad did not use arguments from the Islamic or any aspect of the Asian tradition; in other words, he did not evoke domestic narratives. Instead, he built his argument on established legislation in the modern capitalist economy, such as the anti-trust legislation that outlaws monopolies. 'If even the U.S. has in fact always subjected its own market to strict regulations so as to prevent small investors from being victimized by big wheelers and dealers', he argued, how can it contest the need 'to prevent similar victimization of small financial entities or players in a globalized market?' (Liu 1999: 312–13).

This strategy is of course an effect of dominance. The dominant party normally sets the terms of debate in any situation, and in some respects this affords the dominant party a decisive advantage. At the same time, however, adopting the terms (or narratives) of the dominant party allows the weaker party, in this case Malaysia, to exploit the fundamental heterogeneity and contentiousness of domestic discourses in the West by appealing to different constituencies and thus 'turning their [i.e. the weaker party's] cross-cultural debate *with* the West into a domestic controversy *of* the West' (1999: 304). This, as Liu stresses, is a strategy not of 'reluctant resignation' but of 'shrewd calculation' (1999: 304).[12] It is a subversive strategy presented as one of accommodation and compliance.[13]

Faced with such a strategy, the dominant party is forced to adopt similar tactics. For example, numerous voices in the West continue to stress the importance of 'winning the hearts and minds' of 'ordinary' Arabs and Muslims (in other words, winnable constituencies within those communities) by showing respect for their traditions and explaining things from their perspective.[14] In attempting to legitimize its own position, the dominant party thus finds itself having to legitimize and circulate the discourse of the weaker party, to adopt its terms of debate. Liu refers to such attempts to 'justify *Western* positions in *non-Western* terms' as a strategy of 'counter-domestication' (1999: 306) and suggests that in this 'peculiar mode of cross-cultural argumentation', 'the two opposing parties … venture into the other's "territory" and seek to win the "battle" by provoking a "civil war" behind the opponent's line' (1999: 309). The boundary between dominance and resistance thus becomes even more blurred.

A relatively extreme example of this strategy is discussed in Niranjana (1990). She explains how British officials decided to adopt Indian laws to govern the Indian population. Their starting point, however, was that the Indians were unable to rule themselves and could not administer their own laws (Niranjana 1990: 775). These laws therefore had to be translated into English in order to be used for the Indians' benefit. 'On the evidence of these authoritative translations', Niranjana explains, 'missionaries berated Hindus for not being true practitioners of Indian religion' (1990: 775). This is a good example of what Robert Young means when he argues that the traditional conception of translation as an inferior copy of a superior original is reversed in a colonial setting, where 'the colonial copy becomes more powerful than the indigenous original that is devalued. It will even be claimed that the copy corrects deficiencies in the native version' (2003: 140).

In all these elaborate cycles of dominance and contestation of dominance and the complex interplay between power and resistance, some form of translation is almost always present. This has always been the case, but it is particularly true of the twenty-first century, with its globalized economies and aggressive resurgence of colonial empires. Now, more than ever, '[t]he strategies of containment initiated by translation are deployed across a range of discourses, allowing us to name translation as a significant technology of colonial domination' (Niranjana 1990: 776). But we must remember that translation also offers – and has always offered – major opportunities for contesting and undermining this very domination. Young's point about the colonial copy becoming more powerful than the indigenous original still holds; but we also have numerous examples of translators hijacking this very strategy to give voice to their own constituencies. Khalil Mutran's Arabic translation of Shakespeare's *Othello* in 1912 is one such example. Mutran maintained that 'the story of the Moor is originally an Arabic story, which Shakespeare must have read in Arabic or in translation' and set out to 'redeem it into the language and tradition from which it was dispossessed' (Hanna 2005: 114). Mutran further maintained that the title of his Arabic version, *Utail*, is the correct original Arabic name for *Othello*, and reclaimed Shakespeare himself as a product of the Arabic tradition: 'In Shakespeare, there is definitely something of an Arab ... in all he writes, in general, there is something bedouin, something that anchors itself to the free, genuine human instinct' (1912: 7–8; cited in Hanna 2005: 114). This may seem like an extreme measure, but it is arguably no more extreme than the British appropriation of Indian laws described by Niranjana. The competition over narratives in colonial contexts, it would seem, can take complex and at times somewhat extreme forms. Or, rather, these forms may seem extreme when viewed from our own narrative location today.

In the chapters that follow, the discussion is organized within the framework of narrative theory, starting with typologies of narrative and moving on to features of narrativity and the various ways in which narratives are (re)framed in translation. Cutting across this structural organization of the material, what will hopefully emerge from the discussion is that translators and interpreters, like all social actors, engage with the narrative world in which they are embedded in a variety of ways. Many refuse to reflect on the implications of their choices almost as a matter of principle, opting instead to translate any and all narratives in a detached manner, thus helping to circulate and promote them irrespective of their own narrative location. Others set out to contest dominant narratives and subject them to crticial reflection. Neither can escape being firmly embedded in a series of narratives that define who they are and how they act in the world. And neither can escape responsibility for the narratives they elaborate and promote through their translation and interpreting work.

Core references

Georgakopoulou, Alexandra (1997) 'Narrative', in Jef Verschueren, Jan-Ola Östman, Jan Blommaert and Chris Bulcaen (eds) *Handbook of Pragmatics 1997*, Amsterdam: John Benjamins, 1–19.

Landau, Misia (1997) 'Human Evolution as Narrative', in Lewis P. Hinchman and Sandra K. Hinchman (eds) *Memory, Identity, Community: The Idea of Narrative in the Human Sciences*, Albany: State University of New York Press, 104–18.

Mishler, Elliot G. (1995) 'Models of Narrative Analysis: A Typology', *Journal of Narrative and Life History* 5(2): 87–123.

White, Hayden (1987a [1980]) 'The Value of Narrativity in the Representation of Reality', *Critical Inquiry* 7(1); reproduced in Hayden White (1987) *The Content of the Form: Narrative Discourse and Historical Representation*, Baltimore MD and London: The Johns Hopkins University Press, 1–25.

Whitebrook, Maureen (2001) *Identity, Narrative and Politics*, London and New York: Routledge.

Further reading

Bennett, W. Lance and Murray Edelman (1985) 'Toward a New Political Narrative', *Journal of Communication* 35(4): 156–71.

Bourdieu, Pierre (1998) *Acts of Resistance: Against the New Myths of Our Time*, trans. by Richard Nice, Cambridge: Polity Press.

Chilton, Paul (1982) 'Nukespeak: Nuclear Language, Culture and Propaganda', in C. Aubrey (ed.) *Nukespeak: The Media and the Bomb*, London: Comedia Publishing Group, 94–112.

Ehrenhaus, Peter (1993) 'Cultural Narratives and the Therapeutic Motif: The Political Containment of Vietnam Veterans', in Dennis K. Mumby (ed.) *Narrative and Social Control: Critical Perspectives*, Newbury Park CA: Sage, 77–118.

Ewick, Patricia and Susan S. Silbey (1995) 'Subversive Stories and Hegemonic Tales: Toward a Sociology of Narrative', *Law & Society Review* 29(2): 197–226.

Goodwin, Charles (1994) 'Professional Vision', *American Anthropologist*, 606–33.

Hanna, Sameh F. (2005) '*Othello* in Egypt: Translation and the (Un)making of National Identity', in Juliane House, M. Rosario Martín Ruano and Nicole Baumgarten (eds) *Translation and the Construction of Identity. IATIS Yearbook 2005*, Seoul: IATIS, 109–28.

Hart, Janet (1992) 'Cracking the Code: Narrative and Political Mobilization in the Greek Resistance', *Social Science History* 16(4): 631–68.

Knellwolf, Christa (2001) 'Women Translators, Gender and the Cultural Context of the Scientific Revolution', in Roger Ellis and Liz Oakley-Brown (eds) *Translation and Nation: Towards a Cultural Politics of Englishness*, Clevedon: Multilingual Matters, 85–119.

Liu, Yameng (1999) 'Justifying My Position in Your Terms: Cross-cultural Argumentation in a Globalized World', *Argumentation* 13(3): 297–315.

Séguinot, Candace (1988) 'Translating the Ideology of Science: The Example of the Work of Alfred Tomatis', *TTR: Traduction, Terminologie, Rédaction* 1(1): 103–12.

Tymoczko, Maria (2000) 'Translation and Political Engagement: Activism, Social Change and the Role of Translation in Geopolitical Shifts', *The Translator* 6(1): 23–47.

Young, Robert (2003) *Postcolonialism: A Very Short Introduction*, Oxford: Oxford University Press (Chapter 7: Translation).

Zhang, Longxi (2004) 'History and Fictionality: Insights and Limitations of a Literary Perspective', *Rethinking History* 8(3): 387–402.

3 A typology of narrative

As might be expected, given the academic passion for classification, the extensive literature on narrative in various disciplines abounds with discussions of typologies, dimensions and axes. In the context of political movements, Hart (1992) distinguishes between *ontological* (or subjective) and *mobilizational* (or intersubjective) narratives. Pratt (2003) suggests that identity narratives are organized along two axes. The first is *biographical* and stresses continuity by explaining what a collectivity is in terms of its evolution over time: for example, who the Kurds are as a function of what is narrated as their past, present and future. The second is *vertical* and functions through opposition; it explains who the Kurds are in terms of how they differ from a specific 'other', such as Iraqis or Turks.

For our purposes, the typology proposed by Somers (1992, 1997) and Somers and Gibson (1994) seems the most relevant. They distinguish between ontological, public, conceptual and meta-narratives in an attempt to outline the social functions and political import of narrativity. Their discussion of each category is however very brief, extending to no more than two or three paragraphs in each case. Moreover, as social theorists, Somers and Gibson understandably pay no attention at all to translation and interpreting, nor to discursive issues more broadly. In what follows, I attempt to flesh out the details of their typology and to demonstrate its potential application in translation studies.

3.1 Ontological narratives (narratives of the self)

Ontological narratives are personal stories that we tell ourselves about our place in the world and our own personal history.[1] These stories both constitute and make sense of our lives. Although they ultimately remain focused on the self and its immediate world, they are interpersonal and social in nature, because '[t]he person has to exist, to tell their story, in a social world – they are a situated, located self' (Whitebrook 2001: 24). In concrete terms, this means that 'even the most personal of narratives rely on and invoke collective narratives – symbols, linguistic formulations, structures, and vocabularies of motive – without which the personal would remain unintelligible and uninterpretable' (Ewick and Silbey 1995: 211–12). This is one reason why even a concrete personal story told in one language cannot necessarily be retold or translated into another language unproblematically.[2] The interdependence between the personal and the collective means that the retelling is inevitably constrained by the shared linguistic and narrative resources available in the new setting.

Ella Shohat, an Iraqi Jew whose family left for Israel in the 1950s and who later emigrated to the United States as an adult, describes the effects of rupture between her ontological narrative and the collective narratives available in the USA and Europe as follows:

> not all hyphenated identities are permitted entry into America's official lexicon of ethnicities and races. I could see in people's faces how this corporeally inscribed hyphen, Iraq-Israel, produced a kind of classificatory vertigo, with the result that the hyphen immediately disappeared into an assimilable identity: 'Ah, so you're Israeli!' ... [I]n the United States ... our Asianness disappears, subsumed under the dominant Eurocentric definition of Jewishness (equated with Europe) and Arabness (equated with Islam) as antonyms. Millennia of existence in Iraq are erased in the name of three decades in Israel.
>
> (Shohat 2000: 289)

Ontological narratives, then, are dependent on and informed by the collective narratives in which they are situated. But they are also crucial for the elaboration and maintenance of these same narratives. In the first instance, shared narratives, the stories that are told and retold by numerous members of a society over a long period of time, provide the blueprints for ontological narratives, including the blueprints for the social roles and spaces that an individual can inhabit. Indeed, we are as constrained by these shared narratives as by concrete forms of oppression from which we might suffer on a daily basis. Slavery and apartheid were not just sets of concrete practices that prohibited a given individual at a particular point in time from leaving a geographical space or entering a physical area reserved for whites. They were also storied accounts that inflected the individual's own narrative of who they were and what constituted appropriate – or safe – behaviour on their part, given their place within a pre-existing collective narrative.

Collective narratives, or 'cultural macronarratives', as Hinchman and Hinchman (1997b: 121) call them, thus shape and constrain our personal stories, determining both their meanings and their possible outcomes. They are transmitted through a variety of channels, including (in modern times) television, cinema, literature, professional associations, educational establishments, and a variety of other outlets, as I explain in the section on public narratives on p. 33. At the same time, ontological narratives are by no means inconsequential for the elaboration and maintenance of shared narratives. Society as a whole has a considerable stake in the stories and roles we construct for ourselves, because personal narratives can enhance or undermine the narratives that underpin the social order and hence interfere with the smooth functioning of society. This is why, as Bakan (2004: 134) explains, dominant institutions in society have always 'established roles and identities for their subjects that meshed with their own institutional natures, needs and interests: God-fearing subjects for the church, lords and serfs for feudal orders, citizens for democratic governments'. In Goffman's terms, the interdependence between onto-logical and shared narratives is a function of the fact that 'societies everywhere, if they are to be societies, must mobilize their members as self-regulating participants in social encounters' (1967: 44).[3]

Shared narratives also require the polyvocality of numerous personal stories to gain currency and acceptance, to become 'normalized' into self-evident accounts of the world and hence escape scrutiny. As a good example of how collective narratives promoted by the social order require input from compatible personal narratives, we only need to remember that Germans under the Nazis and white South Africans under apartheid were both encouraged to narrate themselves as racially superior. Only unquestioning subscription by numerous individuals to the assumption of their own superiority (with all its accompanying historical, cultural and political detail) could sustain the collective narrative in each case. Similarly, Longinovic (2004: 4) argues that the political reality of the Balkans that triggered the 1999 NATO-led invasion of the region was not only 'normalized by the media story of history' but also by 'national subjects trained to accept yet another level of insecurity in the name of security, to tolerate military invasions in the name of human rights'. It is this willingness on the part of many individuals to bring their ontological narratives in line with specific collective narratives that sustains the latter and gives them their legitimacy and power. At the same time, personal narratives can be deliberately used to unsettle the social order. They can be 'rescued' and emphasized in order to resist dominant narratives, to elaborate an alternative narra-tive of the world. This is precisely what many feminists attempt to do by giving voice to neglected or suppressed accounts of the female experience of life, such accounts often being mediated through translation. It is also a strategy used by oral historians who attempt to rediscover history 'by rescuing from oblivion individuals who have previously been disregarded' (Reeves-Ellington 1999: 111).

As well as the social order or society as a whole, other individuals with whom we interact also have a stake in our personal narratives, and this too has political conse-quences. Novitz explains that

> there is an intimate connection between the ways in which people construe themselves and the ways in which they are likely to behave. ... It is because of this that we are often concerned enough to challenge the stories that people tell about themselves. We urge them to think again, and in giving them reasons for doing so, we attempt to subvert their sense of self. There is an intricate political process at work here: what I should like to call the politics of narrative identity whereby we assert and maintain our own interests not just by advancing a particular view of ourselves, but by undermining the views that others advance of themselves.

(1997: 146)

Our personal narratives are ultimately important for society and for the individuals we interact with because '[o]ntological narratives are used to define who we are; this in turn is a precondition for knowing what to do' (Somers and Gibson 1994: 61). The stories we tell ourselves guide the way we act and not just the way we think, and any action we take naturally impacts on those around us. At the same time, given that 'we are never more (and sometimes less) than the co-authors of our own narratives' (MacIntyre 1981: 199), the stories other people construct of us are vital for our physical and mental survival and inevitably shape our behaviour. The way others 'story' us can have very concrete implications for our material, professional, social and psychological well-being. It can enhance or destroy our career, make us feel good about ourselves or throw us into despair, improve our social standing or turn us into outcasts. And all this naturally impacts on our own developing narrative of who we are and how we relate to the world around us, on how we 'narrate' ourselves. In the end, we become 'the beneficiaries, victims, or playthings of the narratives that others create and push in our direction' (Novitz 1997: 154).

In the final analysis, we have to negotiate our way around the various incompatibilities or conflicts between our ontological narratives and those of other individuals with whom we share a social space, as well as incompatibilities with collective narratives, in order to be believed, respected, trusted – in short, to 'avoid "ontological abandonment"' (Hinchman and Hinchman 1997b: 121). For those who are suddenly transported into a very different cultural environment and find themselves having to negotiate a major conflict between their personal narratives and those in circulation in their new environment, this could lead to significant trauma. Ingram discusses the effects of this rupture as described in Eva Hoffman's *Lost in Translation* in terms of a negotiation 'between self and culture':

> There is no place for the Polish *Ewa* in the new Canadian context; however, becoming *Eva* calls into question the constructed, social nature of both these identities. Which, the question becomes for Hoffman, is the *real* one?
>
> (1996: 260; emphasis in original)

Interpreters who work with refugees and asylum seekers witness this type of conflict between the migrants' personal stories and the narratives of the receiving culture in very vivid terms (see, for example, Barsky 1993, 1996; Maryns 2005). Asylum seekers are generally offered very little room for negotiating a compromise between their ontological narrative and the institutional and public narratives of the host country. In order to '"construct" themselves as adequate claimants', which can mean the difference between life and death in many cases, they have to 'renounce their previous self and create, successfully or not, an "other" deemed appropriate for the cause' (Barsky 2005: 226). Although interpreters in the asylum-seeking process are explicitly instructed to 'translate exactly' what an applicant says (Inghilleri 2003: 257) and to refrain from 'interpreting' or adapting their story to make it intelligible within the narrative frameworks of the target community, research suggests that at least some interpreters, especially those who belong to the same community as the applicants, tend to 'improve on the applicants' testimonies', and 'give advice during the proceedings concerning the appropriate course of action' (Inghilleri 2003: 258). In other words, they actively attempt to narrow the gap between the personal and collective or institutional narrative.

Gergen and Gergen discuss three types of ontological narratives: the stability narrative portrays the individual's situation as stable, with little or no change over time; the progressive narrative depicts a pattern of change for the better; and the regressive narrative stresses a pattern of decline or change for the worse. They argue that the development of these narrative forms 'is favored by functional needs within the society. Stability narratives are favored by the common desire for the social world to appear orderly and predictable; progressive narratives offer the opportunity for people to see themselves and their environment as capable of improvement; and regressive narratives are not only entailed logically by the development of progressive narratives, but have an important motivational function in their own right'.

(Gergen and Gergen 1997: 175)

Translating and interpreting ontological narratives is often extremely challenging. One interpreter interviewed by the Access to Justice project team at the University of Durham, UK, described the impact of a child abuse case on her emotional well-being:

I used to want to be in tears nearly every night. It was terrible. … when he [deaf child] cried, I cried. When he shouted, I shouted. You know it's very very upsetting – very upsetting. It's one of the worst things I've ever done in my life. And it's awful because I had no-one to share it with.

(Brennan and Brown 1997: 62)

Interpreters at the Truth and Reconciliation trials that took place after the fall of apartheid in South Africa were similarly traumatized by their exposure to very painful ontological narratives of victims and the accompanying narratives of perpetrators:[4]

It has been a gruelling job of work that has taken a physical, mental and psychological toll. We have borne a heavy burden as we have taken onto ourselves the anguish, the awfulness, and the sheer evil of it all. The interpreters have, for instance, had the trauma of not just hearing or reading about the atrocities, but have had to speak in the first person as either a victim or the perpetrator,
They undressed me and opened a drawer and shoved my breast into the drawer which they then slammed shut on my nipple! [or] I drugged his coffee, then I shot him in the head. Then I burned his body. Whilst we were doing this, watching his body burn, we were enjoying a braai on the other side.

This extract from Item 87 of the Chairperson's Foreword to the Truth and Reconciliation Committee Report, Chapter 1, demonstrates the extent and nature of the interpreters' ordeal and suggests that ontological narratives can be among the most demanding and challenging to translate, and particularly to interpret.

3.2 Public narratives

Public narratives[5] are very similar to but not quite the same as what I referred to above as shared or collective narratives. 'Shared' or 'collective' narratives are loose terms that tend to be used outside any specific model. They refer vaguely to any type of narrative that has currency in a given community. Somers and Gibson, on the other hand, draw finer distinctions between public, conceptual and meta-narratives, as we will see below.

In Somers' (1992, 1997) and Somers and Gibson's (1994) model, public narratives are defined as stories elaborated by and circulating among social and institutional formations larger than the individual, such as the family,[6] religious or educational institution, the media, and the nation. Somers and Gibson do not mention the literary system, but literature of course constitutes one of the most powerful institutions for disseminating public narratives in any society. As Jones (2004: 715) explains in relation to the recent wars in Yugoslavia, 'the manipulation of literature often plays a crucial role in the process of ethno-national identity formation by generating "pseudo histories" that create or reinforce national mythologies'.

Somers (1992: 604) gives as examples of public narratives stories about 'American social mobility', the 'freeborn Englishman', and 'the emancipatory story of socialism'. A more recent example might be the numerous and competing public narratives of 11 September 2001, or the war on Iraq launched by the USA-led 'Coalition' in 2003: Who is responsible? Why did it happen? Could it have been avoided? How many died? and so on. Public narratives of 'Western democracy', 'Islamic fundamentalism', 'Christian fundamentalism' and 'gay rights' similarly circulate in many different versions. Individuals in any society either buy into the official or semi-official versions of such public narratives or dissent from them. They dissent when a given public narrative, a narrative elaborated by any group to which they belong (family, religious group, professional group, and so on), 'include[s] aspects which the person as a member of the group cannot easily accommodate in their own story of identity' (Whitebrook 2001: 145).

Public narratives circulating in any society can and do change significantly, sometimes within the span of a few years, even months. For example, Bruner (1997: 269) describes how the dominant public narrative of and about Native Americans in the United States changed quite quickly, 'within a decade after World War II'. In the 1930s and 1940s, the narrative depicted a glorious past, a chaotic present, and a future that necessitated assimilation. The current narrative, by contrast, depicts the past as exploitation, the present as a resistance movement, and consequently the future as ethnic resurgence (Bruner 1997). The first, acculturation narrative, according to Bruner, depicts what it calls the Indian as a romantic, exotic Other, whereas the resistance narrative depicts the Indian as victimized. Which variant of a narrative persists and acquires currency is of course largely a question of the power structures in which the various narrative versions are embedded as well as the determination with which their proponents promote and defend them.

Public narratives about specific individuals who become symbols of a people, a movement, or an ideology can also change drastically over time. Nelson Mandela was widely depicted as a terrorist in the 1960s through to the late 1980s for advocating the use of violent tactics to end apartheid in South Africa. As the international anti-apartheid movement gained strength in the 1970s and 1980s, he became a symbol of resistance, an international hero, and was finally awarded the Nobel Peace Prize in 1993.

Studies of advertising offer numerous examples of the subtle ways in which public narratives are adapted and mediated across cultural boundaries. Munday (2004) discusses the L'Oréal cosmetics campaign, which changed its well-known slogan in 2002 from 'Because I'm worth it' to 'Because you're worth it' in an attempt to soften the impact of the public narrative of free, democratic societies being made up of autonomous, independent individuals with unique attributes. The initial slogan, apparently 'invented as a declaration of "empowerment" by a female American executive of the company' (Munday 2004: 209), had been retained in French, German, Italian and Spanish 'but there had been cultural problems in China, where it was seen as too individualistic, and in France, where it was considered to focus overly on monetary value' (Munday 2004: 209).

Public narratives are also adapted domestically within the same culture in response to evolving reconfigurations of the political and social space. Naudé (2005) offers fascinating examples of the way in which earlier translations of the Bible into Afrikaans participated in sanctioning apartheid in response to the Afrikaner's 'conviction of being God's chosen people and thereby merging their own national identity with that of Old Testament Israel – a people separated from the rest of the nations' (Naudé 2005: 27). The first complete translation (1933) and its revision (1953) stressed the diversity of nations and species and God's intention to separate them. An alternative translation published in 1983, shortly before the Dutch Reformed Church in South Africa retracted the biblical justification for apartheid in 1986, played down the issue of racial and national diversity, as in the following examples (Naudé 2005: 33–4; relevant items highlighted in bold):

Example 1

1933/1953 translation
… sodat die heilige geslag hom met die volke van die lande vermeng het.
[… in order that this holy generation does not intermingle with the **peoples of the countries.**]

1983 translation
Hulle het hierdie volk hom laat vermeng met heidene.
[They allowed this nation to intermingle with the **heathen** (= non-believers).]

Example 2

1933/1953 translation
… dat ons vreemde vroue uit die volke van die land getrou het.
[… that we married foreign women from the **peoples of the land.**]

1983 translation

... ons het met vreemde vroue getrou, vroue uit die heidennasies.

[... we married foreign women, women from the **heathen nations**.]

Example 3

1933/1953 translation

Julle mag julle dogters nie aan hulle seuns gee ...

[You shall not give your daughters to **their sons** ...]

1983 translation

Julle sal julle dogters nie laat trou met die heidene se seuns nie ...

[You shall not allow your daughters to marry the **sons of the heathen** ...]

As Naudé explains, the intermarriage terminology of the earlier version, 'which could be misunderstood as functioning within the political or judicial sphere', is replaced with religious terminology in the 1983 version, thus making it clear that '[i]ntermarriage is not forbidden among nations but between believers and non-believers' (2005: 33).

Just as individuals might have to negotiate the gap between their ontological narratives and the public and institutional narratives of a host country in the context of the asylum-seeking process, they also have to reconcile the public narratives of their own communities with those of the receiving culture. Inghilleri explains that

> While power relations in the asylum context are historically and politically distinctive depending on the country of origin, ... [an] attempt is made to present applicants' accounts of persecution based on the socio-historical conditions of their countries. In asylum interviews, it is fairly typical to hear comments such as, 'This is what rape means over there, society does not accept it', 'In my country, the police cannot be trusted', 'In my country, there is no social order'. On the other hand, applicants may also present rationales for particular actions based on the perceived values of the *host country* in a 'transcultural' gesture of awareness and assimilation of their 'strategic' relevance.
>
> (2005: 78; emphasis in original)

Officials of the Home Office (the British institution which processes and adjudicates asylum-seeking claims) in turn bring their own public narratives to bear on assessing each case, as is evident from the fact that they preface many of the statements with which they challenge claimants' narratives with expressions such as 'It is hard to believe that ... ' and 'It seems reasonable to assume ... ' (Inghilleri 2005: 79).

Literary works and films that threaten to undermine domestic public narratives are often denounced and may even be banned. Dennett (2002: 101) explains that Hemingway's *A Farewell to Arms* was considered anti-Italian and blacklisted in Fascist Italy because it depicted Italy's defeat at Caporetto in World War I. Erich

Maria Remarque's anti-war novel *All Quiet on the Western Front* and Roger Martin Du Gard's *Les Thibault* were similarly censored because of their pacifist messages (Dennett 2002: 101–2). Similar examples can be found in every tradition, and every historical period, though the forms that censorship takes may vary, some being more subtle than others. Omission of blasphemous and taboo references in translation, whether a result of institutional or self-censorship, may similarly be interpreted as an attempt to protect or at least avoid being implicated in undermining dominant public narratives. Indeed, the notion of blasphemy itself, as well as what counts as blasphemous, are both by-products of specific religious narratives of the world, whether Christian, Muslim, Jewish or Buddhist.[7]

Translators and interpreters play a crucial role in disseminating public narratives within their own communities and ensuring that all members of a society, including recent migrants, are socialized into the view of the world promoted in these shared stories. But translators may also be '[l]oyal to dissident ideologies internal to a culture, or to affiliations and agendas external to a culture' (Tymoczko 2003: 201), and this may lead them to position themselves differently in relation to domestic public narratives. For example, in 2004 the Israeli activist group Gush Shalom translated one of its brochures, *Truth Against Truth* (Figure 4), from Hebrew into Russian specifically to appeal to the Russian community in Israel. This was an attempt to 'break ... the national consensus', in other words to challenge internal Israeli narratives about the history of the region and the causes of the current conflict. Gush Shalom's announcement of this initiative read as follows:

> On the eve of Yom Kippur, 60 thousand copies of the brochure 'Truth Against Truth' in Russian will be distributed as an insert in the Russian-language papers 'Vesti' and 'Globus'. Until now, this new brochure has appeared only in Hebrew and English (and has been translated abroad in German and Dutch, with the Arab edition to appear in the coming weeks). It throws completely new light on the Israeli–Palestinian conflict, its origins and phases. The Russian version is an exact copy of the Hebrew original, both in content and form. It, too, bears on its cover the warning: 'Caution! This is a subversive text. It undermines the very foundations on which the National Consensus is based!'[8]

 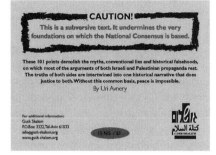

Figure 4 Truth against Truth. Front and back cover of Gush Shalom brochure (English translation)

Translators and interpreters also participate in circulating domestic public narratives beyond their national boundaries, either in an effort to gain a wider following for those narratives or to 'expose' and challenge them by appealing to a foreign audience with a different view of the world. An example of the first is a text entitled 'The Russian–Chechen Tragedy: The Way to Peace and Democracy', which is posted on the website of the Ministry of Foreign Affairs of the Chechen Republic of Ichkeria. The text is posted in English, Russian, French, Spanish, Italian and German. The English translation starts:

> In September 1999, disregarding the lessons of the long and brutal history of the Russian–Chechen conflict, Russian forces reinvaded Chechnya. Since then, the last three years of military impasse and the total devastation in Chechnya have proved what had been obvious to many from the very beginning – that there can be no military solution to the Russian–Chechen conflict. A military solution simply does not exist. The conflict is about a political dispute and therefore can only be resolved by a comprehensive political solution.[9]

This domestic Chechen narrative is articulated and promoted in the languages of other communities in order to compete with alternative Russian narratives that present terrorism in Chechnya as the root of the current conflict.

Numerous examples of translations designed to contest domestic public narratives by challenging them abroad can be found on the website of the Moscow Human Rights News Agency Prima, which distributes news on human rights violations, principally in Russia and the former Soviet Union. Prima's editor-in-chief is a former political prisoner. All news, articles and press releases are translated and published in English, clearly for the benefit of an international rather than domestic audience. For example, one article published on the Prima site, dated 21 February 2005, is entitled 'The Russian Prison'.[10] Written by Pavel Lyuzakov (Remand prison IZ–77/5) and translated by Michael Garrood, it challenges a particular public narrative that depicts current Russian prison authorities as abstaining from using torture, lifting restrictions on the purchase of food in prison shops, and providing televisions and fridges in cells. The article challenges this with an alternative narrative: only remand prisons that the West already knows about, such as Petrovka, have been turned into European-style prisons. The real prisons, such as 'Isolator Five; officially known as Establishment 77/5, located on Vyborg street in Moscow' not only remain 'filthy', 'cold Soviet' prisons but are even worse in terms of the level of oppression and arbitrariness of treatment that the guards inflict on prisoners.

Translators are also becoming increasingly involved in articulating public narratives of groups located outside their own domestic setting altogether. They usually do so because they believe in what these groups stand for and subscribe to their narrative of the world, although it is also true that some (student) translators volunteer to translate such texts in order to gain experience in the field, without being particularly committed to the narratives promoted by the groups in question. The 'Editorial Collective' that produced the book *Zapatistas! Documents of the New Mexican Revolution* (1994) clearly subscribe to the narrative(s) elaborated in this specific text and by the Zapatista movement more broadly. In the Preface, they describe themselves thus:

> This book project was conceived of and coordinated by the Editorial Collective. We are Zapatista solidarity activists, revolutionaries, workers, dreamers. We work for wages and we also work for ourselves. We pay too much rent and don't get enough sleep. We are inspired by the vision of the Zapatistas because we, too, dream of a better world.

The work of this group offers a good example of the involvement of translators in elaborating public narratives relating to foreign rather than domestic constituencies. The original Spanish texts of *Zapatistas!* 'were "farmed out" to volunteers all over the internet', who then produced the English text. The translators are all acknowledged by name, and the Preface also includes an explicit note that indicates awareness of the centrality of translation and translators in disseminating this public narrative beyond Mexico:

> A note on translation:
> We have done our best to create a book that is both easy to read for English speakers and true to the original Spanish. There are several language and translation issues that make this difficult. This book was translated by a large number of volunteers. This effort made the publication of this book possible, but it made consistency in the translations difficult. We think that it is important that the same words be translated in the same way each time, and all of the translations have been checked thoroughly for consistency. Another difficulty in translation was the original Spanish. Most of the Zapatistas are not native Spanish speakers. Their Spanish is sometimes awkward, and the concepts that they use are not always clearly expressed in Spanish, and are even harder to translate into English. Readers should be aware that there are many possible translations for some words, and should keep this in mind as they read the text.

Several of the difficulties outlined in this note are regularly experienced by professional translators working in a variety of contexts. They include the question of terminological consistency and the linguistic quality of the source text. The Zapatistas are mostly native speakers of Quechua, not Spanish, but using Spanish allows them to spread their message more widely.

In sum, then, public narratives may initially be elaborated within a narrow, domestic context (the immediate family, workplace, city or country), but their survival and further elaboration depends on them being articulated in other dialects, languages, and non-domestic contexts. Whether the motivation is commercial or ideological, translators and interpreters play a decisive role in both articulating *and* contesting the full range of public narratives circulating within and around any society at any moment in time.

3.3 Conceptual (disciplinary) narratives

As social theorists, Somers and Gibson (1994: 62) define *conceptual narratives* as 'concepts and explanations that we construct as social researchers', and go on to argue that

> [t]he conceptual challenge that narrativity poses is to develop a social analytic vocabulary that can accommodate the contention that social life, social organizations, social action, and social identities are narratively, that is, temporally and relationally constructed through both ontological and public narratives.
>
> (1994: 63)

However, it seems to me that it is both reasonable and productive to extend this definition to include *disciplinary* narratives in any field of study. Thus, conceptual narratives may be more broadly defined for our current purposes as the stories and explanations that scholars in any field elaborate for themselves and others about their object of inquiry. Ewick and Silbey (1995: 201) explain that in terms of scholarly research, narratives can be 'the object of inquiry, the method of inquiry, or the product of inquiry (the researchers' representation)' and, like Somers and Gibson, they focus on the scholarly discipline of sociology. They go on to map these three distinctions onto three categories: 'sociology *of* narrative', 'sociology *through* narrative', and 'sociology *as* narrative'. Conceptual or disciplinary narratives, as I have opted to define them here, correspond to the third distinction drawn by Ewick and Silbey: narrative as the product of inquiry, the representations elaborated by researchers.[11]

Every discipline, including translation studies, elaborates and thrives on its own set of conceptual narratives. A nineteenth-century scientific theory linking the environment to some hierarchy of racial superiority is one such conceptual narrative, and so is Darwin's theory of natural selection. Some conceptual narratives can have considerable impact on the world at large, as in the case of Cuvier and Darwin, while others remain limited in scope to the immediate community of scholars in the relevant field. A good example of a conceptual narrative in the humanities that exercised considerable influence beyond its immediate disciplinary boundaries is James Mill's *History of British India*, published in 1817. As Niranjana (1990) explains, this *History* relies on the translations of William Jones, Wilkins, Halhed and others to construct an image of the Indians (whether Hindus or Muslims) as insincere and untruthful. 'Throughout the book', Niranjana tells us, 'Mill uses again and again in connection with the "Hindus" the adjectives "wild", "barbaric", "savage" and "rude", thus forming by sheer force of repetition a counter-discourse to the Orientalist hypothesis of an ancient civilisation' (1990: 776). Niranjana goes on to quote the German Indologist Max Mueller as stating that Mill's *History* 'was responsible for some of the greatest misfortunes that had happened to India' (Niranjana 1990: 779). Here, then, is a concrete example of a disciplinary narrative that managed to penetrate the public space and shape public narratives during a specific period of history.

More recent and equally pernicious conceptual narratives that have had considerable impact beyond their disciplinary boundaries include Samuel Huntington's *The Clash of Civilizations and the Remaking of World Order* (1996; see also Huntington 1993) and Raphael Patai's *The Arab Mind* (1973). Samuel Huntington, political scientist at Harvard University, classified world civilizations into distinct groups[12] with 'inherent' cultural characteristics (mostly conflicting with 'good' American values) and predicted that culture would replace ideology as the principal cause of conflict in the twenty-first century. 'Culture', in this narrative, is a non-negotiable given:[13]

> cultural characteristics and differences are less mutable and hence less easily compromised and resolved than political and economic ones. In the former Soviet Union, communists can become democrats, the rich can become poor and the poor rich, but Russians cannot become Estonians and Azeris cannot become Armenians. In class and ideological conflicts, the question was 'Which side are you on?' and people could and did choose sides and change sides. In conflicts between civilizations, the question is 'What are you?'. That is a given that cannot be changed.
>
> (Huntington 1993: 27)

Huntington's narrative 'places the US-led west at the center of political domination' (Longinovic 2004: 4). In a more recent book, *Who Are We? The Challenges to America's National Identity* (2004), Huntington looks at American society through that same neo-conservative cultural prism and elaborates a narrative of an internal clash of civilizations, arguing that the new war is between the country's white majority and its growing Hispanic population. Nelson (2002: 13) points out that '[w]here elites employ a discourse that speaks of challenges and conflict with an *other*, this ... feeds and accompanies violence'. Indeed, in the abstract of his 1993 article on the same theme published in the influential *Foreign Affairs* journal, Huntington explicitly states that '[i]n this emerging era of cultural conflict the United States must forge alliances with similar cultures and spread its values wherever possible. With *alien* civilizations the West must be accommodating if possible, but *confrontational* if necessary' (Huntington 1993; emphasis added).[14]

Huntington's *The Clash of Civilizations* has been a major reference point for the Bush administration, and the narratives it spawned have been directly linked to the official public narratives of 9/11, the wars on Afghanistan and Iraq, and even before all these to the war in the Balkans. Smith (1997: 206) describes how foreign diplomats and politicians depicted the problems in Yugoslavia in the 1990s 'as a matter of the unfathomable mysteries of the Balkans, where hot blooded people went in for ancient hatreds' and 'some Balkan leaders saw themselves fighting on the front lines in a "clash of civilizations"'. In a separate endnote, Smith comments thus on this Huntington-inspired expression: 'The phrase was coined by Huntington (1993) to encapsulate the thesis that future conflict will be defined by irreducible differences between civilizations. Its use in the Balkans to justify ethnocide is a good example of why it is so pernicious' (1997: 212).

It is therefore somewhat disappointing to see Huntington's work and conceptual apparatus quoted superficially and uncritically in the literature on translation, where it is deployed as part of the suspect but popular metaphor of 'in-betweenness' (see Tymoczko 2003 for an excellent critique of this metaphor). An otherwise astute scholar, Wolf (2000) incorporates Huntington's thesis in her work as though it is just another academic theory, and without alerting the reader to its implications:

> It seems that what is at stake is the assumption that Western cultures are based on exclusion and delimitation, that they draw a line between themselves and other cultures, peoples, races and religions. Consequently, they tend to represent their authority primarily through binary oppositions such as the ones mentioned above [us and them, East and West, First and Third World] or others like self/ other, colonizer/colonized, developed/underdeveloped. *The phenomena of visible and invisible 'clashes of civilization' (Huntington 1996), however, result in different forms of acculturation, syncretism, hybridization or pidginization.* A dramatic turn in the representation of the Other that goes far beyond the Manichean division of self and other is being taken. Advocates of this 'turn' in cultural studies recognize the danger in simply reversing these dichotomies, and therefore look to deconstruct them by analyzing the complex processes involved in cultural contact and its various implications, and by emphasizing the concept of 'difference' in the formation of cultural identity. Thus, the key concept in cultural studies is *hybridity*.
>
> (2000: 129; emphasis added)

Huntington's narrative hardly predicts or indeed tolerates hybridization or acculturation. Later in the same article, Wolf (2000: 138) states that '[w]hereas Bhabha's [third] space is a natural creation born of the more or less violent "clash of civilizations," the feminist notion of *intertext* is a conscious creation of a space-in-between'. The use of 'natural' here further suggests an uncritical – if no doubt well-intentioned – acceptance of Huntington's highly pernicious narrative, in spite of Wolf's final plea for the feminist concept of *intertext* on the basis that 'The "clash of civilizations" concept is substituted by a concept of harmony created in the space-in-between, which views voice, sound and rhythm as the main features of writing in the feminine' (2000: 139).

The abstract of a paper presented at a recent translation studies conference in Maastricht (May 2005) seems to recycle Huntington's narrative in an even less critical manner (emphasis in original):

> Translation all too often involves having to mediate between two cultures. The wider apart the two cultures involved, the greater will be the problems to be encountered in translating from one to the other. What is not always recognized though is the fact that, in addition to the familiar gulf between the two cultures, the translator is also often called upon to bridge the ideological chasm separating the two cultures. In fact, cultural differences tend to take over from ideological differences and become practically indistinguishable

from them, especially when there is a clash of civilizations. Or, rather, as Samuel Huntington, who coined the phrase *clash of civilizations*, predicted, ideological differences metamorphose into cultural differences as civilizations enter into a collision course.[15]

So much for the Huntington narrative and its influence within and outside the field of translation. Raphael Patai, who died in 1996, was a renowned cultural anthropologist and Director of Research at the Theodor Herzl Institute in New York. Interestingly, from our point of view as translation studies scholars, Patai was also a translator. One reviewer describes his book *Arab Folktales from Palestine and Israel* (1988) – which consists of his translation, with extensive commentary, of 28 tales from the region – as '[a] meticulous rendering of the Arabic text of folktales into equivalent English expressions which provide the exuberant meaning implied in the Arabic text'.[16] Following the Abu Ghraib torture scandals in April and May 2004, Seymour Hersh of the *New Yorker* described Patai's *The Arab Mind* as 'the bible of the neocons on Arab behavior. In their [the neocons'] discussions ... two themes emerged – ... one, that Arabs only understand force and, two, that the biggest weakness of Arabs is shame and humiliation' (Hersh 2004).[17] Another article in *The Guardian* reported a professor at a US military college describing Patai's book as 'probably the single most popular and widely read book on the Arabs in the US military' and went on to confirm that it is 'even used as a textbook for officers at the JFK special warfare school in Fort Bragg' (Whitaker 2004). Again, we see that narratives elaborated within the confines of academia can and do permeate public discourse and can further sustain long-term meta-narratives, the fourth type of narrative proposed by Somers and Gibson (see 3.4 on p. 44).

A final example of a highly influential conceptual narrative from another domain is what is known in the advertising world as the 'Nag Factor', 'a brilliant new marketing strategy that takes manipulation of children to the extreme' (Bakan 2004: 119). As Bakan explains, advertisers who sell products to adults through their children (for example, packaging a toy with a 24-pack of Labatt Blue beer) rely on conceptual narratives elaborated for them by child psychologists who 'developed a scientific breakdown of different kinds of nags that children use and the differential impacts they have on different kinds of parents' (2004: 119). These narratives describe a world in which children can nag in two main ways: 'with persistence', constantly whining about wanting a certain product without explaining why, or 'with importance', giving strong reasons for wanting the product. Parents on the other hand fall into four categories. 'Bare necessities' parents are well-off but not responsive to their children; they require 'nagging with importance'. The other three groups are 'kids' pals', 'indulgers', and 'conflicted' parents. Kids' pals are younger parents who buy products such as computer games for their children and themselves; 'indulgers' are working parents who buy products for their children to make up for the fact that they don't spend much time with them; and 'conflicted' parents are usually single mothers who claim that they don't like indulging their children but do it anyway. All three categories are amenable to nagging with persistence. Bakan, like many others, stresses that exploiting children in advertising campaigns has a negative effect not just on parents but also on the children themselves.

As with public narratives, translators and interpreters can choose to accept and promote or contest and challenge a given conceptual narrative. St André (2004) describes how Sir George Staunton's English translation of the Qing penal code in 1810 argued directly with James Barrow's claims in his *Travels in China*, published in 1806, that the Chinese are 'fundamentally unjust both in their dealings with each other and with foreigners' (St André 2004: 4), 'sell their children into slavery', 'practice homosexuality', and 'smoke opium and gamble' (2004: 5). Barrow had consistently made references to the Chinese penal code in arguing that it is the injustice of that code that, among other things, 'encourages people to indifference and cruelty toward the unfortunate' (2004: 5). Staunton's translation, by contrast, 'strives to present the Chinese legal code as something comprehensible, reasonable, and just' (2004: 5), produced by a series of Chinese emperors who were '[c]ompassionate, principled' and who 'watched over and guided the development of the legal code so that it continued to meet society's evolving need for justice' (2004: 6). In addition to a sympathetic introduction which stressed that 'the Chinese are people just like us' and that 'any extravagant praise or blame is due to foreigners misunderstanding them' (2004: 6), Staunton's interventions included adding footnotes that directly refuted Barrow's accusations, rearranging and editing tables that detailed types of punishment, fines and degrees of mourning in order to make them more comprehensible to an English reader, and introducing various subtle changes to the syntax and lexis that cumulatively served to make the laws sound more positive and universal.

Interestingly St André explains that in his six-volume *History of British India*, which I discussed briefly on p. 39, James Mill's 'main sources of information concerning interpretations of China (which he uses for purposes of comparison with India)' were James Barrow's *Travels in China* and his *Life of Lord Macartney* (2004: 27). Mill referred to Staunton's translation only once. The 'final irony', St André explains, 'was that Staunton's translation was used by the British as part of the legal apparatus for governing Chinese residents of Hong Kong after 1844' (2004: 27–8). Dennett, quoting the historian John Diggins, provides another interesting example of the unpredictability of the effect and use of translation, this time in the context of Fascist Italy:

> Fascist authorities deliberately published John Steinbeck's *Grapes of Wrath*, assuming its depressing agrarian scenes would demonstrate the virtues of the Corporate State to Italian intellectuals. But the strategy backfired; instead, Italians came to admire a country which allowed authors like Steinbeck and Lillian Smith to write such caustic social criticism.
>
> (Dennett 2002: 114)

Whatever the intentions of a translator or interpreter, there is no guarantee that their work would not ultimately be interpreted 'against the grain', because the uptake and meaning of public and conceptual narratives are always influenced by the specificities of their production *and* reception.

3.4 Meta- (master) narratives

Somers and Gibson (1994: 61) define *meta-* (or *master*) *narratives* as narratives 'in which we are embedded as contemporary actors in history ... Progress, Decadence, Industrialization, Enlightenment, etc.'. Somers (1992: 605) explains that meta-narratives can also be 'the epic dramas of our time: Capitalism vs. Communism, the Individual vs. Society, Barbarism/Nature vs. Civility'.[18] Although he does not write from a narrative perspective, Bourdieu (1998) discusses (and contests) another meta-narrative in which the entire contemporary world is embedded, namely the narrative of economic rationality and what he calls the 'myth' of globalization.

Meta- or master narratives are not to be confused with 'masterplots', defined by Abbott (2002: 42) as 'stories that we tell over and over in myriad forms and that connect vitally with our deepest values, wishes, and fears'. As Abbott explains, masterplots 'undergrid' master narratives, 'are much more skeletal and adaptable' and 'can recur in narrative after narrative' (2002: 43). For example, the well-known narrative of Cinderella has many variants in different cultures, but they all share basic constituent events as well as themes such as injustice and reward; these articulate a masterplot which can be evoked in other narratives and contexts. The notion of 'masterplot' in this sense is closer to that of 'canonical script' and is an important element of *particularity*, one of the features of narrativity I discuss in Chapter 5 (see section 5.1 on p. 78).

A Klee painting named 'Angelus Novus' shows an angel looking as though he is about to move away from something he is fixedly contemplating. His eyes are staring, his mouth is open, his wings are spread. This is how one pictures the angel of history. His face is turned toward the past. Where we perceive a chain of events, he sees one single catastrophe which keeps piling wreckage upon wreckage and hurls it in front of his feet. The angel would like to stay, awaken the dead, and make whole what has been smashed. But a storm is blowing from Paradise; it has got caught in his wings with such violence that the angel can no longer close them. This storm irresistibly propels him into the future to which his back is turned, while the pile of debris before him grows skyward. This storm is what we call progress.

(Benjamin 1999: 249)

To return to Somers and Gibson's notion of meta- or master narrative, it is relatively easy to designate something such as Progress, which would have started out as a simple public narrative, as a meta- or master narrative. We know now, with hindsight, that the narrative has persisted for decades and that the lives of ordinary individuals across the planet have been influenced by it. The Cold War is, perhaps, another such narrative. Even today it continues to have some impact on our lives and on international relations. Thanks to the power of media, Hollywood and Western academia (from James Bond movies to the endless books documenting and analysing every potentially relevant detail), the Cold War narrative, in its many varieties, also travelled far beyond its immediate geographical settings.

An obvious potential candidate for a meta-narrative today is the public narrative of the 'War on Terror', which is aggressively sustained and promoted through a myriad of channels across the entire world, thus rapidly acquiring the status of a super-narrative that cuts across geographical and national boundaries and directly impacts the lives of every one of us, in every sector of society. The choice of *terror* rather than *terrorism* is significant here[19] and offers a good example of the discursive work required for the successful circulation and adoption of narratives in general and meta-narratives in particular. 'Terrorism' refers to one or more incidents that involve violence, with localized and containable impact. 'Terror', on the other hand, is a state of mind, one that can rapidly spread across boundaries and encompass all in its grip. It may be that a narrative must have this type of temporal and physical breadth, as well as sense of inevitability or inescapability, to qualify as a meta- or master narrative. *Terror* indexes these features much better than *terrorism*.

Like other types of narrative, meta-narratives can exist in different versions and are of course open to contestation. This applies even to pervasive and abstract meta-narratives such as those of Progress, Enlightenment and Modernity. Many have argued that 'the idea of progress is one of the most dangerous vestiges of the Enlightenment project because it presumes we can move forward towards a space free from power and domination' whereas 'the march of "progress" has also introduced the gulags, the holocaust, environmental degradation and a frenzied nuclear age' (Fleming 2004: 42).

An interesting question, and one that Somers and Gibson do not address, is how a meta-narrative comes to enjoy the currency it does over considerable stretches of time and across extensive geographical boundaries. Is a certain level of dominance of the community that elaborates a particular public narrative a prerequisite for that narrative's growth into a global meta-narrative? The meta-narrative of the Cold War, for example, like the meta-narrative of the War on Terror, was essentially an invention of the American political elite, soon to be followed by other political elites across the globe. Its global circulation and reach required the kind of economic and cultural muscle that only a super power could muster. Hollywood, a major instrument in elaborating this particular meta-narrative, is a multi-billion-dollar industry.

Political and economic dominance may indeed be the prime factor determining the survival and circulation of political meta-narratives, but what about other types of meta-narrative? How did the Christian, Muslim or Buddhist narratives all come to occupy such a central and enduring position in the history of humanity? Today, at least, Muslim countries have little or no political power, and yet the meta-narrative of Islam probably has wider currency than any other religious narrative, with hundreds of millions of followers worldwide.

Alexander (2002) offers an extremely detailed analysis of the complex array of factors that participated in turning the Holocaust into what we might call a meta-narrative. From being initially 'reported to contemporaries as a war story, nothing less but nothing more' (2002: 17), the element of evil in this historical narrative became so heavily weighted that 'the Holocaust became the dominant symbolic representation of evil in the late twentieth century' (2002: 5) and 'the trauma of the Jewish people' became 'a trauma for all humankind' (2002: 29). One factor in this process was institutional: 'the means of symbolic production were not controlled by a victorious postwar Nazi regime' (2002: 11) and institutional carriers such as the journal *Holocaust and Genocide Studies* actively promoted the new narrative.[20] But in addition to describing the institutional and power structures that enabled this process to take shape, Alexander also offers a fascinating model of cultural trauma that can help explain the elaboration and spread of meta-narratives in general. This model acknowledges that 'no trauma interprets itself' and that all traumatic experience is filtered 'emotionally, cognitively, and morally' through an interpretive grid (2002: 10). The model suggests that any narrative restricted to a specific and situated set of events cannot turn into a meta-narrative. The events depicted have to be heavily weighted in relation to some value such as evil or danger or goodness. But they also have to be configured within a timeless frame, one that does not signal the possibility of a resolution – at least not within our lifetime. As Alexander explains, what we now know as the Holocaust was initially cast within a progressive narrative that blocked the possibility of universalizing the trauma because it continued to link it to a specific historical episode rather than treat it as 'a sacred-evil, an evil that recalled a trauma of such enormity and horror that it had to be radically set apart from the world and all of its other traumatizing events' (Alexander 2002: 27). The 'ascending progressive narrative' was a story of 'redeeming Nazism's victims by creating a progressive and democratic world order' (2002: 29). The Holocaust achieved the status of meta-narrative (in our terms) when

> In place of the progressive story, … there began to emerge the narrative of tragedy. The endpoint of a narrative defines its telos. In the new tragic under-standing of the Jewish mass murder, suffering, not progress, became the telos toward which the narrative was aimed.
>
> (2002: 30)

Alexander goes on to explain that '[t]his transcendental status, this separation from the specifics of any particular time or space, provided the basis for psychological identification on an unprecedented scale' (2002: 30).

The same factors that Alexander describes in such detail in relation to the Holocaust may well be at play in determining the transformation of any narrative into a meta-narrative. Perhaps, as in the case of the Holocaust, a story becomes a meta-narrative when there is 'no "getting beyond" it, when there is 'only the possibility of returning to it: not transcendence but catharsis' (2002: 30).

Another issue worth exploring is the way in which a longstanding, established meta-narrative may be used to lend weight and psychological salience to a developing public or meta-narrative. Neo-conservatives in the American administration repeatedly invoked religious narratives to portray the so-called War on Terror as a war between the Judeo-Christian and Muslim worlds. Much has already been said and written about George W. Bush's use of the term 'crusade' in statements such as 'This crusade, this war on terrorism' shortly after the attacks on New York in 2001. Lt Gen William G. Boykin, Deputy Undersecretary of Defense for Intelligence, similarly announced before a religious congregation in Oregon in 2003 that Muslim extremists hate Americans 'because we're a Christian nation, because our foundation and our roots are Judeo-Christian' (CBS News 2004).

The effects of invoking established meta-narratives, with their own specific histories, to promote new ones can never be predicted, because these histories can release different associations and details in the minds of one's immediate audience as well as the opponents that the evoked meta-narrative is meant to subdue or discredit. The Judeo-Christian vs. Muslim war narrative, including the narrative of the Crusades, inevitably revives narratives of 'jihad', but it may also recall and unleash more specific details. For example, it is interesting to ponder the link between the shocking practice of decapitating hostages in Iraq following the US-led invasion in 2003 and a similar practice by the crusaders over a thousand years ago, where they used to sever the heads of Muslim fighters and use them as missiles, catapulting them over the walls of Jerusalem. Similarly, our minds can easily begin to compare accounts of the massacre that took place in Jerusalem during the First Crusade with accounts of the events in Fallujah in 2004 once the religious and specifically Crusade-related meta-narrative is invoked. Here is an example of an account of the Christian entrance into Jerusalem, by one of the crusaders:

> But now that our men had possession of the walls and towers, wonderful sights were to be seen. Some of our men … cut off the heads of their enemies; others shot them with arrows, so that they fell from the towers; others tortured them longer by casting them into the flames. Piles of heads, hands, and feet were to be seen in the streets of the city. It was necessary to pick one's way over the bodies of men and horses. But these were small matters compared to what happened at the Temple of Solomon [where] … men rode in blood up to their knees and bridle reins. Indeed it was a just and splendid judgment of God that this place should be filled with the blood of the unbelievers, since it had suffered so long from their blasphemies.
>
> (Wallbank *et al.* 1976: 359–60)

Here is a similar eyewitness account of Fallujah on 25 December 2004. This one is not by an invader but by a member of the community on the receiving end of the violence:

> It [Fallujah] was completely devastated, destruction everywhere. It looked like a city of ghosts. Falluja used to be a modern city; now there was nothing. We spent the day going through the rubble that had been the centre of the city; I didn't see a single building that was functioning.

The Americans had put a white tape across the roads to stop people wandering into areas that they still weren't allowed to enter. I remembered the market from before the war, when you couldn't walk through it because of the crowds. Now all the shops were marked with a cross, meaning that they had been searched and secured by the US military. But the bodies, some of them civilians and some of them insurgents, were still rotting inside.

There were dead dogs everywhere in this area, lying in the middle of the streets. Reports of rabies in Falluja had reached Baghdad ...

(Fadhil 2005)

Millions across the world will have read and will continue to read such accounts of the destruction of Fallujah, whether in the original or in translation. Given that the narrative of the Crusades has already been publicly invoked by the invading power, and that the protagonists remain largely the same (the Christian West vs. the Muslim East), echoes of the religious and political narratives of the past will no doubt continue to reverberate in the minds of many.

Finally, it goes without saying that narratives do not travel across linguistic and cultural boundaries, and certainly do not develop into global meta-narratives, without the direct involvement of translators and interpreters. The above eyewitness account published in *The Guardian*, for instance, is by Ali Fadhil, an Iraqi doctor. It is likely that he did not recall or write all this in English, and that somewhere along the line the account has been extensively mediated by one or more translators, even though none is acknowledged in this case. It is also worth pointing out that growing numbers of professional and non-professional translators and interpreters are now actively setting out to elaborate alternative narratives that can challenge the oppressive public and meta-narratives of our time, an issue I have taken up at length elsewhere (Baker, in press, a).

Core references

Somers, Margaret (1992) 'Narrativity, Narrative Identity, and Social Action: Rethinking English Working-Class Formation', *Social Science History* 16(4): 591–630.

Somers, Margaret (1994) 'The Narrative Construction of Identity: A Relational and Network Approach', *Theory and Society* 23(5): 605–49.

Somers, Margaret (1997) 'Deconstructing and Reconstructing Class Formation Theory: Narrativity, Relational Analysis, and Social Theory', in John R. Hall (ed.) *Reworking Class*, Ithaca NY and London: Cornell University Press, 73–105.

Somers, Margaret R. and Gloria D. Gibson (1994) 'Reclaiming the Epistemological "Other": Narrative and the Social Constitution of Identity', in Craig Calhoun (ed.) *Social Theory and the Politics of Identity*, Cambridge MA and Oxford: Blackwell, 37–99.

Whitebrook, Maureen (2001) *Identity, Narrative and Politics*, London and New York: Routledge.

Further reading

Alexander, Jeffrey C. (2002) 'On the Social Construction of Moral Universals: The "Holocaust" from War Crime to Trauma Drama', *European Journal of Social Theory* 5(1): 5–85.

Bakan, Joel (2004) *The Corporation: The Pathological Pursuit of Profit and Power*, London: Constable & Robinson Ltd.

Baker, Mona (2005) 'Narratives *in* and *of* Translation', *SKASE Journal of Translation and Interpretation* 1(1): 4–13. Available online at www.skase.sk (accessed 15 December 2005).

Barsky, Robert (1996) 'The Interpreter as Intercultural Agent in Convention Refugee Hearings', *The Translator* 2(1): 45–63.

Bruner, Edward M. (1997) 'Ethnography as Narrative', in Lewis P. Hinchman and Sandra K. Hinchman (eds) *Memory, Identity, Community: The Idea of Narrative in the Human Sciences*, Albany: State University of New York Press, 264–80.

Burman, Erica (2003) 'Narratives of Challenging Research: Stirring Tales of Politics and Practice', *International Journal of Social Research Methodology* 6(2): 101–19.

Diriker, Ebru (2005) 'Presenting Simultaneous Interpreting: Discourse of the Turkish Media, 1988–2003', *AIIC Webzine*, March–April. Available online at www.aiic.net/ViewPage.cfm/page1742.htm (accessed 25 September 2005).

Geesey, Patricia (2000) 'Identity and Community in Autobiographies of Algerian Women in France', in Amal Amireh and Lisa Suhair Majaj (eds) *Going Global: The Transnational Reception of Third World Women Writers*, New York and London: Garland Publishing, 173–205.

Gergen, Kenneth J. and Mary M. Gergen (1997) 'Narratives of the Self', in Lewis P. Hinchman and Sandra K. Hinchman (eds) *Memory, Identity, Community: The Idea of Narrative in the Human Sciences*, Albany: State University of New York Press, 161–84.

Inghilleri, Moira (2005) 'Mediating Zones of Uncertainty: Interpreter Agency, the Interpreting Habitus and Political Asylum Adjudication', *The Translator* 11(1): 69–85.

Lambertus, Sandra (2003) 'News Discourse of Aboriginal Resistance in Canada', in Lynn Thiesmeyer (ed.) *Discourse and Silencing: Representation and the Language of Displacement*, Amsterdam and Philadelphia PA: John Benjamins, 233–72.

Maryns, Katrijn (2005) 'Displacement in Asylum Seekers' Narratives', in Mike Baynham and Ana De Fina (eds) *Dislocations/Relocations: Narratives of Displacement*, Manchester: St Jerome Publishing, 174–96.

Naudé, Jacobus A. (2005) 'Translation and Cultural Transformation: The Case of the Afrikaans Bible Translations', in Eva Hung (ed.) *Translation and Cultural Change*, Amsterdam and Philadelphia PA: John Benjamins, 19–41.

Niranjana, Tesjawini (1992) *Siting Translation: History, Poststructuralism, and the Colonial Context*, Berkeley: University of California Press.

4 Understanding how narratives work

Features of narrativity I

In the previous chapter, I discussed four types of narrative that mediate our experience of the world and outlined the political import of narrativity in broad terms. In this chapter and the following one, we move on to the question of how narratives function in terms of how they construct the world for us. The political import of narrativity will remain a major thread running through this and the following chapters.

Somers and Gibson (1994) and Somers (1992, 1997) focus on four defining features of what they call 'reframed narrativity'. Bruner (1991) discusses a more extensive range of features,[1] some of which overlap with or extend the four features outlined by Somers and Gibson, while others are less useful for our current purposes. I combine the two accounts where necessary in order to offer a more coherent and detailed model of analysis, bearing in mind our current focus on translation and interpreting. This chapter covers the four core features identified by Somers and Gibson, namely temporality, relationality, causal emplotment and selective appropriation. The remaining features, mostly derived from Bruner, are examined in Chapter 5.

4.1 Temporality (Bruner's narrative diachronicity)

Somers and Gibson (1994) and Bruner (1991) use two different terms – temporality and narrative diachronicity, respectively – to refer to the same feature. In both cases, temporality is understood as constitutive of narrativity rather than as an additional or separable layer of a 'story'.

> I take temporality to be that structure of existence that reaches language in narrativity and narrativity to be the language structure that has temporality as its ultimate referent. Their relationship is therefore reciprocal.
>
> Ricoeur (1981b: 165)

Temporality does not mean that events are recounted in the 'correct' order to reflect their unfolding in 'real' or chronological time.[2] It means that narrative is 'irreducibly durative' (Bruner 1991: 6), that the elements of a narrative are always placed in *some* sequence, and that the order in which they are placed carries meaning. Neither Somers and Gibson nor Bruner discuss this feature in any detail, but it seems helpful to tease out some of its implications and explore the way it impacts the work of translators and interpreters.

First, temporality means that sequence is an organizing principle in interpreting experience. The set of events, relationships and protagonists that constitute any narrative – whether ontological, public or conceptual – has to be embedded in a sequential context and in a specific temporal and spatial configuration that renders them intelligible. Even when they are 'characterizable in seemingly nontemporal terms (as a *tragedy* or a *farce*)', argues Bruner, 'such terms only summarize what are quintessentially patterns of events occurring over time' (1991: 6). For Bruner, space itself is an aspect of temporal ordering:

> Even nonverbal media have conventions of narrative diachronicity, as in the 'left-to-right' and 'top-to-bottom' conventions of cartoon strips and cathedral windows. What underlies all these forms for representing narrative is a 'mental model' whose defining property is its unique pattern of events over time.
>
> (1991: 6)

In recounting ontological narratives, as in autobiographical writing and various types of interviews, 'temporal organization is seldom strictly chronological' (McCormick 2005: 152); Bourdieu (2000: 298) similarly asserts that 'anybody who has ever collected life histories knows that informants constantly lose the thread of strict chronological order'. Most people, it seems, tend to recall events in a combination of thematic and chronological order, often without precise temporal reference. The lack of precision in temporal reference then is not unusual in everyday life, and may be due to a variety of factors, including trauma and memory lapses. And yet, many institutional authorities insist on a strict chronological ordering of events, hence forcing the narrator to repackage their experience to suit the institution's norms of presentation. The statement read out by the immigration official in Canada at the beginning of a refugee hearing includes the following instruction to the claimant: 'During your statement, try to keep a chronological order of the events, and please be as precise as you can concerning the dates, the places and the names of any persons stated during your examination' (Barsky 1993: 140). This forced restructuring of memory can leave the narrator with a deep sense of disorientation.

Barsky also explains that interpreters in the asylum system sometimes have to 'interpret the meaning of time for persons from cultures where time is measured or evaluated differently' (1993: 152). Time and space are not objective realities. Absolute time and space are historical products and are heavily mediated by the social environment, including the economy. Witness the radical restructuring of our perception of time and space in the past few decades as a consequence of technological advances that have reconfigured both our physical ability to move in space and the speed and scope of disseminating information.

Going back to the issue of imposing a specific temporal structure on a narrative account, the translators responsible for the 1969 version of Milan Kundera's *The Joke* cut, paste and reordered the chapters to make them fit into a strict chronological order (Kuhiwczak 1990). At least one of the two translators admitted in a letter to the *Times Literary Supplement* that he 'found the lack of strict chronological order in the book misleading, and even bewildering' (Kuhiwczak 1990: 125). Bolden (2000) discusses several examples from the medical sphere where interpreters turn open questions that call for simple yes/no answers into requests for precise temporal information, without the doctor necessarily being aware of the intervention.[3] In the following example (adapted from Bolden 2000: 396–7), the interpreter is mediating between a Russian-speaking patient and an English-speaking doctor at a large urban hospital in the Midwestern part of the USA. Boldface indicates interpreter utterances in Russian that are not accessible to the doctor:[4]

DOCTOR   Ah: : : ar- are you ah h-having a problem with uh chest pain?
INTERPRETER   **Do you have a chest pain?**
PATIENT   Well how should I put it, who knows. It … Sometimes it does happen.
INTERPRETER   **Once a week, Once every two weeks.**
PATIENT   No this thing happens then depending on – on the circumstances of life
INTERPRETER   **Well at – at this particular moment do your life circumstances cause you pain once a week or – or more often?**
PATIENT   Sometimes more often.
INTERPRETER   **Sometimes more often.**
INTERPRETER   Once or twice a week maybe.

Bolden argues that interpreters in this type of context selectively topicalize aspects of patients' responses that relate to specific medical contingencies, in other words to information that allows them to describe symptoms within a specific coding scheme for history-taking. The temporal dimension of the patient's narrative is clearly deemed to be crucial and is inherent in the very idea of 'history-taking' as part of a medical consultation.

Second, as a corollary of the above, the sequence in which a narrative is presented is constitutive of that narrative in the sense that it directs and constrains interpretation of its meaning. The way we order elements in a narrative, whether temporally or spatially, creates the connections and relations that transform a set of isolated episodes into a coherent account. Consider the following versions of a diary entry from Alan Bennett's *Writing Home*:

Version 1
11 May, Yorkshire. A day or two after the accident at Chernobyl, Barry Brewster, our local doctor, called all the local farmers and told them to keep their cows indoors and alerted all the schools to stop them drinking the milk. He rang the Department of Health and various other authorities wanting information about the likelihood of contamination but got no help whatsoever.

In the appropriate co-textual and contextual environment, this version could easily suggest that Barry Brewster is an impulsive, irresponsible doctor, and that his action would almost certainly have caused unnecessary panic among the public. No wonder the Department of Health refused to deal with him. In other words, the lack of response from the Department of Health can plausibly be interpreted here as a consequence of Brewster's rash intervention. What makes this interpretation plausible is that Doctor Brewster's intervention is mentioned first, without syntactic or lexical signals that indicate a reverse temporal order. Now consider Alan Bennett's actual entry:

Version 2

11 May, Yorkshire. A day or two after the accident at Chernobyl Barry Brewster, our local doctor, rang the Department of Health and various other authorities wanting information about the likelihood of contamination. Getting none, and indeed no help whatsoever, he called all the local farmers and told them to keep their cows indoors and alerted all the schools to stop them drinking the milk. On such people will survival depend.

(1997: 200–1)

Here, Dr Brewster's intervention is presented as responsible *and* a consequence of the Department of Health's indifference to public safety. The order in which events take place matters, and this order is a function of the narratives people elaborate about the events in question.

Spatial ordering of elements – often meant to reflect some form of temporal ordering – is likewise constitutive of a narrative, as can be seen in Paul Fitzgerald's 'Big Bad World' cartoon (Figure 5), which appeared on page 32 of the April 2005 issue of the *New Internationalist*.

This spatial order tells a story. My reading of it goes something like this. Freedom, justice and hope are consistently being abused and violated. All reasonable avenues for seeking these basic human rights have been blocked. This has left the victims of injustice with only one option: terrorism. There is nowhere else for people to go. In other words, this narrative portrays terrorism as the inevitable outcome of systematic and widespread violations of human rights. Now consider how this story could be altered completely through a rearrangement of the elements, with the door marked 'terrorism' being placed in initial position. An alternative reading of the

Figure 5 Paul Fitzgerald's 'Big Bad World' cartoon, *New Internationalist* (April 2005)

reordered image would then be that terrorism threatens freedom, justice and hope. Its prevalence today is forcing governments to introduce measures that restrict civil liberties, allow them to hold prisoners without trial, bomb countries such as Afghanistan and Iraq, and torture those they suspect of terrorism in order to extract information that can help protect the rest of society. But there is no alternative, since the road to justice, freedom and hope will continue to be blocked if governments do not put a stop to terrorism. This is a narrative that can be and is used by politicians to justify a variety of measures such as the Patriot Act[5] in America, which, among other things, gives the FBI the power – without any probable cause – to access an individual's medical, student, library or any other records and the power to prevent holders of these records from informing the individual in question that their records have been accessed.

> The Patriot Act contains an entire article on translators, who are clearly recognized as a vital element of the so-called War on Terror narrative:
>
> SEC. 205. EMPLOYMENT OF TRANSLATORS BY THE FEDERAL BUREAU OF INVESTIGATION.
> (a) AUTHORITY – The Director of the Federal Bureau of Investigation is authorized to expedite the employment of personnel as translators to support counterterrorism investigations and operations without regard to applicable Federal personnel requirements and limitations.
> (b) SECURITY REQUIREMENTS – The Director of the Federal Bureau of Investigation shall establish such security requirements as are necessary for the personnel employed as translators under subsection (a).
> (c) REPORT – The Attorney General shall report to the Committees on the Judiciary of the House of Representatives and the Senate on –
> (1) the number of translators employed by the FBI and other components of the Department of Justice;
> (2) any legal or practical impediments to using translators employed by other Federal, State, or local agencies, on a full, part-time, or shared basis; and
> (3) the needs of the FBI for specific translation services in certain languages, and recommendations for meeting those needs.

Third, it follows from the previous point and the examples above that the process of locating events and characters in space and time is not independent of another important feature of narrativity that I will discuss shortly, namely causal emplotment. Temporality is not just about the past and the present but also, and crucially, about the future. Narratives always project a chronological end that is also a moral end, a purpose, a forecast, an aspiration. This is why narratives guide behaviour and action. 'We act', Polletta argues, 'by locating events within an unfolding life-story' (1998: 140). Landau makes a similar point in relation to scientific narratives:

[s]electing events and arranging them sequentially involves considerations of causality as well as of chronology. The question of what happens next often cannot be answered separately from the questions of how and why it happened and how it all turns out. Thus, although scientific explanations may invoke specific laws to account for events (for example, the principles of natural selection, uniformitarianism, or genetics), such explanations must be distinguished from the explanatory effects produced simply by the sequential ordering of events.

(1997: 116)

Fourth, temporality also means that everything we perceive, our narratives of the world, are 'history laden' (Somers and Gibson 1994: 44) and that history, in turn, is a function of narrativity. 'We are members of the field of historicity as storytellers', Ricoeur says, and thus '[t]he game of telling' is itself 'included in the reality told' (1981b: 294). Ricoeur argues that this may explain why in many languages the word for 'history' is characterized by 'rich ambiguity of designating both the course of recounted events and the narrative that we construct' (1981b: 294).

Historicity means that the narratives of today encode and re-enact those of the recent as well as distant past.[6] This can work for or against the narrator. As an example of the negative impact of failure to attend to this feature in the context of relatively recent events, consider the following text.

'It was one of the worst things I've seen in my lifetime.' Carlton Brown, a normally unflappable commodities broker, was deeply troubled by what he had seen on September 11, 2001. 'All I could think about was getting them the hell out,' he says. 'Before the building collapsed, all we were thinking was, let's get those clients out' – out of the gold market, that is. ... Fortunately, he says, 'in the next couple of days we got them all out ... everybody doubled their money.'

(Bakan 2004: 111)

What most readers are likely to find shocking in the above comments is the lack of sensitivity to the immediate historical moment, the public narrative of which is dominated by details of human suffering rather than stock market crashes, although those too constitute an element that could have been but was not publicly emphasized. All the associations we developed over the past few years in relation to this particular historical moment set up immediate expectations of a focus on human suffering, so that the unexpected preoccupation with financial issues comes across as extremely callous. Our interpretation of this stock exchange narrative and our assessment of the individual narrating it are both inevitably constrained by the larger historical events in which they are embedded.

The controversy described in Sutton (1997) over a text he translated for *Ronda Iberia* in 1994 illustrates another facet of historicity: the way in which history is a function of our narration of the past from the vantage point of our location in the present. Here is the item that sparked the controversy (relevant terms highlighted in source and target texts):

La Vaquilla
20 de enero. Fresnedillas de la Oliva (Madrid)
La sostiene un sólido y complicado entramado, milagrosamente conservado a pesar de la proximidad de la devoradora capital. La a menudo vampirizadora influencia de Madrid no ha servido, en esta ocasión, para acabar con la fiesta. En ella toman parte **los judíos o motilones**, unos cuarenta jóvenes a cuyo cargo corre toda la organización, vestidos con monos de vivos colores y con cencerros o zumbas a la espalda. A su lado, la vaca, provista de un armazón de madera rematado en prominente cornamenta, con la que embiste al alcalde y al alguacil. La nota grotesca la ponen la hilandera (llamada cabalmente guarrona) y el escribano, que, armados con un libro repleto de imágenes pornográficas, hacen pagar a propios y extraños el tributo.

The Wild Cow
20th January. Fresnedillas de la Oliva (Madrid)
This fiesta is sustained by a solid set of traditions, miraculously preserved despite the proximity of the all-devouring capital. This time, Madrid's vampirising influence has failed to ruin the festival. The protagonists are **the 'Jews' or 'Friars'**, a group of some forty young men dressed in bright boiler suits with cowbells on their backs. The cow, which is led on by them, has on its head a wooden frame ending in two prominent horns, with which he charges the mayor and his bailiff. A grotesque note is provided by the 'spinner' (also called the 'dirty old sow') and the 'scribe', who carry around a pornographic book while demanding the payment of tribute from locals and visitors alike.

(Sutton 1997: 67–8)

Sutton explains that he had no choice but to translate *judíos* by 'the obvious one-to-one translation, "Jews"' but that he was nevertheless 'careful to place it in inverted commas' (1997: 68). For *motilones*, he could find no semantic equivalent in English with the same range of meanings. One possibility was to translate it as 'the shorn-heads' or 'the cropped-tops'. However, as Sutton explains, this choice would have been disastrous since 'any textual juxtaposition of Jews and cropped heads instantly conjures up the holocaust' (1997: 68). He thus opted for a secondary meaning of *motilones* which, according to the *Diccionario de uso del español*, is also 'a pejorative name for a friar' (1997: 68). Sutton further capitalized the word *Friar* and placed inverted commas around it to neutralize the pejorative connotation of the Spanish word and signal that this is a one-off usage (1997: 69). Nevertheless, the Simon Wiesenthal Center found the article, and the fiesta it depicts, highly offensive to the Jewish community, demanded an apology from *Ronda Iberia*, a commitment from the magazine to publish an article in a future edition on the Center's Museum of Tolerance in Los Angeles, and 'a pledge to "purge the contents of such festivals as 'The Wild Cow' of their racist stereotypes"' (Sutton 1997: 69). In the correspondence that followed, the executive director of *Ronda Iberia* assured the Wiesenthal Center that 'there is no antisemitic content in this fiesta' and explained that the fiesta is 'extravagant and difficult to interpret' and that 'even if it had an antisemitic root, something it is impossible to demonstrate, this has been lost over the years' (Sutton 1997: 69–70). The Center, in turn, accused the executive director of *Ronda Iberia* of a 'lack of sensibility and knowledge of history' (1997: 69). The campaign against *Ronda Iberia* progressed to include a news report broadcast on 23 January 1995 by Canal+ in which images from the fiesta were intermingled with images from the Holocaust. This led to a lawsuit initiated against Canal+ by the Town Hall of Fresnedillas, a major national debate in the leading Spanish newspaper *El Mundo* over the meaning of the fiesta, and the American ambassador eventually having to apologize to the mayor of Fresnedillas.

From the point of view of the Jewish community, the fiesta scenes could not easily be divorced from the medieval practice of staging passion plays that portrayed Jews as responsible for the death of Christ, which were often followed by mob violence against members of the Jewish community.[7] It is also this historical practice that partly triggered the controversy surrounding Mel Gibson's 2004 film, insensitively titled *The Passion*. For the Spanish community, on the other hand, the 'Wild Cow' is just another popular festival. Indeed, Sutton wonders why, by the same token, 'Arab readers of *Ronda Iberia* have not complained about the Moors and Christians [*sic*] festivals that take place all over Spain in September' (1997: 74) and suggests that '[i]t is tempting to speculate, for instance, that Arabs view the Moors and Christians [*sic*] festivals as representations of an honourable military defeat, whereas the "Wild Cow" is clearly interpreted by the Wiesenthal Center as celebrating a humiliation' (1997: 75). Interestingly, Sutton notes, throughout this prolonged controversy no one commented on the use of *Friars*.

Historicity is also a resource that narrators draw on in order to enhance identification with a current narrative and enrich it with implicit detail. A text about the 2001 US invasion of Afghanistan and its aftermath, for example, can draw parallels with past narratives of China and Hong Kong in order to elaborate not only the concrete details of the new narrative but, more importantly, its moral import:

Saturday, December 11, 2004
A New Opium War
Ben Masel

If you look at the changes in the political economy of Afghanistan, you may conclude that this is neither a 'war on terror' that Washington says it is nor a pipeline war as some of its critics allege. It looks as if it is the latest Opium War, regardless of intentions of all parties (Afghans, Americans, Europeans, and others) involved. ...

Afghanistan was not always the world's largest producer of opium. The first turning point was Washington's support for Afghan mujahideen fighting against the Soviet Union. Before the American intervention, Afghanistan had an economy largely based upon subsistence agriculture: 'As late as 1972, economists estimated that the cash economy constituted slightly less than half of the total' (Barnett Rubin, 'The Political Economy of War and Peace in Afghanistan,' 1999). The war against the Soviets and Afghan Communists changed it.

The mujahideen commanders – a new elite whose rise in Afghanistan was underwritten by US, Pakistani, and Saudi monies – 'pressured the peasants to grow opium, a cash crop they could tax. It was also during this period that the production of opium started to increase' (Rubin, 1999).

The US intervention in Afghanistan was a chapter in the long history of opium and empire. Sugar, tea, coffee, tobacco, and opium …

(Masel 2004)

How many layers of this new narrative we are able to penetrate, or appreciate, will depend in part on how familar we are with the narrative of the Opium Wars of 1839–42 and 1856–60. The first of these wars led to Hong Kong being ceded to the British in 1843 and the second to China being forced in 1858 to sanction Christian missionary activities and legalize the import of opium. The hostilities began with British merchants smuggling opium to China and came to a head when the Chinese government decided to prohibit the importation of opium and then confiscated and destroyed a large shipment in Guangzhou. But Britain was waiting for an excuse to attack China in order to end its restrictions on foreign trade. The second Opium War was triggered by an allegedly illegal Chinese search of a British ship in Guangzhou, and this time British troops were joined by French, Russian and American troops. All these elements of the historical narrative of China, if accessible to the reader, give Masel's contemporary narrative of Afghanistan certain dimensions and moral implications that constitute its historicity. The link between the sanctioning of Christian missionary activities in the nineteenth-century narrative of China and the role played by Christian fundamentalists in driving American foreign policy in some versions of the contemporary narrative of Afghanistan and Iraq, for example, can give Ben Masel's account a certain moral depth that enhances the opportunities for identification and action among certain sections of his audience.

In a more interesting example of historicity being put to creative use in an activist agenda, this version of the narrative of black suffering directly draws on what has proven to be an extremely effective historical narrative of Jewish suffering:[8]

Beyond the conscious capitalization of *Holocaust* to signal a(nother) unique and equally horrifying episode of history, there are several lexical items and strings of items that take the analogy with the Jewish Holocaust beyond the question of numbers killed and suffering endured. Items such as *memorial, monuments, apologies, Diaspora, testimony, descendants* and *survivors* activate various facets of the Jewish narrative and make them available for the practical negotiation of black suffering in the real world. We are encouraged to think of ways of compensating the 'survivors' of the Black Holocaust in the same way that survivors of the Jewish Holocaust have been and continue to be compensated, to campaign for public apologies from governments and groups implicated in *this* Holocaust, to build memorials, educate the descendants of black survivors, and so on. *Diaspora* also signals the potential of a return to some original homeland. And naturally, while many black activists and their supporters will experience this narrative as empowering, members of the Jewish community may see it as threatening, possibly even offensive, since it indirectly undermines the status of unique suffering that the Holocaust narrative has

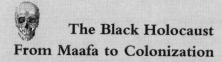

The Black Holocaust
From Maafa to Colonization

BLACK   (black), adj. 3a. of, pertaining to the various populations characterized by dark skin pigmentation, specifically the dark-skinned
peoples of Africa, Oceania, and Australia.

HOLOCAUST (hol e kost), n. 1a. a great or complete slaughter or reckless destruction of life.

The Black Holocaust is one of the more underreported events in the annals of human
history. The Black Holocaust makes reference to the millions of African lives which
have been lost during the centuries to slavery, colonization and oppression. The Black
Holocaust makes reference to the horrors endured by millions of men, women, and
children throughout the African Diaspora. In sheer numbers, depth and brutality, it is
a testimony to the worst elements of human behavior and the strongest elements of
survival.

Yet no monuments have been made and apologies have been few. Worse still, most of
the descendants of those who suffered, struggled and died, are unaware of this Holocaust while others seek to ignore it. One can only imagine the terrible damage placed
upon the psyche of a people who seek to ignore or forget the tragedies of their past.

The next few pages will give but a cursory glance at this Holocaust. As you read
remember that it is more than simply numbers and facts. It is a memorial to those who
could not live to tell their tale. It is a tribute to those who struggled and died so that
others may live. It is a reminder to the descendants of the survivors who have now
forgotten or do not know. In this manner we can honor those who have gone before
us and perhaps take a step towards real healing and understanding.

arguably achieved. On a textual level, it undermines the capitalized *H* in *Holocaust*
and dilutes its impact. Those involved in translating literature of this type – and
there are many activist translators who do (see Baker, in press, a) – will want to
consider how this feature of historicity may be preserved or activated when the text
is carried over into another culture in order to better serve their own and their
author's activist agenda.

As I explained in Chapter 2, narratives are articulated in a variety of media. Figure
6 offers an example of a visual articulation of a narrative that, like the Black Holocaust story above, appeals to another historical setting to drive home the horror and
consequences of a contemporary injustice.

Figure 6 Members of the Grassroots Palestinian Anti-Apartheid Wall Campaign pose as indigenous Americans, Ramallah, 8 April 2004

The caption below the photo on the *Stop the Wall* site reads as follows:

> These are not real indigenous Americans protesting about the reserves in the USA, or a tourist attraction. They are Palestinians from the new reserves (Ghettos) being created by the Apartheid Wall and its gates, tunnels, roads and locks. The silent, but deeply symbolic protest, emphasized that we will never accept our heritage, culture, life and land to be extinguished as happened to the indigenous Americans. They are also announcing the beginning of the week long conference held in Ramallah on the fate of Jerusalem. They are here to stress that their resistance will never stop against the Apartheid Wall. They will lay down their lives in the struggle for their lands and freedom. These ghettos suggest our path to victory and freedom might be distant. Long-term resistance may be the only solution for our freedom. Or to the contrary, we can look forward to a future like the indigenous Americans. That's exactly what the Zionists want to enforce upon our people.[9]

Apart from invoking the narrative of another community that has been uprooted and decimated by colonial settlers, the narrative of indigenous Americans – rather than, for example, Australian aborigines – serves another purpose here, since it underlines the role played by the USA in the Palestinian narrative of dispossession. This message is reinforced in the posters held by the activists in the photo, all of which address 'Mr. Bush', thus indicating their conviction that he – as a representative of the USA – is responsible for and/or holds the key to ending their dispossession.

As a resource, historicity is equally available to dominant parties and allows them to elaborate their own meta-narratives. Keeble offers a good example from the first invasion of Iraq in January 1991. The choice of the term *Allied* to describe the group of countries involved in the invasion, he argues,

> draws nostalgically on Second World War rhetoric. Like all the Hitler analogies directed at Saddam Hussein, it represents an ideologically motivated use of history by the US-led powers and their propaganda media to silence many other histories – in particular the imperial roles of the US and UK in the Middle East and more globally … And it seeks to legitimise the massacres by drawing a parallel between the Allied fight against evil Hitler with the … war against Saddam.
>
> (Keeble 2005: 43)

Finally, anthropological and scientific narratives often encode an implicit relationship between linearity as a temporal or spatial continuum and 'development' in the sense of progress from lower to higher states of existence. This background narrative allows dominant political institutions 'to impose linear historical narratives on different civilisations', which in turn 'legitimises and extends colonial domination' (Niranjana 1990: 775).

4.2 Relationality (hermeneutic composability)

Both *relationality* (in Somers and Gibson's terminology) and *hermeneutic composability* (in Bruner's framework)[10] mean that it is impossible for the human mind to make sense of isolated events or of a patchwork of events that are not constituted as a narrative:

> This hermeneutic property marks narrative both in its construction and in its comprehension. For narratives do not exist, as it were, in some real world, waiting there patiently and eternally to be veridically mirrored in a text. The act of constructing a narrative … is considerably more than 'selecting' events either from real life, from memory, or from fantasy and then placing them in an appropriate order. The events themselves need to be *constituted* in the light of the overall narrative.
>
> (Bruner 1991: 8)

Relationality has direct implications for translation and interpreting. Clifford (1998: 689) points out that in Maurice Leenhardt's[11] translation of the Bible into Houailou (a Melanesian language), 'there could be no simple importation of a Western divinity into a Melanesian religious landscape'. The relationality of narratives cannot allow such straightforward importation of 'parts' from other narratives. Another anthropologist, Godfrey Lienhardt, considered 'the problem of describing to others how members of a remote tribe think' as 'one of translation', and insisted that '[i]t is when we try to contain the thought of a primitive[12] society in our language and categories, without also modifying these in order to receive it, that it begins in part to lose the sense it seemed to have' (1967: 97). In the process of importing elements from another narrative, both the original narrative and our own narrative are inevitably *reconstituted*.

Kuhn (1999: 36) offers another useful example from the scientific domain. He explains that both Aristotelian and Newtonian theories make generalizations about matter and motion, and both use concepts of force, quantity of matter and weight in elaborating these generalizations. However, some of the Aristotelian generalizations are incompatible with Newtonian physics 'so that enriching the Newtonian conceptual vocabulary with Aristotelian terms (or vice versa) would build contradictions about observable natural phenomena *into language itself* (emphasis in original), with the result that 'a language which contained such contradictions could not successfully deal with nature' (1999: 36).

Although Clifford, Lienhardt and Kuhn do not use the notion of narrative in arguing their points, the examples they discuss nevertheless demonstrate the implications of relationality as conceived within narrative theory. They illustrate the impossibility of elaborating a coherent narrative – be it religious, anthropological or scientific – on the basis of a patchwork of elements from different narratives. A narrative consists of different parts that make up a whole, but the viability and coherence of that whole depends on how the parts 'mesh together', how they are 'made to live together' (Bruner 1991: 8). Were it possible to isolate parts of a narrative and interpret them without reference to a constructed configuration and to their social and cultural setting, and were it possible to interpret other narratives without simultaneously accommodating them to our own narratives and accommodating our own narratives to them, translation and ethnography would indeed be much simpler and less involved acts of mediation. But narrativity being what it is, the translator and ethnographer both necessarily reconstruct narratives by weaving together relatively or considerably new configurations in every act of translation, and re-siting these new configurations in different temporal and spatial settings. Each new configuration modifies and reinterprets the narratives that went into its making. One consequence of this process is that translating a narrative into another language and culture inevitably results in a form of 'contamination', whereby the original narrative itself may be threatened with dilution or change. This explains why missionaries involved in the colonization of communities such as the Philippines insisted that translators retain some key words such as *Dios* and *Virgen* in Latin or Castilian (Rafael 1993).[13] Replacing these terms with native ones, which come loaded with their own relational profiles, risked 'conflating "pagan" religious beliefs and practices with Catholic ones' (Rafael 1993: 29). But retaining key concepts in a foreign language cannot suppress relationality and its consequences. For one thing, foreign words simply get pressed into service as another resource for addressing existing needs, as elaborated in local narratives. Rafael provides evidence for this:

> Hearing the untranslated terms of Christianity, native converts recognized them for what they were: opaque signifiers with no prior signifieds in Tagalog. Such terms formed momentary blanks in the semantic progression

of the vernacular. To seize upon untranslatable signs was to mark the recurrence of such gaps and to see in them a whole range of possible associations that had only the most tenuous connection to the original message of the priest. In other words, the very untranslatability of Christian signs could be reread in different ways by native converts. Rather than making indisputably apparent the authority of God's Sign and that of the priest, such terms presented the possibility of dodging the full weight of the missionary's intent.

(Rafael 1993: 117)

Kahf (2000) discusses an interesting consequence of using a term in a translation that is already loaded with relational meaning in the target culture, thus seriously disrupting the source narrative. The source text in question is Huda Sha'rawi's *Mudhakkirati* (*My Memoirs*, 1981), translated into English by Margot Badran in 1986 as *Harem Years: Memoirs of an Egyptian Feminist*. Huda Sha'rawi (1879–1947) was a pioneer of the women's rights movement in the Arab world and an advocate of social change in Egypt. The translator apparently decided to use the English word *harem* instead of the standard transliteration of the Arabic word *harim* because she felt the latter would be unfamiliar to the reader. Kahf makes two points in relation to this choice. First, that the use of an unfamiliar word in this context would have been preferable because it would have 'jolted the reader out of the comfortable pattern of expectations and created a more challenging and transformative reading experience' (Kahf 2000: 165). Second, and more importantly, Sha'rawi only uses the word *harim* once in 457 pages, whereas the English version uses it 25 times in the Introduction alone and many more times in endnotes and captions. The word *harem* (or *harim*) then

> is not an operative term in the Arabic memoirs because it does not delineate a meaningful category for Sha'rawi. *Harem* is the word of the outside looking in. Sha'rawi's terms represent the narrative perspective of the writerly self looking out and moving about the world in ways that seem natural to her (and which are hardly more restrictive than the orbits of the average Victorian or Edwardian woman of the same class).
>
> (Kahf 2000: 165)

The main effect of this strategy is that the Arabic narrative is *haremized*, with issues such as the seclusion of women becoming the main focus, although this is not an organizing principle of the source narrative. The use of *harem* also directs the gaze of the English reader to a very different interpretation of visual material in the source text:

> One photo placed in the section on holidays is captioned, 'Huda [*sic*] and friend pose in Egyptian peasant dresses. Dressing up was a favourite pastime in the harem' (47). The second sentence reminds the reader of the framing notion 'harem,' although the word is not in the accompanying text at all. What the caption alludes to is the convention that *ennui* was a defining characteristic of 'harem life' and required especial effort at amusement to relieve. This notion of

'the harem' as a site of trivial amusements infantilized the women who were the objects of the observation.

(Kahf 2000: 165)

Thus the use of this one element from the narrative world of the target culture triggers a set of interpretations that are a function of its own relational context in the public narratives of the target readers.

Translators and interpreters at times also avoid the use of a direct semantic equivalent of an item in the source text or utterance when that equivalent is or has become embedded in a different and potentially negative set of narratives in the target culture. This is again a function of relationality, since it is impossible to extract an item from a given narrative or set of narratives and treat it as an independent semantic unit. The following English subtitles from Mohammad Bakri's film documentary *Jenin Jenin*,[14] which was released in 2002 following Israel's attack on the Jenin camp in the Occupied West Bank, illustrate the point.[15] The speakers are all Palestinian men and women of different ages and educational backgrounds, who describe the destruction of the camp in April 2002, some also recalling similar attacks on their homes during the first *intifada*. The relevant items are highlighted in bold:

Example 1

"لسه بندوّر شهدا من تحت الأرض".

Backtranslation
   We are still pulling **martyrs** from underneath the ground.
English subtitle
   We are still pulling **victims** out of the rubble.

Example 2

"متخلفين عقليًا استشهدوا عندنا، معاقين استشهدوا عندنا، أطفال استشهدوا عندنا، نساء استشهدوا عندنا".

Backtranslation
   We have mentally retarded people who have been **martyred**; we have disabled people who have been **martyred**; we have children who have been **martyred**, we have women who have been **martyred**.
English subtitle
   They **killed** some mentally disabled people, children and women in the camp.

Example 3

"خلال دائرة قطرها 30 متر بس وجدنا عشر شهداء".

Backtranslation
   Within a circle of no more than 30 metres in circumference, we found ten **martyrs**.

Figure 7 Screen shot from *Jenin Jenin*

English subtitle
In an area of 30 metres we discovered 10 **corpses**.

In another shot, a Palestinian doctor describes how, as his area was being shelled by Israeli planes during the first *intifada*, he tended to many injured people and managed to save many lives, only to discover when the shelling stopped that his own son (Ameed) had been shot and was lying somewhere nearby bleeding to death:

Example 4

"بعد ماتوقف اطلاق النار بدا الجيران بالصياح، ويقولوا عميد استشهد، عميد استشهد".

Backtranslation
After the shooting stopped, the neighbours began to shout, saying Ameed has been **martyred**, Ameed has been **martyred**.

As in the previous examples, the English subtitles for this frame suppress all references to martyrdom:

After the cease-fire the neighbours started shouting that Ameed my son was **dead**.

In all the above examples, the subtitlers avoid translating the Arabic word *shaheed* and all its derivatives by its standard equivalent in English, namely *martyr*.[16] It seems reasonable to suggest that these choices are motivated by a desire to avoid associations of Islamic fundamentalism, terrorism and suicide bombing that this word now readily evokes as part of the anti-Muslim and anti-Arab narratives circulating in the West. Many Arab speakers who use the word *shaheed*, including Palestinians interviewed in this documentary, are totally opposed to any acts of violence on either side. *Shaheed*, in Arabic, is embedded in a very different and far less 'militant' set of narratives. It is generally used to refer to anyone who is killed violently, especially in war. Ihab Al-Shereef, the Egyptian ambassador who was kidnapped and killed in Iraq in July 2005, was widely referred to in the Egyptian media as *shaheed*.[17] *Shaheed*, then, is not necessarily – or even mainly – part of a narrative of violent resistance. It is broadly used in everyday discourse to refer to anyone on the receiving end of violence in a situation of conflict, whether or not they choose to be involved in that situation. But whatever its current use in the source culture, its standard semantic equivalent in English inevitably activates a set of Western narratives that provide a different and, in this case, most undesirable interpretive frame for those who must rely on English subtitles to understand the documentary.[18]

Like other features of narrativity, relationality functions both as a constraint and as a resource for elaborating new narratives. It can be drawn on to inject a target text or discourse with implicit meanings derived from the way a particular item functions in the public or meta-narratives circulating in the target context, thus obscuring or downplaying its relational load in the source environment. Tekiner provides an interesting example in his discussion of the standard English translation of the Hebrew word *ezrahut*, which he disputes:

> Zionist uses of the term 'nation,' 'national,' and 'nationality' are indeed difficult to understand and to explain because they derive from concepts that are unfamiliar to Americans. Moreover, their true meanings are deliberately obscured by usually incorrect translations from Hebrew into English.
>
> The prime example of deception, from which the others flow, is the accepted translation of Israel's Law of Citizenship as 'Nationality' Law. In the original Hebrew text, the word is *ezrahut*, the correct translation is 'citizenship.'
>
> It would not occur to the average English speaking observer to object to translating *ezrahut* as 'nationality' because 'citizenship' and 'nationality' are interchangeable terms in the United States, as well as in most democratic societies. In Israel, however, they are two separate and very different statuses. Citizenship (*ezrahut*) may be held by Arabs as well as Jews while nationality (*le'um*), which bestows significantly greater rights than citizenship, may be claimed by Jews alone.
>
> (Tekiner 1990: 20)

Tekiner's analysis of the choice of *nationality* as an equivalent of *ezrahut* in the case of Israel offers a very concrete demonstration of the way in which relationality can function as a resource rather than a constraint. It also highlights the real world consequences of the narrative choices made in individual instances of translation and interpreting, and the institutional stakes in these choices.

4.3 Causal emplotment

While relationality means that every event has to be interpreted within a larger configuration of events, *causal emplotment* 'gives significance to independent instances, and overrides their chronological or categorical order' (Somers 1997: 82). It is only when events are emplotted that they 'take on narrative meaning', because it is then that they are 'understood from the perspective of their contribution and influence on a specified outcome' (Polkinghorne 1995: 5). In other words, emplotment allows us to *weight* and *explain* events rather than simply list them, to turn a set of propositions into an intelligible sequence about which we can form an opinion. It thus charges the events depicted with moral and ethical significance. Because causal emplotment is inherent in narrativity, some scholars argue that narrativity 'is intimately related to, if not a function of, the impulse to moralize reality' (White 1987a: 14). This impulse manifests itself in causal emplotment.

In concrete terms, causal emplotment means that two people may agree on a set of 'facts' or events but disagree strongly on how to interpret them in relation to each other. For instance, one narrative of the Middle East conflict depicts Israeli-targeted assassinations as a response to Palestinian terror attacks, while another narrative depicts Palestinian suicide bombing as a desperate and inevitable outcome of Israeli state terrorism. Proponents of the two competing narratives may accept that the individual events (or episodes) took place, and even agree on the details of each event (who did what, where and when), but disagree strongly on how the events relate to each other and what motivates the actors in each set of events. Similarly, Benford's (1993) study of the 1980s nuclear disarmament movement demonstrates that members of the various groups that aligned themselves with the broad narrative of nuclear disarmament disagreed vociferously about the reasons for the nuclear threat: some believed it to be the result of a general decline in morality, others thought it was the defence industry or capitalism more generally that was driving it, and still others believed it was the USA, or the Soviet Union, or that it was simply the result of runaway technology. The different groups were not contesting the individual elements of the narrative: no one disputed the interests of the defence industry, or the fact that technology was developing at a mad pace, nor that the USA and the Soviet Union were vying for control. But they disagreed on how all these elements related to each other and on their exact relationship to the nuclear threat. Causal emplotment thus allows us to take the same set of events and weave them into very different 'moral' stories. It is perhaps the most important feature of narrativity, because it is identifying a cause for a set of events that helps us determine what course of action we should take, and this in turn allows us to appeal to others who see their 'own sentiments or interests reflected in that choice of a social scene' (Bennett and Edelman 1985: 160).

Emplotment is often signalled merely through sequence and the ordering of events. The following is one of the many victim accounts presented to South Africa's Truth and Reconciliation Commission following the collapse of apartheid. This particular account is reproduced in Antje Krog's much acclaimed *Country of My Skull*:

That morning I did something I had never done before. My husband was still at his desk busy with the accounts of our business. I went up to him and stood behind his chair. I put my hands under his arms and tickled him ... he looked surprised and unexpectedly happy.

'And now?' he asked.

'I am going to make tea,' I said.

While I poured water on the tea bags, I heard this devastating noise. Six men stormed into our study and blew his head off. My five-year-old daughter was present ... That Christmas I found a letter on his desk: 'Dear Father Christmas, please bring me a soft teddy bear with friendly eyes ... My daddy is dead. If he was here I would not have bothered you.' I put her in a boarding school. The morning we drove there we had a flat tyre. 'You see,' she said, 'Daddy does not want me to go there ... He wants me to stay with you ... I have watched him die, I must be there when you die ... ' She is now a teenager and has tried twice to commit suicide.

(Krog 1998: 43)

Causal emplotment in this ontological narrative is realized merely through sequence and temporal ordering. Without any explicit linguistic signals, we interpret the teenage daughter's attempts at suicide as an outcome of the trauma of witnessing her father's murder. There is no need to spell out the connection between the two sets of events. Another implicit causal link may be read into the sequence 'That Christmas I found a letter on his desk: "Dear Father Christmas, please bring me a soft teddy bear with friendly eyes ... My daddy is dead. If he was here I would not have bothered you."' and 'I put her in a boarding school', suggesting – perhaps – that putting the daughter in a boarding school was an attempt to effect some distance between her and those painful memories, to allow her to get over them.

Another aspect of emplotment has to do with weighting events and endowing them with significance, perhaps as crises of a particular magnitude or as turning points in the context of the overall narrative. Landau (1997) explains that because of its emphasis on natural selection, the Darwinian narrative often casts what it depicts as a series of critical moments within a framework of transformation through struggle, even though, she argues, no event is inherently a crisis or a transition. Moreover, 'once events acquire such meaning, they may become associated with moments of crisis or transition found in other kinds of narratives, such as "fall and redemption," or "empire and decline," and thus can take on connotations reaching far beyond their original contexts' (Landau 1997: 116). In Alexander's (2002) highly detailed study of the development of the Holocaust narrative as we know it today, we can see how that set of events was first treated as a crisis, some aberration that constituted a serious breach of morality but could nevertheless be rationally exam- ined, taken heed of, and then prevented from ever happening again. Identified as a crisis, the events in question could be placed in the context of a progressive narrative that promised a resolution and a better future. But once the event was reconstituted as a turning point, there could be no going back to a pre-Holocaust world, and there could be no redemption – 'with the decline of the progressive narrative, ... as

"Holocaust" became the dominant representation for the trauma', Alexander argues, 'it implied the sacral mystery, the "awe-fullness," of the transcendental tradition' (2002: 28–9). Something similar to this, perhaps, is happening with the September 11 narrative. There is growing evidence that it is being actively constituted as a turning point in the history of the modern world.

It is this feature of weighting, rather than the details of the event itself, which is often the subject of contestation by individuals and groups situated outside what is or has become the dominant narrative. In the case of the weighting of September 11, one of the best known public attempts at contestation came from Emmanuel Ortiz, a third-generation Chicano/Puerto Rican American poet. Written on the occasion of the first anniversary of the attack on the Twin Towers, Ortiz's 'A Moment of Silence' (Ortiz 2002) sparked considerable controversy at the time because it framed the events of 9/11 in the context of alternative historical turning points that are marginalized in our current narratives but can be weighted more heavily if factors such as the number of lives lost or the length and nature of human suffering were taken into consideration. The poem starts with this verse:

Before I start this poem, I'd like to ask you to join me
In a moment of silence
In honor of those who died in the World Trade Center and the Pentagon
        last September 11th.
I would also like to ask you
To offer up a moment of silence
For all of those who have been harassed, imprisoned, disappeared, tortured,
        raped, or killed in retaliation for those strikes,
For the victims in both Afghanistan and the U.S.

The poet here signals his detachment from the official public narrative even before the first verse is over. The verses that follow feature an extension of the duration of silence with every historical event depicted as more worthy of being treated as a turning point: a full day of silence for tens of thousands of Palestinians killed by US-backed Israeli forces; six months of silence for the Iraqis who died as a result of eleven years of sanctions; two months of silence for the blacks under apartheid in South Africa; nine months of silence for the dead in Hiroshima and Nagasaki; a year of silence for the millions of dead in Vietnam.

The weighting of events and various elements of a narrative, including characters, can be changed in translation to produce a different pattern of causal emplotment. Kahf (2000) again offers us an interesting illustration of this in her discussion of the way Margot Badran's *Harem Years* 'is shaped by a "horizon of expectations" for writing by and about Arab and Muslim women' (2000: 148) in the English-speaking world. One of the features of the English version is its exaggeration of the importance of Europe and European characters in the original text, *Mudhakkirati*:

The *Harem Years* text frequently uses the given name of Rushdi Basha's wife, Eugenie Le Brun, which has the effect of highlighting her Europeanness rather than the fact that she was the wife of a prominent Egyptian. In *Mudhakkirati*, Sha'rawi never calls her friend anything but 'Haram [the wife of] Rushdi Basha.' This is a reflection of Sha'rawi's respect for propriety, titles, and seniority, but it also draws the reader's attention to Mrs. Rushdi's investiture in her Egyptian context. Sha'rawi's memoirs certainly draw a picture of a close friendship with Mme Rushdi, and Badran transmits Sha'rawi's sense that her friend had a deep and lasting effect on her. ' … even after [Mme Rushdi's] death I felt her spirit light the way before me' (Badran, 82). The significance of this passage, with its emphasis on Sha'rawi's friendship with the European woman, is granted more weight in the English version than in the Arabic by its positioning. The passage closes Part Three of the English text, whereas in the Arabic text it is embedded within a chapter. In contrast, the English text omits a similar sensation that Sha'rawi recounts after the death of another friend, Egyptian feminist Malak Nassef: … In *Mudhakkirati*, Sha'rawi mentions her love and admiration for the Princess Amina, wife of the Khedive Tawfiq, before her mention of Mme Richard, a European friend of her mother; the translated text reverses the order in which they are mentioned.

(Kahf 2000: 158–9)

Patterns of causal emplotment can thus be subtly changed in translation through the cumulative effect of relatively minor shifts that lend a different weighting to the elements of the original narrative.

Patterns of causal emplotment can also be drastically reconfigured, deliberately or otherwise, simply through the choice of equivalents in translation and interpreting. In an FBI terrorism case against Sami Al-Arian[19] and seven others, which started in February 2004 and was based almost entirely on evidence in Arabic, major arguments broke out over the translations of numerous words in the transcripts of speeches, wiretaps and seized videos. The court heard that '"Jihad" has several meanings, including "striving for the utmost," as well as "holy war," depending on the context. And talk of "slaughtering and butchering" – especially during the winter holidays – might refer to what's for dinner' (Laughlin 2005).

Caught between the Defence and Prosecution, the FBI translator, Tahsin Ali, tried to steer a middle path. He was obliged to defend some of his choices in some instances and admit that some Arabic words are open to alternative interpretations in others:

> Both sides agreed that 'chickpeas' added up to 'hummus.' But they parted on whether 'hummus' was code for the terrorist group 'Hamas.' They also couldn't agree on whether an Arabic word that sounded like 'ka-tuh-yee' referred to 'brigades' or 'pancakes.' As a general rule, federal prosecutors argued that the defendants' words had violent meanings, or were code for something sinister related to terrorism, while defense attorneys argued that they were mild, innocuous words.
>
> The translator fell somewhere in the middle.
>
> He flipped through his English–Arabic dictionary and the original Arabic in

transcripts to explain why he sometimes capitalized the words 'jihad' and 'intifada' and sometimes didn't.

'I capitalized the event – the battle – but not the general word, "jihad",' he said.

He said uncapitalized 'jihad' meant 'striving to the utmost to achieve a goal.' Uncapitalized 'intifada' was a 'general uprising.' Capitalized 'Intifada' was the Palestinian uprising.

...

Defense attorney Stephen Bernstein asked if 'martyrdom' always meant 'suicide for a cause.' Ali replied that it could mean getting killed by the enemy.

(Laughlin 2005)

Ultimately, reconfiguring patterns of causal emplotment is not simply a function of translator/interpreter choices, in most cases. Different forms of intervention by other agents, combined with translational choices, often contribute to the elaboration of the reconfigured narrative, as in this case:

One of the lessons of the day was in English: a primer on the meaning of the word 'redacted.'

That meant 'left out,' Ali told jurors, referring to missing lines in a foot-tall stack of transcripts. [Defense attorney Linda] Moreno began adding up the numbers of lines from page to page that prosecutors had redacted. Her point: Prosecutors are focusing upon information that they hope will make their case. Defense attorneys hope to show that information was excluded that gives a fuller, more reasonable picture of defendants.

When the number of redacted lines went over 500, U.S. District Judge James S. Moody stopped Moreno to instruct jurors about the missing information.

'There is a lot more that you haven't heard than what you have heard,' he said.

(Laughlin 2005)

As can be seen from this and the previous example from Kahf, patterns of causal emplotment are also closely connected with another feature of narrativity, namely selective appropriation, to which I now turn.

4.4 Selective appropriation

Somers and Gibson (1994) argue that narratives are constructed according to evaluative criteria that enable and guide selective appropriation of a set of events or elements from the vast array of open-ended and overlapping events that constitute experience. White (1987a: 10) similarly suggests that '[e]very narrative, however seemingly "full," is constructed on the basis of a set of events that might have been included but were left out'.

To elaborate a coherent narrative, it is inevitable that some elements of experience are excluded and others privileged. But what guides this process of selection? Somers suggests that this process is thematically driven:

Themes such as 'husband as breadwinner,' 'union solidarity,' or 'women must be independent above all' will selectively appropriate the happenings of the social world, arrange them in some order, and normatively evaluate these arrangements.

(1992: 602)

Similarly, Polkinghorne (1995: 7) states that the selection of events to be woven into a narrative is guided by the plot, which he defines as the 'thematic thread' that allows the narrator to depict individual elements of a story as part of an unfolding narrative that culminates in an outcome. Even annals, which do not have an overt narrative form, select the events to be recorded along general themes such as major battles, famines or violence, and thus manage to portray 'a world in which need is everywhere present, in which scarcity is the rule of existence, and in which all of the possible agencies of satisfaction are lacking or absent or exist under imminent threat of death' (White 1987a: 11).

But there is more to selective appropriation than simply the theme or central subject of a narrative. White (1987a) mentions that the annalist recorded the Battle of Poitiers of 732 but did not record another very important battle in the same year: the Battle of Tours. Even if the annalist had known of this battle, White asks, 'what principle or rule of meaning would have required him to record it?' (1987a: 9). His answer is as follows:

> It is only from our knowledge of the subsequent history of Western Europe that we can presume to rank events in terms of their world-historical significance, and even then that significance is less world historical than simply Western European, representing a tendency of modern historians to rank events in the record hierarchically from within a perspective that is culture-specific, not universal at all.
>
> (White 1987a: 9–10)

It is not just a question of theme or central subject of the narrative then but also a question of our location in time and space, and our exposure to a particular set of public, conceptual and meta-narratives that shape our sense of significance. Manuel Jerez *et al.* describe an interesting instance of student translation that illustrates this process of selectivity:

> También ha podido observar cómo en ejercicios de interpretación consecutiva, dos estudiantes que interpretan un mismo discurso omiten un mismo dato, en este caso una referencia histórica: en una clase reciente un discurso enumeraba los crímenes de los nazis durante la Segunda Guerra Mundial y se refería a la matanza de seis millones de judíos, de una Quinta parte de la población polaca y de 25 millones de soviéticos. Esta última cifra se omitía en ambos casos, llegando una estudiante a afirmar que había dudado de lo que había oído por parecerle disparatado pese a ser tan <histórico> como los otros dos.
>
> [I have also witnessed how, during consecutive interpreting training sessions, two students interpreting the same source speech omit the same item of

information, in this case a historical reference: in a recent session, the source speech listed the murders that the Nazis were responsible for during the Second World War and referred to the massacre of six million Jews, a fifth of the Polish population and 25 million Russians. This last figure was omitted in both cases [target versions], one student pointing out that she had doubted what she had heard as it seemed nonsensical, despite it being just as 'historical' as the other two].

(2004: 70)

Selective appropriation, whether conscious or subconscious, has an immediate impact on the world. In commenting on the way in which British travel accounts of the exploration of Africa in the late eighteenth and first half of the nineteenth century 'largely eliminate[d] current inhabitants from the environment', Pratt (1994: 208) concludes that 'one cannot help seeing in these depopulated verbal landscapes of the travel books the ideological preparation for the real depopulation that was to come'. This is why the selection and weighting of events in any narrative is often the core of contestation of that narrative. We can see an example of this in the following critique of the dominant narrative of Yugoslavia:

> During the 90s, the Former Yugoslavia incarnated the specter of the civilizational clash announced by Huntington, provided for by the effect of translation and the global media in search of the properly simplified political narrative. This dominant translation reduced the multiplicity of meanings inherent in the Balkan original to the imploding Yugoslavia, to the heated passions and irrational violence between ethnic groups which were divided by acculturated religious differences. The name of Yugoslavia became emblematic for the entire Balkan region, as the global media gaze obscured the complexities by foregrounding the stories of tribal hatred and urging military action to bring the most militant ones to heel. This translation became so dominant in the global vision of the Balkans that it somehow omitted the plurality of the region it was supposedly working to restore.[20]

(Longinovic 2004: 3–4)

Another troubling example of selective appropriation, with the direct involvement of translators, concerns an advocacy group called MEMRI. On 12 August 2002, Brian Whitaker published an article in *The Guardian* under the title 'Selective Memri' which started as follows:

> For some time now, I have been receiving small gifts from a generous institute in the United States. The gifts are high-quality translations of articles from Arabic newspapers which the institute sends to me by email every few days, entirely free-of-charge. ... The emails also go to politicians and academics, as well as to lots of other journalists. The stories they contain are usually interesting. ... Whenever I get an email from the institute, several of my Guardian colleagues receive one too and regularly forward their copies

to me – sometimes with a note suggesting that I might like to check out the story and write about it.

(Whitaker 2002)

MEMRI, as Whitaker found out, was set up by Col. Yigal Carmon, a former member of the Israeli intelligence service.[21] The stories it selects for translation 'follow a familiar pattern: either they reflect badly on the character of Arabs or they in some way further the political agenda of Israel' (Whitaker 2002). Harris (2003) similarly insists that 'MEMRI engages in the practice of publishing selective and decontextualized excerpts of the Arabic press in ways that can present opponents of [Israel's] occupation as religious extremists or anti-Semites'.[22] And the Mayor of London, Ken Livingstone, describes MEMRI as a 'very well-funded' organization 'which specialises in finding quotes from Arab media for circulation in the West. The translation and selection of quotes tend to portray Islam in a very negative light' (Livingstone 2005: 4).

MEMRI's own site (httpl://memri.org) describes the organization as follows – interestingly making explicit use of the bridge metaphor often invoked to portray translation as an inherently empowering and ethical practice:

> The Middle East Media Research Institute (MEMRI) explores the Middle East through the region's media. MEMRI bridges the language gap which exists between the West and the Middle East, providing timely translations of Arabic, Farsi, and Hebrew media, as well as original analysis of political, ideological, intellectual, social, cultural, and religious trends in the Middle East.
>
> Founded in February 1998 to inform the debate over U.S. policy in the Middle East, MEMRI is an independent, nonpartisan, nonprofit, 501 (c)3 organization. MEMRI's headquarters is located in Washington, DC with branch offices in Berlin, London, and Jerusalem, where MEMRI also maintains its Media Center. MEMRI research is translated to English, German, Hebrew, Italian, French, Spanish, Turkish, and Russian.

We might note in passing here that of the three source languages targeted by MEMRI (Arabic, Farsi and Hebrew), only Hebrew is listed among the set of target languages in which translations are provided. The press reports on the organization's work, proudly quoted by MEMRI on its site, confirm Whitaker's, Harris' and Livingstone's analysis of the type of narrative that MEMRI's translations seek to promote through careful selective appropriation:

> 'MEMRI, the indispensable group that translates the ravings of the Saudi and Egyptian press … ' *Weekly Standard, April 28, 2003*

> 'I am full of admiration for the work MEMRI has done … in its dedicated exposure of Arab antisemitism. Until MEMRI undertook its effort to review and translate articles from the Arab press, there was only dim public awareness of this problem in the United States. Thanks to MEMRI, this ugly phenomenon has

been unmasked, and numerous American writers have called attention to it.'
U.S. Rep. Tom Lantos, May 1, 2002

'www.memri.org – What they do is very simple, no commentary nothing else. What they do is they just translate what the Saudis say in the mosques, say in their newspapers, say in government pronouncements, say in their press.'
October 1, 2002, BBC

It is also worth noting that MEMRI translations constituted the main source of 'evidence' in a dossier submitted to the Metropolitan Police in 2004 calling for the expulsion of Dr Yusuf al-Qaradawi from Britain. Dr al-Qaradawi was President of the Muslim Association of Britain at the time and widely considered among 'the most authoritative Muslim scholars in the world' (Livingstone 2005: 2).

Acknowledging that all stories are selective representations of reality, Bennett and Edelman (1985: 164) explain that '[t]he issue with selectivity is whether a representation funnels emerging reality back into stereotypical terms, or whether it introduces new information in terms of unfamiliar dilemmas, puzzles, and contradictions of the sort that promote critical thought and a self-consciousness of problem-solving behavior'. They further argue that '[m]ost stock political formulas drive out the stuff of critical thought and action and replace it with self-fulfilling ideas and habituated action imperatives' (1985: 164).

In rebutting Whitaker's attack the following day, MEMRI's founder explained that '[m]onitoring the Arab media is far too much for one person to handle. We have a team of 20 translators doing it'. Harel reports heavy reliance on translators in similar Israeli programmes of 'propaganda, psychological warfare and sometimes disinformation' in *Haaretz*, one of the most prestigious Israeli newspapers:

> In October 1999, Aluf Benn revealed in Haaretz that members of the [psychological warfare] unit used the Israeli media to emphasize reports initiated by the unit that it managed to place in the Arab press. He reported that the news reports focused on Iranian and Hezbollah involvement in terror activity.
>
> Psychological warfare officers were in touch with Israeli journalists covering the Arab world, gave them translated articles from Arab papers (which were planted by the IDF) and pressed the Israeli reporters to publish the same news here.
>
> That was meant to strengthen the perception of the Iranian threat in Israeli public opinion.
>
> (Harel 2005)

Selecting, and in some cases 'inventing', texts that help elaborate a particular narrative of an 'enemy' culture, then, is a well-documented practice that often relies heavily on the services of translators and interpreters. The narratives that these translators and interpreters help weave together, relying mainly on the feature of selective appropriation, are far from innocent. But deliberate selective appropriation is of course a feature that both sides can exploit more or less effectively, depending largely on the resources they have available at their disposal. In his *Guardian* article, Brian Whitaker proposed that Arabs should also use translation to fight back against demonization programmes of this type:

> As far as relations between the west and the Arab world are concerned, language is a barrier that perpetuates ignorance and can easily foster misunderstanding. ... All it takes is a small but active group of Israelis to exploit that barrier for their own ends and start changing western perceptions of Arabs for the worse. ... It is not difficult to see what Arabs might do to counter that. A group of Arab media companies could get together and publish translations of articles that more accurately reflect the content of their newspapers.
>
> (Whitaker 2002)

About a year or so later, an organization called Arabs Against Discrimination was set up, almost as a direct response to Whitaker's suggestion (www.aad-online.org). This organization too relies very heavily on translation to promote a counter-narrative of what they believe Arabs stand for as well as expose patterns of racism and discrimination in Israeli society. How we decide which type of selective appropriation is legitimate depends on our narrative location, including our sense of causal emplotment in the Middle East narrative in this case. Chapter 7 engages more directly with the issue of how we assess individual and competing narratives to determine whether they are worthy of our adherence.

A final and related factor that guides our processes of selective appropriation is our own 'values' – the values we subscribe to as individuals or institutions – and our judgement as to whether the elements selected to elaborate a given narrative support or undermine those values. The very concept of 'values' assumes that whatever is adopted as such by an individual or group is seen in a positive light, even if from our particular narrative vantage point we might consider it wrong or even reprehensible. Bakan (2004) cites many corporate executives who argue vehemently against big business adopting good causes for their own sake. Milton Friedman, a Nobel laureate and a leading economist, 'believes the new moralism in business is in fact *immoral*' (Bakan 2004: 33; emphasis added), and even Hank McKinell, the Chief Executive of Pfizer, who believes his company is dedicated to doing as much good in the community as possible, 'concedes that corporate self-interest is, and must be, the primary motivation behind his company's good deeds' (Bakan 2004: 47). Profit for the shareholders then heads the list of values for corporate businesses, irrespective of the individuals who run them. This means that in all practices and narratives elaborated by corporations, 'certain values get emphasized while others get de-emphasized', according to the overriding principle of profit (Danny Schechter, award-winning journalist specializing in corporate work; in Bakan 2004: 51). No doubt certain 'facts', 'events' and 'arguments' also get emphasized or de-emphasized according to the same principle. The same process arguably informs the way we select elements to weave any type of narrative – ontological, public or conceptual.

Temporality, Relationality, Causal Emplotment and Selective Appropriation represent the core features of narrativity. All four derive mainly from the work of

Somers (1992, 1994, 1997) and Somers and Gibson (1994). The next chapter will cover additional features discussed, albeit very briefly, in Bruner (1991).

Core references

Bruner, Jerome (1991) 'The Narrative Construction of Reality', *Critical Inquiry* 18(1): 1–21.

Somers, Margaret (1992) 'Narrativity, Narrative Identity, and Social Action: Rethinking English Working-Class Formation', *Social Science History* 16(4): 591–630.

Somers, Margaret (1994) 'The Narrative Construction of Identity: A Relational and Network Approach', *Theory and Society* 23(5): 605–49.

Somers, Margaret (1997) 'Deconstructing and Reconstructing Class Formation Theory: Narrativity, Relational Analysis, and Social Theory', in John R. Hall (ed.) *Reworking Class*, Ithaca and London: Cornell University Press, 73–105.

Somers, Margaret R. and Gloria D. Gibson (1994) 'Reclaiming the Epistemological "Other": Narrative and the Social Constitution of Identity', in Craig Calhoun (ed.) *Social Theory and the Politics of Identity*, Cambridge MA and Oxford: Blackwell, 37–99.

Further reading

Damrosch, David (2005) 'Death in Translation', in Sandra Bermann and Michael Wood (eds) *Nation, Language, and the Ethics of Translation*, Princeton NJ and Oxford: Princeton University Press, 380–98.

Harvey, Keith (2003a) *Intercultural Movements: 'American Gay' in French Translation*, Manchester: St Jerome Publishing.

Jacquemet, Marco (2005) 'The Registration Interview: Restricting Refugees' Narrative Performance', in Mike Baynham and Anna De Fina (eds) *Dislocations/Relocations: Narratives of Displacement*, Manchester: St Jerome Publishing, 197–220.

Jacquemond, Richard (1992) 'Translation and Cultural Hegemony: The Case of French-Arabic Translation', in Lawrence Venuti (ed.) *Rethinking Translation*, London and New York: Routledge, 139–58.

Kahf, Mohja (2000) 'Packaging "Huda": Sha'rawi's Memoirs in the United States Reception Environment', in Amal Amireh and Lisa Suhair Majaj (eds) *Going Global: The Transnational Reception of Third World Women Writers*, New York and London: Garland Publishing, 148–72.

McMurran, Mary Helen (2000) 'Taking Liberties: Translation and the Development of the Eighteenth-Century Novel', *The Translator* 6(1): 87–108.

Pratt, Mary Louise (1994) 'Travel Narrative and Imperialist Vision', in James Phelan and Peter J. Rabinowitz (eds) *Understanding Narrative*, Columbus: Ohio State University Press, 199–221.

Rafael, Vicente L. (1993 [1988]) *Contracting Colonialism: Translation and Christian Conversion in Tagalog Society Under Early Spanish Rule*, Durham NC and London: Duke University Press.

5 Understanding how narratives work

Features of narrativity II

In addition to the four core features discussed in the previous chapter, some of the features identified in Bruner (1991) are worth examining in some detail. These include: particularity, genericness, normativeness (including canonicity and breach), and narrative accrual.

5.1 Particularity

Bruner's discussion of this feature of narrativity is extremely brief, extending to no more than a single paragraph; he also conflates it with *genericness*, another feature he discusses separately (see 5.2 on p. 85). In what follows I take a closer look at the implications of particularity and attempt to disentangle it from genericness, even though Bruner himself uses the term 'genre' indiscriminately under both headings, and without defining it.

Starting with issues of definition, by particularity Bruner (1991: 6–7) means that narratives refer to specific events and people but nevertheless do so within a more general framework of 'story types', which give the specific happenings their meaning and import. It is 'by virtue of embeddedness in genre', Bruner explains, that 'narrative particulars can be "filled in" when they are missing from an account' (1991: 7). By 'genre', in this particular instance, Bruner seeems to mean *generic story outline* (or *plot, story* or *histoire* in narratological terms) rather than genre in the sense of text type such as 'novel', 'editorial', 'ballad', and so on. Generic story outlines in this sense are 'master plots', as understood by narrative grammarians and to some extent by folklore scholars – skeletal stories that combine a range of raw elements in different ways. Broadly speaking, an individual narrative derived from a given storyline may vary in specifics (names, settings, nuances of character) but will ultimately be a variant of that skeletal storyline.[1] In folklore studies, the motifs that constitute the raw elements of folk narratives are painstakingly indexed to trace their development and different realizations across cultures and languages. A coding 'B', for instance, would indicate the presence of the motif 'Animals' in the plot, 'Q' would indicate 'Rewards and Punishments', and 'X' would indicate 'Humour'. Other combinations can then be derived from these headings; for instance 'L' indicates the plot motif of 'reversal', and 'L162' is the motif number for the plot element 'Lowly heroine marries prince'. In another indexing system for whole tales known as the Aarne-Thompson Typology, a complete tale is referred to as a *type* while the term *motif* refers to a single action or narrative procedure. Drawing on one or both systems, folklore scholars are thus able to make an explicit link between a local version of a given story and the 'canon' to which it belongs:

> The Palestinian version of the Cinderella story ... is not called Cinderella, but nevertheless it belongs to Aarne-Thompson type 510, which is the designated number for the Cinderella cycle of stories. This simple fact is one of the most important aspects of the tale's translatability, for one does not only translate a particular but also a universal. The universal fact, the fact that there is a canon with articulated plots which exhibit sufficient regularity to be classified into numbered types, puts the canon at the heart of the process of translation. If the canon did not exist, the translatability of the tale would be hampered.
>
> (Muhawi 1999a)

Folktales aside, all our narratives ultimately derive from sets of skeletal storylines with recurrent motifs, and these sets may differ in their entirety or in specific details across cultures. In translation, source texts and even entire genres are often adapted to evoke culturally popular storylines, as in the case of Kuroiwa Ruikō's translations of Western detective novels into Japanese in the late nineteenth century. Silver (2004) demonstrates how Ruikō adapted his plots to bring them closer to a storyline known as the *dokufu-mono* or 'poison-woman story', a brand of *gesaku* writing that was very popular during the Meiji period. One of the main motifs in this storyline was 'reward for virtue and punishment for evil' (Silver 2004: 192). Emile Gaboriau's *L'Affaire Lerouge* (1866) tells the story of a lawyer named Noel, the bastard son of a wealthy count who pretends to be his legitimate heir and attempts to deprive his half-brother of his inheritance. Noel murders a nurse who knows that he is an illegitimate son, and is found out. In the final pages of the novel, which Ruikō completely rewrites in line with *gesaku* conventions, the police have Noel trapped in the apartment of his lover Juliette. The source text, an English translation of *L'Affaire Lerouge*, features the following exchange between the lovers:

> 'There must be some escape!' [Juliette] cried, fiercely.
> 'Yes,' replied Noel, 'one way. ... They will pick the lock. Bolt all the doors, and make them break them down; it will gain time for me.'
> Juliette ... sprang forward to do this. Noel leaning against the mantel took out his revolver, and placed it against his breast.
> But Juliette ... perceiving the movement, threw herself headlong upon her lover to prevent his purpose, but so violently that the pistol was discharged. The shot took effect, the ball passing through Noel's stomach. He gave a terrible cry.
> Juliette had made his death a terrible punishment; she had only prolonged his agony.
> He staggered but did not fall, supporting himself by the mantel, while the blood flowed copiously.

'You shall not kill yourself,' she cried, 'you shall not. You are mine; I love you'.

(Silver 2004: 194–5)

Ruikō, who renames the protagonists as Minoru and Rie, completely reconfigures this ending as follows:

'[E]scape with me to America!' [Minoru said.]

The young woman, completely overcome, could not even muster a tear. She was silent for a time, her head bowed, but then seemed to make up her mind.

'I misjudged you badly. A man should not talk about running at a time like this, when everything is in shambles. Please ... take your life gracefully here and now, and say you are mine. If you kill yourself gracefully, my love will never change. I will die together with you. If after hearing me say this, you still say you are unsure, and that you want to escape, I will shoot you right now. ... Well – which is it to be? Will you die together with me? Or will you be killed by my hand? Based on your answer I will become either your wife forever or your enemy.'

'Forgive me, Rie. I am yours forever.'

'Together then?'

'A graceful suicide.'

'I could not be gladder.'

(Silver 2004: 195)

The story thus ends in a Japanese-style love suicide. Silver offers other examples of the way Ruikō adapted Western detective novels to *gesaku* conventions and suggests that 'the popularity of Ruikō's translated detective novels may have depended in part upon their largely accidental congruence with the earlier native form' (2004: 192).

Our non-fictional narratives of the world, insofar as they can be separated from the narratives elaborated in folktales or fictional genres in general, are also based on skeletal storylines. One such storyline discussed by Bennett and Edelman in the US context is

the saga of the government and its agents confronting formidable 'facts of life,' such as the deceitfulness of Communists, the immorality of criminals, or the aversion to honest work that swells the ranks of of welfare recipients and the hard-core unemployed. ... Although measurable progress is scant against the entrenched enemies of society, most chapters in the ongoing saga of 'embattled society' conclude with hopeful proposals for defending the good life against yet another onslaught by its implacable foes.

(1985: 156)

Bruner suggests that skeletal storylines enable us to make sense of individual narratives and fill in any missing details. For example, in most cultures the boy-woos-girl narrative provides a master plot for numerous individual stories and triggers certain sequences or assumptions that relate to (secret) dating, the giving of gifts, girl initially resisting boy's advances, and so on. Even when left implicit, these particularizations of the narrative can be active in the form of taken-for-granted assumptions, because they form part of the default framework in which the specific narrative is embedded. When US Supreme Court Justice Louis Brandeis likened corporations to Frankenstein monsters in 1933, he was not just using a rhetorical ploy to capture the attention of his audience. Having signalled an analogy with a specific variant of a monster-out-of-control storyline, his audience could easily infer that '[g]overnments create corporations, much like Dr Frankenstein created his monster, yet, once they exist, corporations, like the monster, threaten to empower their creators' (Bakan 2004: 149).

Motifs and skeletal storylines within which the particularity of a narrative is realized shape our interpretation of events and discourses in other ways. For example, Abbott (2002: 44) argues that the masterplot of a black man punished unjustly for stepping out of his place served O. J. Simpson well when he was tried for the murder of his white American wife and found not guilty in 1995. From a very different perspective, Pratt (1994) demonstrates in her groundbreaking study of travel narratives of the eighteenth and nineteenth centuries and the imperial visions that underpinned them how these travel stories drew on the classic quest motif, or skeletal storyline in our terms. This storyline depicts the hero setting forth into a harsh and dangerous environment in order to recover for his community those treasures that rightfully belong to it. The plot, Pratt argues, 'fit well with European imperial design' because it was 'already firmly instilled in the consciousness of every European who had ever heard a fairy tale' (1994: 201) and was therefore a powerful resource for legitimizing exploration. Interestingly, Pratt argues that the earlier accounts of exploration were very personal in tone and revolved around the ambitions and industry of the individual explorers recounting the story as they experienced it or as they wished to inform their fellow Europeans about it. In other words, the particularities of those earlier narratives were embedded in a different skeletal storyline. Pratt explains the movement into higher levels of abstraction as realized in the quest motif in later narratives of exploration as follows:

> The notion of a benevolent civilizing mission comes into play later, one suspects, when there is a full-fledged imperial mission that needs mystifying. So it was with the Spaniards in America three hundred years before, and so it is today, in White House pronouncements where 'democracy' and 'freedom' replace 'prosperity' and 'salvation' as the goods equated with imperial intervention.
>
> (1994: 205)

Skeletal storylines come equipped with character types 'whose motivation and personality are an integral and often fixed element of the masterplot' (Abbott 2002: 148). In the legal domain, for example, the court projects particular qualities on different types of defendants and witnesses; masterplots can then 'absorb the complexity of a defendant's human nature into the simplicity of type' (2002: 148). Moreover, character types are not restricted to individual characters; they can also reflect characteristics of an entire group. Colonial narratives often depict the colonized either as underdeveloped and in need of protection and guidance from a more developed society, or as bloodthirsty and dangerous, or both. The traditional anthropological narrative depicted the anthropologist as a mobile representative of an advanced society and the community under study as stable, timeless, primitive, even though the community in question may well have had a long history of displacement and migration (Baynham and De Fina 2005: 88). The moralizing storylines of the middle classes in sixteenth- and seventeenth-century Europe depicted women as 'innately more moral than men, ... correct, decorous, angelic creatures whose impact on brutish men ... must be to civilize them, to educate them in the softer, kinder, gentler ways of Jesus Christ' (Robinson 1995: 155–6). In the nineteenth century, orientalist narratives of the East represented its people as licentious and immoral; today, Western narratives of the region represent the same people, especially Eastern women, as sexually repressed and in need of liberation. All these character types feature prominently in the stock of stories that underpin the narratives of the time.

5.1.1 The resonance of recurrent storylines

Recurrent storylines can have special resonance for particular groups or cultures, with the result that members of these groups will tend to find individual narratives that echo these storylines highly credible. In an article entitled 'Redemption and American Politics', McAdams (2004) argues that the Republicans won the 2004 US elections because they were better storytellers than the Democrats,[2] and specifically because they used a popular narrative of redemption to frame their electoral campaign:

> the Republican Party has groomed candidates and honed messages that resonate deeply with a story of life that Americans hold dear. It is the narrative of *redemption* – a story about an innocent protagonist in a dangerous world who sticks to simple principles and overcomes suffering and hardship in the end. This is a story that many productive and caring American adults – Democrats, Republicans, and Independents – love to tell about their own lives. Republicans, however, have found ways of talking about public life and political issues that reinforce this story.
>
> (McAdams 2004: B14)

As a research psychologist, McAdams, along with his students, had been studying the stories people tell about themselves – their ontological narratives – and had found that American adults, whether liberal or conservative, 'tend to describe their own lives as variations on a general script' that McAdams refers to as 'the redemptive self':

> The story of the redemptive self in American life has two key themes. The first is the belief that as a young child, I was fortunate, blessed, or advantaged in

some manner, even as others around me experienced suffering and pain. I am the innocent protagonist, chosen for a special, manifest destiny. As I journey forth in a dangerous world, I hold to simple truths, basic values of goodness and decency.

...

The second major theme in the story of the redemptive self is overcoming hardships and adversity. Especially caring and productive American adults often tell stories about their lives in which emotionally negative events lead directly to reward. These stories take many different forms. Stories of atonement describe a religious move from sin to salvation. Stories of upward social mobility depict the socioeconomic move from rags to respectability and riches. Stories of recovery tell how sick or addicted protagonists regained their health or sobriety. Stories of liberation chart the move from feeling enslaved to feeling free. From Franklin to Oprah, from Horatio Alger to 12-step programs, American folklore and culture have provided a treasure trove of redemptive narratives from which we all (unconsciously) borrow in fashioning the stories of our own lives.

(McAdams 2004: B14)

The Republicans' success in exploiting this powerful storyline to appeal to the American electorate in 2004 becomes more understandable when the connection between the ontological and political narrative is spelled out:

The attacks of September 11 and the 'war on terrorism,' ... play perfectly into the story of the redemptive self. Terrorism and war show us that the world is a dangerous, unredeemed place. In times of crisis, the good American protagonist must call upon the deepest reservoir of unwavering conviction and hope.

A dangerous world is indeed the kind of world that the good and strong hero of the redemptive self seems unconsciously to expect. Under conditions of adversity, he will fight the good fight. He will keep the faith. In the end, his suffering will give way to redemption. And along the way, he may even help to redeem others.

(McAdams 2004: B14)

Somers and Gibson (1994: 73–4) point out that '[t]he extent and nature of any given repertoire of narratives available for appropriation is always historically and culturally specific', which means that the narrative of redemption will not necessarily have much resonance outside the American context, nor of course for all constituencies within that context.

5.1.2 Subverting familiar storylines

Familiar storylines can be deliberately satirized to communicate social or political messages. The highly successful films *Shrek* and *Shrek2* take a typical fairytale storyline and subvert it to very good effect. As the tagline of the first of the two films put it, 'The Prince isn't charming. The Princess isn't sleeping. The sidekick isn't helping. The ogre is the hero. Fairy tales will never be the same again'.[3] *Shrek2* ends with Fiona, the princess who turned ugly when she was kissed by an ogre rather than a prince, refusing to take the magic potion that would return her to her former beauty and opting instead to remain as she is with the ogre she loves. The moral of the narrative is clear: life is not about outward beauty and material possessions. This take on the traditional fairytale narrative exhorts us not to judge others by their appearance. The lead character Shrek, in particular, directly challenges our stereotypes:

> At first glance, he's an ugly one. Shrek, that is, a green ogre with trumpet-shaped ears and a seemingly ferocious temper who's never afraid to rid himself of unneeded body gases. ... But in no time, we realize he's a sweetheart, a pushover, a softie who just acts mean and ornery because, well, everyone *thinks* he's mean and ornery.
>
> (Howe 2001)

Here is an example of a more ambivalent take on a popular and highly topical storyline; this particular example relies on a translation-specific practice, namely subtitling, to achieve effect. A comic video clip entitled *News from Iraq* circulated on the Internet in October 2004 and has since been available to download from a site called *Visit4info.*[4] It shows an English-speaking female reporter interviewing what appear to be Iraqi fighters in Tikrit, the former stronghold of Saddam Hussein. The reporter's introduction is typical of the media hype we have come to expect:

> Once a stronghold of forces loyal to captive dictator Saddam Hussein, the city of Tikrit, here in Northern Iraq, is now firmly under the control of American forces. Or is it? These members of the Iraqi resistance movement still loyal to Saddam Hussein think otherwise.

The first hint of ambivalence can be seen in the choice of *Iraqi resistance movement.* This is highly unrepresentative of official media coverage in the English-speaking world, where the standard term used tends to be *insurgents*, or at its least subjective simply *fighters*. The choice also collapses all political players in that region into one category (resistance fighters who are loyal to Saddam Hussein), thus parodying the highly simplistic neo-conservative storyline which portrays the struggle in Iraq as being one of evil (Saddam and his followers) versus good (America and its allies). This caricature of the various Iraqi groups fighting the Occupation is emphasized by the fact that the faces of all the Iraqis shown in the clip are covered; their 'faceless-ness' is in line with their portrayal as a single group with a single objective.

Although the Iraqi being interviewed speaks perfectly understandable English, everything he says is repeated in (English) subtitles across the screen. At first, the Iraqi man appears quite serious, announcing in a somewhat over-rehearsed monotonous tone that betrays the 'mock show' nature of the clip: 'The Americans tell lies. Each day our forces grow stronger, each day we move closer to our goal of driving the infidel ... ' The use of *infidel* contrasts with the reporter's superficially positive choice of *resistance movement* and continues the neo-conservative caricature of placing various groups, including both secular and religious political players, into the same category. This Iraqi 'resistance fighter' then stops, points to the subtitles on the screen, and asks 'Wh ... what are they?'. The reporter answers 'Nothing, carry on'. He tries to ignore the subtitles and carries on with the rhetoric of 'driving the infidels from our motherland'. But then he stops sharply again and asks, now in a more clearly comical fashion, 'Are they subtitles?'. From thereon the interview deteriorates as this 'resistance fighter' gets more comical, questioning the need for his English to be subtitled and insisting that he 'studied English at the bloody American University in Cairo'. The reporter attempts to appease him by saying that she can understand his English, but this produces an even more comically outraged reaction: 'oh ... you ... you see how they condescend to us with their subtitles'.

After a few such exchanges, and especially as he notes that the speech of another of his fellow 'resistance fighters' is not accompanied by subtitles, he cannot contain his (comical) outrage and moves out of the screen shot. The reporter goes back to addressing the audience, describing the dangerous situation in Iraq in a very serious tone, and the clip closes with the Iraqi fighter moving back into the shot, comically gesticulating in the background and shouting that he can't understand the reporter's English.

This is a more ambivalent attempt to subvert a storyline of good and evil as they fight it out in a dangerous world, with our 'free', serious, democratic media bringing the latest episode in this noble fight into our living rooms. Rather than subverting a particular take on the good and evil fight in the context of Iraq, this video clip seems to undermine the entire narrative of serious, valiant heroes of any kind, and on any side. In the course of doing so, it also draws attention to and ridicules particular positions within the dominant media discourse. For example, the fracas over the subtitling draws attention to the tendency of Western media to represent the Other, especially the Arab Other, as unintelligible and in need of translation – literally and metaphorically.

5.2 Genericness

Bruner's definition of genres (1991: 14), insofar as he provides one, is very brief – they are 'recognizable "kinds" of narrative: farce, black comedy, tragedy, the *Bildungsroman*, romance, satire, travel saga, and so on'. Examples of non-literary genres – which are not discussed by Bruner – can be added to this list and might include editorials, legal contracts, eyewitness reports, shopping lists, menus, academic articles, magazine interviews and documentaries, among many others. These established frameworks of narration 'provide both writer and reader with commodious and conventional "models" for limiting the hermeneutic task of making sense of human happenings – ones we narrate to ourselves as well as ones we hear others tell' (1991: 14).

Bruner also distinguishes beween what he calls the 'plot form' of a genre and the form of telling associated with it and recognizes that 'to translate the "way of telling" of a genre into another language or culture where it does not exist requires a fresh literary-linguistic intervention' (1991: 14). This way of telling is not a cosmetic, outer layer that merely glosses the content of the narrative. Conventionalized ways of telling 'predispose us to use our minds and sensibilities in particular ways' (1991: 15).

Genre, then, is a conventionalized framework that guides our interpretation in a number of different ways. To start with, generic identification endows a narrative experience with coherence, cohesiveness and a sense of boundedness. It allows us to recognize it as an instantiation of a recognizable communicative practice that is meaningful and discrete. It also encourages us to project certain qualities onto the narrative experience: factuality, seriousness, humour, glamour. A poem is not expected to be 'factual', but a scientific article is. These expectations are of course culture-specific. An academic lecture may feature stretches of humour in the English-speaking world and still be taken seriously and treated as 'factual' in content, but in other cultures the use of humour may undermine the veracity of the narrative elaborated in the lecture. Nida (1998: 27) mentions a similar cross-cultural problem relating to the Bible. One translator, Nida explains, paid special attention to the poetic character of some sections of the Bible but still printed them in prose because 'he wanted people to realize that what was written was true'. Poetry, it seems, is strongly associated with fictional content in many cultures.

Genres encode participant roles and power relations. Only a weak, marginalized party under some form of threat from a more powerful opponent would resort to the genre of 'petition'. Issuing a petition is in itself an attempt to elaborate a narrative in which the party being appealed to is portrayed as powerful but unfair or ill-advised in some sense, and the party doing the petitioning (which may include hundreds and even thousands of signatories) is marginalized but morally superior and able to draw on 'people power'.[5] Press releases, on the other hand, are usually associated with groups that, if not necessarily powerful, are either thought of as legitimate or wish to project themselves as such. Press releases are typically issued by government officials and large corporations, but they are also increasingly being issued by activist groups who are positioned outside the mainstream of society. As a genre, the press release is part of a narrative that portrays those who issue the release as a coherent and legitimate entity endowed with some form of authority, be it one derived from what Bourdieu would call social capital or from a moral position. It may thus project a position of institutional authority or of moral challenge, but it does not project a position of subservience.

Translators need to be aware of the contribution of generic form to the elaboration of particular narratives since the way in which a particular genre may encode or signal participant roles does vary across cultures, and so do the real world consequences of elaborating one's narrative within a particular genre.

5.2.1 Genre-specific signalling devices

Some genres are associated with specific signalling devices, or contextualization cues in Gumperz's terms (Gumperz 1992). These devices index a textual instantiation of the genre in question and/or trigger a set of expectations and inferences associated with it.

They may be lexical – as in the case of 'Once upon a time', and similar expressions that preface fairytales in many languages – or syntactic, as in the use in academic abstracts of the present and past tense, respectively, to distinguish between what is stated in the article itself and what was actually done in the research on which the article reports (Baker 1992: 100). Or they may be structural. Muhawi explains that 'three fold repetition is one of the basic tropes of plot in folktales. A formula has to be repeated three times to be effective, ... a hero must try three times before he succeeds' (1999b: 229).

Signalling devices, or contextualization cues, may also be visual, including typographical features such as the use of italics, the choice of colour, or a particular style of drawing that might signal the genre as a cartoon, hence encoding a non-factual and humorous or satirical narrative. The cover of Sherry Simon's well-known book *Gender in Translation*, published by Routledge in 1996, is vertically split into two colour areas: the lefthand side, which occupies more space than the righthand side, is blue. The righthand side, occupying less space, is pink. The back cover is entirely blue. In the English-speaking world, newborn babies and small children are often dressed in blue if they are male and in pink if they are female, and the cover therefore encodes part of the Western academic narrative of gender for readers: we live in a male-dominated world. In other cultures, these colours do not have the same meanings, and the narrative of a male-dominated world as elaborated in Western feminist genres therefore has to be signalled differently, or not at all, on the main cover.

Signalling devices associated with different genres then are often culture-specific. This culture-specificity extends to the fact that some genres, in different parts of the world, may be 'gendered'. Muhawi (1999a, 1999b, in press) argues that the Arab folktale is a gendered genre, explaining that in the Arab world,

> the tellers of folktales are women. Not only have women been the tellers, but women have also been the traditional audience for folktales. The Arabic folktale is a woman's art form narrated by women for women, and it is her speech that has conditioned this art form over the ages.
>
> (Muhawi 1999a)

This has consequences for the way in which a genre may be translated, either to retain or subvert the gendered voice of the author, depending on the specificities of a given context and the broader agenda in which the translation is embedded. Harvey (1998, 2003a) offers interesting examples of the translation of what we might call the 'sexualized' genre of gay fiction.

Different genres, including the verbal and non-verbal activities embedded in them, are also often associated with specific formal features such as length, duration, thematic content, pitch and loudness, level of formality, and setting. These features, again, are not cosmetic. At one extreme, compliance with them could determine whether a given behaviour is intelligible at all. MacIntyre gives a good example which illustrates the impact of setting:

> If in the middle of my lecture on Kant's ethics I suddenly broke six eggs into a bowl and added flour and sugar, proceeding all the while with my Kantian

exegesis, I have *not*, simply in virtue of the fact that I was following a sequence prescribed by Fanny Farmer, performed an intelligible action.

(1981: 194–5)

Beyond the question of intelligibility, these features also contribute to the elaboration of individual narratives set within the relevant generic boundaries. An eyewitness report is expected to focus on grave and usually very painful incidents, and hence whatever is presented as falling within this genre is implicitly injected with these meanings. On the other hand, a political speech delivered in a soft tone is likely to be exprienced as ineffective, or 'wishy washy' in common parlance.

Nevertheless, the fit between an individual text and the genre in which it is moulded is rarely complete. For one thing, different people make their own decisions as to how closely they wish to conform to or deviate from genre conventions, and this in itself signals certain aspects of their ontological narratives – whether they want to project themselves as disciplined, adventurous, confident or skilful, for instance. Moreover, playfulness and the subversion of conventions is practically a convention in its own right in some genres. Advertising is a case in point. An Alfa Romeo advert which appeared in the British magazine *Radio Times* in September 2002 consisted of a list of features set out as a menu, as follows:

Menu

The New Alfa 156 Range
1.8 T. Spark
2.0 T. Spark
2.0 Selespeed
2.5 V6 24v/Q-System
2.4 JTD
and the
New 1.6 T. Spark
New standard specification
Four airbags
Climate control
Leather steering wheel
Titanium effect console★
3 Year Alfacare Dealer Warranty
Two new versions

Lusso	Veloce
Leather upholstery	Recaro sports seats
Radio/CD player	or Leather upholstery
Third rear headrest and	Body colour side skirts
3 point centre seatbelt	Sports suspension
15" Alloy wheels	16" Alloy wheels
Headlamp washers	Carbon effect console

A picture of the car appears underneath the above text, followed by: 'Salivating yet?'

This is an instance of creative, genre-based manipulation that supports rather than subverts commercial narratives consistent with the genre of advertising. In other words, playfulness is an in-built convention of the genre itself in this case and hence has no subversive import as such.

5.2.2 Parodying and subverting genres

The Alfa Romeo advert exploits generic conventions to elaborate typical advertising narratives, not to subvert any dominant narratives or undermine ones that we expect to encounter in the advertising genre. Hatim and Mason refer to this type of fluidity in marking and exploiting genre boundaries as 'multifunctionality' and suggest that translators 'will seek to preserve in translation the generic ambivalence' of the resulting texts (1990: 141). But genre conventions can also be strategically exploited to undermine dominant narratives elaborated in the same or a very different generic medium. Instead of the usual copyright page we are used to seeing in a wide range of published material, *Zapatistas! Documents of the New Mexican Revolution* (1994) features a section entitled 'Anti-Copyright' in the Table of Contents. This directly challenges the conventions of the broad macro-genre of commercial publications:

Text anti-copyright © 1994 Autonomedia, editors,
        and contributors.
This book may be freely pirated and quoted for
        non-commercial purposes,
provided that a portion of any income derived
        thereby returns to
the Indigenous and campesino communities of
        Southern Mexico.
Please inform the editors and publishers at:

Autonomedia
POB 568 Williamsburg Station
Brooklyn, New York 11211–0568 USA

.... .

A portion of the proceeds from the publication of
this book will be donated to the Zapatistas.

ISBN: 1–57027–014

The parodying of dominant narratives of the day to undermine existing relations of power or prestige in society is a very common tactic of activism that often relies on our understanding of generic forms and conventions to make its point. In terms of conceptual narratives, for instance, there are several humorous periodicals that parody the genre of scientific journals in order to undermine the narrative of scientific research as cutting edge, urgent, meaningful and highly consequential. Examples of

Figure 8 AIR (Annals of Improbable Research): Front cover of the January/February 2002 issue

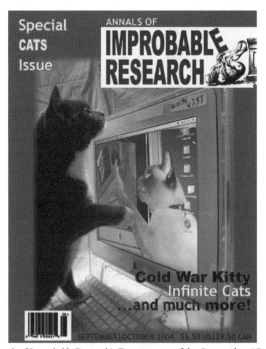

Figure 9 AIR (Annals of Improbable Research): Front cover of the September/October 2004 issue

HM Department of Vague Paranoia

PREPARING FOR EMERGENCIES
WHAT YOU NEED TO KNOW

Welcome to the Preparing for Emergencies website.

In an effort to worry the public and convince them to vote for us again next year, and because George Bush asked us to, this website includes the common sense advice found in the Preparing for Emergencies booklet, and information on what the government is doing to protect the country as a whole. (Hint: we're praying *really, really* hard.) National editions of the booklet will be available here when we can be arsed to get translators to put them into your crazy moon languages.

From 2nd August, translations of the booklet into 16 languages will be available on this website. They will be in: Arabic, Bengali, Chinese, English, Farsi, French, Greek, Gujarati, Hindi, Kurdish, Punjabi, Somali, Turkish, Urdu, Vietnamese and Welsh. In the meantime, just assume that we don't care about you.

You will also be able to order copies of the booklet in audio tape, large print, and Braille formats. We wouldn't have bothered, but Blunkett insisted. *

* David Blunkett, then Home Secretary of Britain, is blind.

Figure 10   *Preparing for Emergencies* (www.preparingforemergencies.co.uk)

this satirical exploitation of scientific genres include the *Journal of Insignificant Research*[6] and the *Journal of Irreproducible Results*.[7] The *Annals of Improbable Research (AIR)*[8] even sponsors an alternative 'Ig Nobel Awards' ceremony, which is held at Harvard every autumn, just before the 'real' ceremony in Stockholm. The acronym *AIR* itself of course recalls the expression 'hot air' in English, defined in the *Cobuild English Dictionary* as 'claims or promises that are made to impress people but which will probably never happen'. It contributes to debunking the narrative of science as consequential.

A similar strategy, which involves parodying the same generic format to undermine academic narratives, is employed in constructing the elaborate website of the *University of Bums on Seats* (www.cynicalbastards.com/ubs/index.html), whose Vice-Chancellor is aptly named Prof. Alan Dubious (MAd, TOTP, DipSHiT).

Genre conventions can also be exploited to undermine dominant public narratives of the day. Another mock website, *Preparing for Emergencies*, hijacks an actual information booklet of the same title distributed to British households in 2003, with translated versions available in a range of languages. The mock site reproduces even the visual format, exact colours and exact layout of the leaflet. Only the text is different.[9]

As a corollary to undermining dominant public narratives, genre conventions can also be exploited to ridicule prominent public figures associated with those narratives. Hart Seely's well-known satirical narrative of Donald Rumsfeld as a great poet

The Unknown

As we know,
There are known knowns.
There are things we know we know.
We also know
There are known unknowns.
That is to say
We know there are some things
We do not know.
But there are also unknown unknowns,
The ones we don't know
We don't know.

Feb. 12, 2002, Department of Defense news briefing

Clarity

I think what you'll find,
I think what you'll find is,
Whatever it is we do substantively,
There will be near-perfect clarity
As to what it is.
And it will be known,
And it will be known to the Congress,
And it will be known to you,
Probably before we decide it,
But it will be known.

Feb. 28, 2003, Department of Defense briefing

A Confession

Once in a while,
I'm standing here, doing something.
And I think,
'What in the world am I doing here?'
It's a big surprise.

May 16, 2001, interview with the New York Times

is based on recasting Rumsfeld's actual pronouncements in a range of official genres such as briefings and interviews as poetry.

The mock narrative of Rumsfeld as a great poet is discursively and visually elaborated in several venues, including the Slate website (which published the original 'poems'), the *Guardian* newspaper in Britain, and later in book form (Seely 2003b). Each venue contributes to the further elaboration of the narrative in its own way, always relying on the generic manipulation of Rumsfeld's pronouncements, as well as our familiarity with the generic conventions and discourse of journalism and literary criticism, to achieve effect. For example, the Slate website features an article by Hart Seely that simulates the discourse of serious journalism:

The Poetry of D.H. Rumsfeld
Recent works by the secretary of defense
By Hart Seely
Posted Wednesday, April 2, 2003, at 10: 03 AM PT
Secretary of Defense Donald Rumsfeld is an accomplished man. Not only is he guiding the war in Iraq, he has been a pilot, a congressman, an ambassador, a businessman, and a civil servant. But few Americans know that he is also a poet.

Until now, the secretary's poetry has found only a small and skeptical audience: the Pentagon press corps. Every day, Rumsfeld regales reporters with his jazzy, impromptu riffs. Few of them seem to appreciate it.

But we should all be listening. Rumsfeld's poetry is paradoxical: It uses playful language to address the most somber subjects: war, terrorism, mortality. Much of it is about indirection and evasion: He never faces his subjects head on but weaves away, letting inversions and repetitions confuse and beguile. His work, with its dedication to the fractured rhythms of the plainspoken vernacular, is reminiscent of William Carlos Williams'. Some readers may find that Rumsfeld's gift for offhand, quotidian pronouncements is as entrancing as Frank O'Hara's.

(Seely 2003a)

The opening statement of Hart Seely's book *Pieces of Intelligence: The Existential Poetry of Donald H. Rumsfeld* (Seely 2003b) simulates the discourse of literary criticism, including prefaces to important works of literature, but the front cover immediately betrays the satirical nature of the book's content:

The poetry of D. H. Rumsfeld (as he is known to the literary cognoscenti) demands to be read aloud. Like the epics of Homer, or modern African-American street poetry, Rumsfeld's oeuvre originated as oral improvisation … During news briefings and media interviews, Rumsfeld quietly inserts haiku, sonnets, free verse, and flights of lyrical fancy into his responses, embedding the verses within the full transcripts of his sessions.

All these generic manipulations contribute to the elaboration of the immediate mock narrative of Rumsfeld as a great poet. This, in turn, satirically evokes a

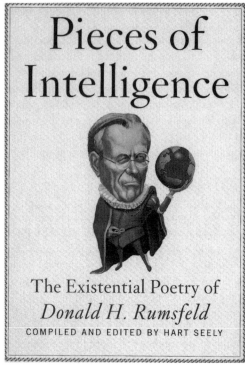

Figure 11 Book cover of Hart Seely's *Pieces of Intelligence: The Existential Poetry of Donald H. Rumsfeld*

narrative of Rumsfeld as an incoherent and shoddy speaker and, more importantly, of the political leadership of America as confused, complacent, and a source of ridicule rather than inspiration.

Perhaps the most radical form of genre-based subversion of dominant narratives is 'culture jamming', 'the practice of parodying advertisements and hijacking billboards in order to drastically alter their images' (Klein 2000: 280). This is an activist means of responding to our ongoing loss of space and privacy, our loss of control over our environment. 'Adbusters', as they are known, argue that since most of us are not in a position to buy back these spaces and display our own messages, we are

Figures 12 and 13 A variant of culture jamming – graffiti and slogans on Israel's separation wall

entitled to talk back to the images of corporate culture. Adbusters elaborate 'counter-narratives that hack into a corporation's own method of communication to send a message starkly at odds with the one that was intended' (Klein 2000: 281). The graffiti and political statements that now adorn large sections of the wall erected by Israel to isolate the Palestinian population in various parts of the West Bank and Gaza may be seen as a variant of this strategy of 'culture jamming'.

5.2.3 The policing of genres

At various points in history and in various parts of the world some genres have tended to be more 'policed' or tightly controlled than others, with higher levels of regimentation generally serving the interests of those in power. Indeed, translation itself was once carefully policed as a genre. During the Reformation, women could only translate religious works (Krontiris 1992: 10). When Margaret Tyler decided to translate a secular work, the Spanish romance *A Mirrour of Princely deedes and Knighthood*, in 1578, she had to entreat the reader in the Preface to forgive her this trespass (Krontiris 1992: 17).

The policing of genres influences our lives in more or less significant ways. To be valid in many countries, an official translation of a document that belongs to a specific set of genres such as birth certificates and academic degrees must feature a certifying formula, which is stipulated by law, and this formula varies from country to country (Mayoral Asensio 2003: 84). Though highly regimented, the impact of this type of controlled generic environment is relatively limited. A more extreme example is the ruling by the US Treasury's Office of Foreign Assets Control (OFAC) in September 2003 that the Institute for Electrical and Electronic Engineers (IEEE) can only publish scientific papers from Iranian authors in its journals if the articles are reproduced 'as is', that is without any editing of style or content, and without translation. The IEEE had requested

> concurrence that no license is needed for its member volunteers to ask questions or provide comments to authors in Iran concerning the manuscripts submitted to the U.S. Entity, and for its member volunteers to prepare the manuscript for publication, including translation, reordering of paragraphs or sentences, correction of syntax, grammar, spelling and punctuation, replacement of inappropriate words, and preparing the text for printing.[10]

In his response to the Institute dated 30 September 2003, the Director of OFAC confirmed that the activities described above 'would constitute the provision of prohibited services to Iran, regardless of the fact that such transactions are part of the U.S. Entity's normal publishing activities'.[11]

The more regimented or closely policed a genre at any point in time, the more tightly those in authority can control access to it by various members of society as well as control the 'narrative space' of those involved in the relevant event. In the Arab world, all written genres are expected to use Standard Written Arabic rather than any of the varieties spoken in different Arab countries. When Mustapha Safouan decided to translate Shakespeare's *Othello* into *'amiyya* (the Egyptian vernacular) in 1998, he was aware that the artificial gap between Standard Written Arabic and the vernacular is imposed and policed by the dominant powers in the Arab world in order to 'disempower both the masses and the intellectuals' (Hanna 2005: 119). The choice of the Egyptian vernacular as a medium for translating a canonized tragedy serves not only to give voice to the disempowered masses but also to liberate Arab consciousness 'from a pre-fabricated unity that suppresses difference and downgrades diversity' (Hanna 2005: 119).

5.2.4 Generic shifts in translation

The literature on translation abounds with examples of source texts that have either been accommodated to the target culture conventions of a given genre or carried over as is without due regard to differences in generic conventions. Shibamoto Smith (2005) offers several examples of the latter in relation to Western and Japanese category romances. For one thing, the physical appearance and general demeanour of both heroes and heroines in these romances are very different: Western heroes are 'spectacularly masculine, sexually hyper-experienced, and reserved, if not cold' and Western heroines are 'extraordinarily beautiful', 'unusually intelligent and/or unusually honest and moral' (2005: 99). Japanese heroes, on the other hand, are 'just ordinary, nice men, who act in relatively ordinary ways' and the Japanese heroine 'is not necessarily a great, sexually compelling beauty' (2005: 100). These differences, according to Shibamoto Smith, are not generally mediated in the translation of Harlequin romances into Japanese, with the result that the Japanese-speaking characters in these imported romances 'inhabit "western" social fields and react in ways that – whatever their suitability in those social fields – are not the ways that Japanese true lovers speak, behave, and come to their own *happiiendingu* "happy ending" in domestically produced romance novels' (2005: 99).

A source text may also be translated into a different genre altogether, sometimes resulting in the creation of a new genre in either the source or target cultures. Critical comments and introductory material to late nineteenth-century English translations were used to reframe Irish comic tales of the Ulster Cycle as historical or topographical documents (Tymoczko 1999: 210).[12] Polezzi (2001: 206ff.) explains that there is no specific genre of travel writing in Italian but that translations have 'produced' a body of Italian travel literature, or at least an image of it, for the benefit and consumption of foreign audiences. Generic shifts in English translations of Italian books on Tibet include adapting the titles to the conventions of British travel writing, ultimately reconfiguring the source narrative within a very different genre in the target context (Polezzi 1998: 331). What started out as 'scientific or semi-scientific writing' in Italian becomes 'popular adventure travel' in English.

Reeves-Ellington's (1999) description of her own approach to translating oral history texts offers several examples of the impact of generic shifts in translation. The following version of an excerpt from the speech of a 75-year-old, university-educated Bulgarian woman follows the conventions of academic writing, a reasonable strategy given that the excerpt in question was intended for use in a research paper about Bulgarian women's narratives of work:

One of the saddest moments of my life was my mother's early death. She died from heart disease when she was 45 years old and I was still in high school. But I think the harsh village life killed her. She worked as a teacher, and she had village work and field work to do. Conditions were unimaginably harsh. The land was so mountainous and infertile. And then she had to help her mother-in-law. Quite simply the harsh village life had an adverse effect on her, and she passed away very early.

(Reeves-Ellington 1999: 114)

This version adapts the oral narrative to the conventions of written prose in general and the genre of anthropological research papers in particular, and generally aims to improve clarity by removing ellipsis and minor errors, reducing instances of repetition and shortening long sentences. As Reeves-Ellington explains, '[i]nasmuch as such excerpts are regularly embedded as microtexts within research papers, the translated excerpt meets audience expectations and achieves generic intertextuality within the rhetorical range of the target language' (1999: 116). However, this version clearly suppresses the individual voice of the speaker, dilutes the energy and dynamism of the ontological narrative, and all but eliminates the emotional impact of the original. This becomes clearer if we compare it with an alternative version provided by Reeves-Ellington, one that treats the same features of orality as poetic elements:

My mother.
I told you, didn't I
that one of the *harshest* moments of my life
which I think *most harshly* affected my fate
was my mother's early death.
My mother died when I was still a girl in high school.
My mother died when she was 45 years old
from heart disease.
But I think
my mother died because of the *harsh village life*.
Unimaginably harsh conditions.
And school work
And village work
And those fields
Mountainous
Infertile
She had to help with that
That and her mother-in-law.
Quite simply
the *harsh village life* affected her very badly
and she passed away very early
my mother.

(Reeves-Ellington 1999: 118)

This version adopts a transcription system that allows the translator to reproduce speech delivery patterns to effect what Ellington-Reeves calls 'displaced generic intertextuality: the poetic transcription is familiar to target-text readers but occurs in an unexpected context, that is, a research paper on a topic of history' (1999: 118–19). Ellington-Reeves retains repetitions such as *my mother* and *harsh/harshest/harshly* not only because they are a feature of the speech of this particular informant but also because the repeated phrases are 'among the formulas used in South Slav traditional epic songs and ballads … [as] evident in any contemporary collection of Bulgarian women's folk songs' (1999: 117).

5.3 Normativeness/canonicity and breach

For Bruner, breaches of canonical scripts are what makes a narrative worth telling, which implies that material that does not involve some form of innovation or breach does not constitute a narrative in his view. Indeed, in discussing 'normativeness' – separately – as a feature of narrativity, Bruner argues that '[b]ecause its 'tellability' as a form of discourse rests on a breach of conventional expectation, narrative is necessarily normative' (1991: 15). It seems reasonable, given the approach adopted in this book, to suggest that breach is not a prerequisite to narrativity but rather inherent in it; that it is part of the inbuilt potentiality of narrative.[13] It also seems sensible to discuss canonicity/breach and normativeness as a single feature rather than separately as Bruner does.

In Chapter 2, I explained that all narratives, including scientific ones, participate in processes of legitimation and justification that are ultimately political in import. This normative function underlines the central role that narrative plays in policing cultural legitimacy. Since the normative function of narrativity is a theme that runs throughout this book, and as I have already discussed several examples of 'an implicit canonical script' being 'breached, violated, or deviated from' (Bruner 1991: 11) to disrupt the legitimacy of a canonical storyline or genre, the discussion below is restricted to aspects of the normative import of narrative that I have not directly dealt with so far, especially normative participation and intelligibility.

Normativeness is a feature of all narratives, not just dominant ones. Socialization into *any* narrative order therefore 'will have its repressive side' (Hinchman and Hinchman 1997b: 235). Polletta (1998: 155) demonstrates that narratives are 'prone to reproducing hegemonic understandings even when used by oppositional movements', and explains this by the fact that their intelligibility derives from their conformity to familiar plots, or storylines in our terms. One such plot in modern Western movement stories tends to 'attribute insurgency to individual, independent actors' (Polletta 1998: 155) rather than the relationships which make up the fabric of society and within which individual actors are firmly embedded. Thus participants in social movements may end up reproducing much of the same narrative world they set out to challenge.

Polletta (1998: 142) explains that while theorists of narrative 'differ on just how many plots there are, and just how universal they are', they nevertheless agree that 'stories not conforming to a cultural stock of plots typically are either not stories or are unintelligible'. This means that even breaches of canonical storylines have to be effected within circumscribed, normative plots if they are to be intelligible at all.

Ewick and Silbey (1995: 221) thus stress that one of the conditions of challenging hegemony is 'knowing the rules' by which both hegemonic powers and those who wish to subvert them have to play. In practice, this might mean, for example, that rather than shielding a marginalized client from the workings and assumptions of the court and asking them to simply answer the questions that the attorney has already decided on, an attorney might explain the nature of the court game to the client. Rather than *scripting* the client, an attorney might explain to them that there *is* a script and what that script entails. Rather than 'concealing the socially constructed nature of the proceeding', an attorney might enable a marginalized client 'to participate in that construction' (Ewick and Silbey 1995: 221).

The intelligibility and resonance of particular storylines vary across time and cultures, as we saw in Section 5.1 on p. 78. The normativeness of narrative, as Bruner explains, 'is not historically or culturally terminal. Its form changes with the preoccupations of the age and the circumstances surrounding its production' (1991: 16). Translators are generally conscious of this and their mediation often centres on making the target text intelligible while retaining the particular breach encoded in it. An interesting example of this process that I have discussed elsewhere (Baker, in press, b) can be seen in the choice of subtitles in Mohammad Bakri's documentary *Jenin Jenin*, released in 2002 following Israeli 'incursions' into the Jenin camp in the Occupied West Bank.[14] At one point in the documentary, an old Palestinian man expresses his shock at what happened and the world's apparent indifference and reluctance to intervene. He ends his contribution by saying,

"أنا عار ف و الله العظيم، و الله العظيم، بيتنا ما صار بيت".

which literally means 'What can I say, by God, by God, our home is no longer a home'. The subtitle for this frame is:

What can I say? Not even Vietnam was as bad as this.

In order to communicate the gravity of the situation to a world public whose conception of gravity is conditioned by the political dominance of the USA – in other words, to make the *Jenin Jenin* narrative intelligible to a Western, and particularly American, audience – the subtitlers recontextualize the event by evoking a narrative which is assumed to have moral resonances for those viewers. The indigenous storyline within which the original utterance is framed, and which is evoked by the use of 'home', is one of repeated evictions from the lands of the narrator's ancestors, repeated loss of home after home, dispersal of Palestinians across the world, the familiar site of endless refugee camps into which generation after generation is being squeezed and which they are forced to regard as 'home'. In 2002, this storyline had very little resonance in the USA in particular, and the subtitlers seem to have judged it as unintelligible to Western audiences. It is replaced here with a historical episode that is deemed intelligible to Americans and internationally and that evokes a storyline which is familiar to them.

This example illustrates both breach and normativeness. The tragedy of Jenin is compared to Vietnam, rather than Kashmir for instance, in order to be made

Figure 14 Screen shot from *Jenin Jenin*

intelligible in the context of American political dominance. At the same time, a breach of the then dominant narrative of Israel being a small defenceless country under threat and the USA playing the role of an honest broker in the area is explicitly signalled. The subtitlers could have evoked a more recent event which has even more currency among the target viewers, namely 9/11, but in opting for Vietnam they simultaneously identify America as aggressor and perpetrator of violence, rather than honest broker, even as the Jenin tragedy is reframed to make it intelligible to American audiences. The subtitlers thus succeed in both ensuring intelligibility *and* retaining the breach encoded in the very making of the film.

Finally, normativeness is not restricted to the policing of narratives. It also functions to pressure us directly and indirectly into taking part in those narratives, into playing normatively defined roles within them, even in cases where there may apparently be no obvious motivation for doing so. Social movement scholars such as Polletta (1998), for instance, wonder what it is that compels activists to subscribe to certain narratives and participate in activities that are emotionally demanding and often physically dangerous. Their explanation of this phenomenon revolves around the normative dimension of participation:

> Highly regarded roles within communities may come to be linked with activism in a way that makes participation a requirement of the role. In the early part of the civil rights movement, activism was linked with – normatively

required of – churchgoers; in 1960, *student* became linked to activist, became a 'prized social identity' that supplied the selective incentives to participation.

(Polletta 1998: 143)

5.4 Narrative accrual

Bruner (1991: 18) talks about *narrative accrual* as the manner in which we 'cobble stories together to make them into a whole of some sort' (1991: 18). One of the ways in which this is achieved, according to Bruner, is through 'the imposition of bogus *historical-causal entailment*' – as in claiming that the assassination of Archduke Franz Ferdinand caused the outbreak of the First World War (1991: 19). Repeated (earlier) claims that the second US-led invasion of Iraq in 2003 was triggered by the 9/11 attacks on New York may be considered another example of bogus historical-causal entailment, if we accept that no link between Saddam's regime and those events has ever been confirmed. Another strategy for achieving narrative accrual, according to Bruner again, is *coherence by contemporaneity*, whereby events are assumed to be connected simply because they happen at the same time (1991). In modern times, narrative accrual in both these senses may be regarded as 'the result of a whole labour of symbolic inculcation in which journalists and ordinary citizens participate passively and, above all, a certain number of intellectuals participate actively' (Bourdieu 1998: 29).

Burner's definition of narrative accrual, insofar as he does provide one, is too restricted. For our purposes, we might redefine narrative accrual more broadly as the outcome of repeated exposure to a set of related narratives, ultimately leading to the shaping of a culture, tradition, or history. This history may be personal, as in the case of ontological narratives. It may also be public, including institutional and corporate narratives, thus ultimately leading to the elaboration of meta-narratives. And it may be conceptual, where we might speak of narrative accrual shaping the history of a discipline or of a particular concept that cuts across disciplines. In all these cases, the issue of what is bogus and what is not lies outside the scope of this revised definition of narrative accrual.

Our ontological narratives are no more than variants on the stock of stories available in our culture; these stories continually gather more detail, acquire more depth, and proliferate through the process of narrative accrual. Our understanding of our own life and of what to do and how to do it to survive in society is a by-product of the stock of stories to which we are exposed from childhood onwards. 'Deprive children of stories', MacIntyre argues, 'and you leave them unscripted, anxious stutterers in their actions as in their words' (1981: 201). Bruner explains that once they achieve a certain level of currency within a culture, narrative accruals begin to have the force of a constraint. 'Culture', he explains, 'always reconstitutes itself by swallowing its own narrative tail' (1991: 19). Whether intended to function as such or not, narrative accruals do establish interpretive and behavioural canons, and it is these 'forms of canonicity that permit us to recognize when a breach has occurred and how it might be interpreted' (1991: 20). Our ontological narratives are simultaneously constrained and empowered by this process. Firmly anchored in a collective past, 'our sense of belonging to this canonical past ... permits us to form our own narratives of deviation while maintaining complicity with the canon' (1991: 20). MacIntyre makes a similar point when he describes the narrative view of the self – as opposed to Sartre's and Goffman's treatment of the self as detached, with no history – as follows:

> the story of my life is always embedded in the story of those communities from which I derive my identity. I am born with a past; and to try to cut myself off from that past, in the individualist mode, is to deform my present relationships. The possession of an historical identity and the possession of a social identity coincide.
>
> (1981: 205)

Public narratives promoted by powerful institutions such as the state or media not only highlight those elements they selectively appropriate, but also force them on our consciousness through repeated exposure, a process that Bourdieu describes as 'symbolic dripfeed' (1998: 30). The legal system functions in a similar way. Bruner explains that '[i]nsofar as the law insists on such accrual of cases as "precedents," and insofar as "cases" are narratives, the legal system imposes an orderly process of narrative accrual' (1991: 20). The example of the legal system is useful in that it also demonstrates how the process of narrative accrual is partly a function of dominance. Even instances of dissent and contestation within the legal system ultimately contribute to reinforcing the overall legal narrative over time. For example, *Plessy v. Ferguson* (163 U.S. 537, 1896) centred on the issue of whether segregation of blacks in separate railway cars according to the Louisiana statute at the time was constitutional. The majority opinion in this case was in favour of upholding the statute, with the only dissenter being Justice Harlan. As Mertz's (1996) account of the case demonstrates, Justice Harlan's dissent reinforced both the overall legal narrative and the existing social structure at the time. To contest the opinions expressed in the current case, he had to appeal to previous legal cases and to the Thirteenth Amendment, thus contributing to the process of narrative accrual in this domain by circulating and giving credence to certain variants of the legal narrative. In terms of the existing social structure, Justice Harlan was careful for his dissent not to appear threatening to the white sector of society or the balance of power between the races. He thus presented the problem largely as one of impracticality and potential inconvenience for the dominant party rather than abuse of the weaker party's rights: 'If a colored maid insists upon riding in the same coach with a white woman whom she has been employed to serve, and who may need her personal attention while travelling, she is subject to be fined or imprisoned for such an exhibition of zeal in the discharge of duty' (cited in Mertz 1996: 146).

Accrual of any form of narrative, including public narratives, is achieved through various channels and is not entirely the preserve of the dominant institutions of society. Activists and marginalized groups elaborate their narrative versions through a whole range of forums and media. They circulate leaflets, issue press releases, launch petitions, organize marches in which they hold posters, shout slogans, and

engage in a multiplicity of other forms of protest. The same process of canonicity and breach embedded in narrative accrual and evident in the *Plessy v. Ferguson* case discussed above can be seen at play here too. Cartoons such as Paul Fitzgerald's (Figure 5, p. 53) and even protest window stickers, T-shirts and badges[15] that satirize and challenge the dominant take on security cannot but contribute to elaborating the broader narrative of terror even as numerous activist groups set out to undermine it. It is ultimately this feature of narrative accrual that enables the spread of meta- or master narratives of progress, enlightenment, global terror, Western democracy, and so on, even as various groups in society set out to challenge and undermine some of those very narratives.

Features of narrativity discussed in this and the previous chapter are not discrete; they inevitably overlap and are highly interdependent. Historicity (an aspect of temporality, section 4.1), narrative accrual, and canonicity and breach cannot be neatly separated, nor is it productive to treat them as discrete features. The same applies to all other features of narrativity: temporal and spatial sequences participate in elaborating patterns of causal emplotment; causal emplotment in turn is partly realized through selective appropriation, and so on. The discussion of these features under separate headings is merely intended to clarify some of the complex ways in which narrativity mediates our experience of the world.

Core references

Alexander, Jeffrey C. (2002) 'On the Social Construction of Moral Universals: The "Holocaust" from War Crime to Trauma Drama', *European Journal of Social Theory* 5(1): 5–85.

Bennett, W. Lance and Murray Edelman (1985) 'Toward a New Political Narrative', *Journal of Communication* 35(4): 156–71.

Bruner, Jerome (1991) 'The Narrative Construction of Reality', *Critical Inquiry* 18(1): 1–21.

Ehrenhaus, Peter (1993) 'Cultural Narratives and the Therapeutic Motif: The Political Containment of Vietnam Veterans', in Dennis K. Mumby (ed.) *Narrative and Social Control: Critical Perspectives*, Newbury Park CA: Sage, 77–118.

Ghosh, Bishnupriya (2000) 'An Affair to Remember: Scripted Performances in the "Nasreen Affair"', in Amal Amireh and Lisa Suhair Majaj (eds) *Going Global: The Transnational Reception of Third World Women Writers*, New York and London: Garland Publishing, 39–83.

Reeves-Ellington, Barbara (1999) 'Responsibility with Loyalty: Oral History Texts in Translation', *Target* 11(1): 103–29.

Silver, Mark (2004) 'The Detective Novel's Novelty: Native and Foreign Narrative Forms in Kuroiwa Ruikō's *Kettō no hate*', *Japan Forum* 16(2): 191–205.

Further reading

Ewick, Patricia and Susan S. Silbey (1995) 'Subversive Stories and Hegemonic Tales: Toward a Sociology of Narrative', *Law & Society Review* 29(2): 197–226.

Gergen, Kenneth J. and Mary M. Gergen (1997) 'Narratives of the Self', in Lewis P. Hinchman and Sandra K. Hinchman (eds) *Memory, Identity, Community: The Idea of Narrative in the Human Sciences*, Albany: State University of New York Press, 161–84.

Hermans, Theo (1982) 'P.C. Hooft: The Sonnets and the Tragedy', *Dispositio: Revista Hispánica de Semiótica Literaria* VII (19–20): 95–110.

Muhawi, Ibrahim (1999b) 'On Translating Palestinian Folktales: Comparative Stylistics and the Semiotics of Genre', in Yasir Suleiman (ed.) *Arabic Grammar and Linguistics*, Richmond: Curzon Press, 222–45.

Pratt, Mary Louise (1994) 'Travel Narrative and Imperialist Vision', in James Phelan and Peter J. Rabinowitz (eds) *Understanding Narrative*, Columbus: Ohio State University Press, 199–221.

6 Framing narratives in translation

Translators and interpreters face a basic ethical choice with every assignment: to reproduce existing ideologies as encoded in the narratives elaborated in the text or utterance, or to dissociate themselves from those ideologies, if necessary by refusing to translate the text or interpret in a particular context at all. Given that they are normally in a position to turn down an assignment, 'accepting the work ... implies complicity' (Séguinot 1988: 105).[1] Beyond this basic choice, translators and interpreters can and do resort to various strategies to strengthen or undermine particular aspects of the narratives they mediate, explicitly or implicitly. These strategies allow them to dissociate themselves from the narrative position of the author or speaker or, alternatively, to signal their empathy with it.

This chapter examines some of the many ways in which translators and interpreters – in collaboration with publishers, editors and other agents involved in the interaction – accentuate, undermine or modify aspects of the narrative(s) encoded in the source text or utterance. Having outlined the relevant features of narrativity in chapters 4 and 5, I now turn to the broad concept of *framing* to explore how these features may be renegotiated to produce a politically charged narrative in the target context. The assumption throughout is that translators and interpreters are not merely passive receivers of assignments from others; many initiate their own translation projects and actively select texts and volunteer for interpreting tasks that contribute to the elaboration of particular narratives. Neither are they detached, unaccountable professionals whose involvement begins and ends with the delivery of a linguistic product. Like any other group in society, translators and interpreters are responsible for the texts and utterances they produce. Consciously or otherwise, they translate texts and utterances that participate in creating, negotiating and contesting social reality.

6.1 Framing, frame ambiguity and frame space

The related notions of *frames*, *frameworks* and *framing* are used in a variety of ways by researchers working within different scholarly traditions. They are also often used in conjunction with the concept of *schema* or *schemata*. The latter generally denote those 'expectations about people, objects, events, and settings in the world' that participants bring with them to the interaction (Tannen and Wallat 1993: 60). This definition of schemata overlaps considerably with Goffman's notion of framework, especially when he talks about 'a group's framework or frameworks' as 'its belief system, its "cosmology"' (1974: 27). Frames, on the other hand, emerge out of the interaction itself as participants develop 'a sense of what activity is being engaged in, how speakers mean what they say' (Tannen and Wallat 1993: 60). The above definition of framework then suggests a set of static beliefs and expectations, whereas the definition of frames stresses the dynamic nature of interaction.

Although Goffman endows individuals with agency in arguing that a participant does not just perceive frames but 'also takes action, both verbal and physical, on the basis of these perceptions' (1974: 345), he and many of his followers clearly focus on questions of interpretation rather than active and conscious intervention to frame an event for others; hence Goffman's interest in how 'an individual's framing of activity establishes meaningfulness *for him*' (1974: 345; emphasis added). In much of the literature on social movements, by contrast, framing is treated as an active process of signification; frames are defined as structures of *anticipation*, strategic moves that are consciously initiated in order to present a movement or a particular position within a certain perspective. Framing processes are further understood to provide 'a mechanism through which individuals can ideologically connect with movement goals and become potential participants in movement actions' (Cunningham and Browning 2004: 348). I follow this particular scholarly tradition here in defining framing as an active strategy that implies agency and by means of which we consciously participate in the construction of reality.

A good example of the way in which processes of framing are encoded in translation is discussed in Behl (2002). The frame in question is that of 'revelation' in the context of religious traditions. Behl tells us that the seventeenth-century Zoroastrian ethnographer Mubad Shah demonstrated the importance of this frame in his *Dabistan-i Mazahib* (School of Religious Faiths), in which he divided and ranked religious sects largely according to whether their religion is revealed or non-revealed. As Behl explains, one of the main ways in which the Islamic community then came to distinguish itself from the Hindus is by pointing out that the latter had no revealed book, that 'they had not received divine revelation (*wahi*) from heaven' (2002: 91). The frame was thus set for any subsequent dialogue with the Hindus: 'We have the truth because it came down from heaven and is present in the form of a book; therefore, in order to prove that they have a truth and it is the same truth, we must prove that a similar condition obtains among the Hindus' (2002: 91–2). The main task for any translator, such as Prince Dara Shikoh (1615–1659), who wanted to effect a dialogue between the two communities was therefore to demonstrate that the Hindus too had heavenly books that expressed the same mystical truth.[2] In other words, Prince Shikoh had to actively frame Hindu religious texts as 'heavenly' and 'revealed'. Of all the other frames within which this dialogue could have been contextualized, that of 'revelation' was deemed the most effective.

Translation may be seen as a frame in its own right, whether in its literal or metaphorical sense. Draper uses translation as a metaphor in his discussion of rhetorical strategies used to frame political violence since September 2001:

the United States has justified its post-September 11 actions by translating all original violence, that is the many and diverse forms of violence it does not support, into the target language of 'terrorism,' and has consequently encouraged other major global powers such as Russia and India to translate violent opposition similarly. Such a mode of translation involves a transmission of the pure instance of violence into the discourse of terrorism. This transmission is always accompanied by the work of forgetting and elision of the historical context of the violence in order to evacuate it of all meaning. Translating a violent act as terrorism thus reifies the act as a commodity of pure negativity, a commodity which can then be inscribed with whatever moral or political connotations the translator deems expedient. Such a translation can thus be effectively marketed to domestic and international audiences. The global translatability of the Terror discourse can be seen from the remarkable popularity of the notion of terrorism demonstrated not only by the countries allied with the United States but even by its most intractable enemies. Osama bin Laden, for instance, was quick to label Americans [as] proponents of 'bad terror' while putting himself on the side of 'good terror.'

(Draper 2002)

In other words, terror is deliberately exploited as – or 'translated into' – what we might call a 'master frame' to streamline the narratives of US political opponents and divest them of all historicity as well as potentially understandable, if not justifiable, motivation.

Translation may also be treated as a frame in a less metaphoric sense. In his discussion of performance vs. literal communication, both of which he regards as interpretive frames that guide the way we make sense of messages, Bauman (2001: 168) goes on to list an additional number of such interpretive frames.[3] This list includes '*translation*, in which the words spoken are to be interpreted as the equivalent of words originally spoken in another language or code'.

This chapter will attempt to demonstrate that beyond this basic framing function, translation acts as an interpretive frame in many more ways, some of which remain concealed from direct observation by most readers and/or hearers. In other words, translation 'is not simply an interpretive frame but a performance that encompasses any number of interpretive frames' (Muhawi, in press).

6.1.1 Frame ambiguity

The same set of events can be framed in different ways to promote competing narratives,[4] with important implications for different parties to the conflict; this often results in *frame ambiguity*. For example, forms of violent conflict may be framed as 'war', 'civil war', 'guerrilla warfare', 'terrorist acts', or even 'low intensity conflict' (Chilton 1997: 175). Smith (1997) illustrates this process in relation to the Chechen conflict and the events in Bosnia-Hercegovina. Those who support the Chechen cause insist that their conflict with Russia is an inter-state war or a war of independence, since '[t]o say otherwise would be to acknowledge what the war was fought to refute – Russia's sovereignty over the territory of Chechnya' (Smith 1997: 204). In the case of Bosnia-Hercegovina, framing what happened there between 1992 and 1995 as civil war is similarly unaccept-able to the government and its supporters, one of the reasons being that the civil war frame does not allow for the recognition of certain types of war crimes that would be recognized within the inter-state war frame (Smith 1997: 205).[5] Framing, in other words, has concrete consequences for those affected by the process.

Frame ambiguity, 'the special doubt that arises over the definition of the situation' (Goffman 1974: 302), is often experienced by different parties to a conflict as a by-product of competing attempts to legitimize different versions of the relevant narra-tive. Drawing on this notion, Blum-Kulka and Liebes conducted 22 interviews with 36 Israeli soldiers who served in the Occupied Territories and identified three ways in which they framed the Palestinian *intifada*:

> The two polar frames that emerge are that of *Law and Order*, which frames the army in the transformed and unfamiliar role of a riot police in charge of 'the repression of disturbances,' and *War*, which preserves the traditional role of the army and frames the *intifada* as another outbreak of the ongoing conflict ... The third frame might be called *State Terror*, in that it identifies Israel's actions in the *intifada* as illegitimate aggression which triggers thoughts of refusing to serve [in the army].
>
> (Blum-Kulka and Liebes 1993: 45)

These different ways of framing the *intifada* lead to different actions on the part of the individual soldiers, but Blum-Kulka and Liebes also found that many soldiers oscillate between two or more frames; in other words they continue to have doubts about the definition of the situation.

If frame ambiguity is a feature of everyday life, then we should expect this to be reflected in the texts and utterances we translate and interpret, but this ambiguity is often resolved or obscured in translation. Bongie's (2005) analysis of *The Slave-King*, the English translation of Victor Hugo's novel *Bug-Jargal*, offers one example of this phenomenon. While Hugo's text reveals an ambivalent attitude to slavery, the English version resolves this frame ambiguity and presents the reader with a narra-tive that is unequivocally anti-slavery. I will shortly discuss some examples of how this effect is achieved discursively (see section 6.3.1 on p. 115).

Frame ambiguity can also be exploited in translation. In Baker (in press, b), I discussed an interesting controversy over the meaning of one word, *wilaya*, in a tape from Osama Bin Laden aired by al-Jazeera on 29 October 2004, in the thick of the US elections. In principle, *wilaya* can mean either 'state' in the sense of nation/ country or 'state' in the modern-day sense of electoral region. Al-Jazeera translators opted broadly for the first sense, while the translators of MEMRI, the neo-conser-vative media institute whose translation activities I discussed under 'Selective Appropriation' on p. 78, opted for the second sense:

Al-Jazeera translation[6]

In conclusion, I tell you in truth, that your security is not in the hands of Kerry, nor Bush, nor al-Qaida. No.

Your security is in your own hands. And every **state** that doesn't play with our security has automatically guaranteed its own security.

MEMRI Translation (square brackets, bracketed material and italics in original)[7]

Your security is not in the hands of Kerry or Bush or Al-Qa'ida. Your security is in your own hands, and any **[US] state [*wilaya*]** that does not toy with our security automatically guarantees its own security.

MEMRI insisted that Bin Laden 'threatened each U.S. state, [and] ... offered an election deal to the American voters – a sort of amnesty for states that don't vote for Bush', and that '[t]he U.S. media have mistranslated the words "ay wilaya" (which means "each U.S. state") to mean a "country" or "nation" other than the U.S. ... while in reality bin Laden's threat was directed specifically at each individual U.S. State'.[8] Juan Cole, Professor of History at the University of Michigan and owner of the activist website *Informed Comment* (www.juancole.com), contested this interpretation:

> Bin Laden says that such a 'state' should not trifle with Muslims' security. He cannot possibly mean that he thinks Rhode Island is in a position to do so. Nor can he be referring to which way a state votes, since he begins by saying that the security of Americans is not in the hands of Bush or Kerry. He has already dismissed them as equivalent and irrelevant, in and of themselves.[9]

MEMRI and other like-minded media outlets then worked hard at exploiting the potential frame ambiguity triggered by the use of *wilaya* to activate what we might call the 'interference in US elections' frame. Activists opposed to their type of politics worked equally hard to dismiss this potential frame ambiguity and undermine neo-conservative attempts at manipulating it.

6.1.2 Frame space

Frame ambiguity aside, it is important to note that treating framing as an active and conscious strategy does not mean that it is not subject to various types of constraint or that agency is not restricted by the context in which it is exercised. Goffman's notion of *frame space* is very useful here and lends itself to being elaborated in line with our current focus.

Participants in any interaction play different roles (announcer, author, translator, prosecutor, lecturer, military officer, parent), engage in the interaction in different capacities (speaker, reader, primary addressee, overhearer, eavesdropper), and take different positions in relation to the event and other participants (supportive, critical, disinterested, indifferent, uninformed outsider, committed). The sum total of all these possibilities constitute what Goffman calls the frame space of a participant.[10] This frame space is 'normatively allocated', which means that a contribution is deemed acceptable when it stays within the frame space allocated to the speaker or writer and unacceptable when it falls outside that space (Goffman 1981: 230). Goffman offers an interesting example of a particular aspect of the workings of frame space which should help elucidate the relevance of this notion for translators and interpreters:

> consider that characteristically, prime-time national network announcers – newscasters, disc jockeys, program M.C.s – deliver lines that technically speaking are almost flawless, and that they operate under a special obligation to do so, whether fresh talk, aloud reading, or memorization is involved. Indeed, although ordinary talk is full of technical faults that go unnoticed as faults, broadcasters seem to be schooled to realize our cultural stereotypes about speech production, namely, that ordinarily it will be without influences, slips, boners, and gaffes, i.e., unfaultable. Interestingly, these professional obligations, once established, seem to generate their own underlying norms for hearers as well as speakers, so that faults we would have to be trained linguistically to hear in ordinary talk can be glaringly evident to the untrained ear when encountered in broadcast talk. May I add that what one may here gloss as a 'difference in norms' is what I claim to be a difference in prescribed frame space.
>
> (1981: 240)

Like announcers, translators and interpreters act within a frame space that encourages others to scrutinize every aspect of their linguistic and – in the case of interpreters – non-linguistic behaviour. Their frame space also circumscribes the limits of their discursive agency, although as with any type of constraint it is almost always possible to evade or challenge these limits. One of the best ways of undermining the restrictive effect of frame space in translation is to adopt a strategy of temporal and spatial framing that obviates the need to intervene significantly in the text itself. This strategy is discussed in detail later in this chapter (section 6.2 on p. 112).

Translators and interpreters can make use of various other routines that allow them to inject the discourse with their own voice (in other words to actively frame its narrative) while signalling their intention to stay within the prescribed frame space for their activity. On the surface, these routines may signal that any deviation from the prescribed frame space is either unintended or 'offends the perpetrator's own sense of propriety and is not to be heard [or read] as characteristic of him' (Goffman 1981: 231). Aphra Behn's preface to her English translation of Fontenelle's *Entretiens sur la pluralité des mondes habités* makes use of the traditional routine of apology to evade possible criticism for stepping outside her frame space as translator:

> I have endeavoured to give you the true meaning of the Author, and have kept as near his Words as was possible; I was necessitated to add a little in some places, otherwise the book could not have been understood.
>
> (1688: 76; cited in Knellwolf 2001: 102)

Behn's preface later makes clear the real reason for her intervention, without admitting the link between her distaste for Fontenelle's project and the necessity 'to add a little', which makes her step outside her frame space:

> The Design of the Author is to treat of this part a Natural Philosophy in a more familiar Way than any other hath done, and to make every body understand him … But if you would know before-hand my Thoughts, I must tell you freely, he hath failed in his Design; for endeavouring to render this part of Natural Philosophy familiar, he hath turned it into Ridicule; he hath pushed his wild notion of the *Plurality of the Worlds* to that height of Extravagancy, that he most certainly will confound those Readers, who have not Judgement and Wit to distinguish between what is truly solid (or, at least, probable) and what is trifling and airy.
>
> (1688: 76–7; cited in Knellwolf 2001: 103)

Behn clearly disapproved of Fontenelle's attempt to render natural philosophy familiar and comprehensible to lay readers 'who have not Judgement and Wit to distinguish between what is truly solid … and what is trifling and airy', in the manner of today's popular science. From her perspective, Fontenelle simplified complex ideas 'at the expense of their truth claims' (Knellwolf 2001: 104). The public and conceptual narratives within which her own perspective is embedded portray science as power, as an expert domain in which serious matters are researched and debated with precision by an informed elite, and as set apart from the triviality and ignorance of lay society. Her 'little' additions and rewordings then may be seen as framing strategies designed to bring the source text in line with her own narrative position, to make it fit within a prescribed frame space for scientific discourse.

In the rest of this chapter I will attempt to outline and exemplify in more detail a number of ways in which (re)framing may be effected in translation, including the way in which this process draws on features of narrativity such as temporality, selective appropriation and genericness to reconfigure patterns of emplotment and influence the narrative perspective of the reader or hearer. Processes of (re)framing can draw on practically any linguistic or non-linguistic resource, from paralinguistic devices such as intonation and typography to visual resources such as colour and image, to numerous linguistic devices such as tense shifts, deixis, code switching, use of euphemisms, and many more. When Kostas Venetsanos, the publisher of the 1969 Greek translation of Machiavelli's *The Prince*, was instructed by the censors to delete parts of the text that were deemed subversive, he implemented the changes but left white margins where the cuts had been made and increased letter spacing to add emphasis to other parts that were equally or even more subversive (Sotiropoulou 1996: n.p.; in Asimakoulas, 2005). This visual feature, which is meaningless in itself, functioned as a framing strategy in this context, drawing the reader's attention to the effect of censorship, accentuating the sense of oppression experienced by readers living under the ruthless rule of the junta, and creating a sense of collusion between the Greek publisher and translator, and their readers.

Given the open-ended list of devices that can be used to frame or reframe narratives in translation, the discussion that follows is inevitably illustrative rather than comprehensive. I limit myself here to temporal and spatial framing, framing through selective appropriation, framing by labelling, and repositioning of participants – four key strategies for mediating the narrative(s) elaborated in a source text or utterance.

6.2 Temporal and spatial framing

Temporal and spatial framing involves selecting a particular text and embedding it in a temporal and spatial context that accentuates the narrative it depicts and encourages us to establish links between it and current narratives that touch our lives, even though the events of the source narrative may be set within a very different temporal and spatial framework. This type of embedding requires no further intervention in the text itself, although it does not necessarily rule out such intervention.

Jones is evidently aware of the interpretive dynamics of temporal and spatial location when he expresses concern over translating Vasko Popa during the Kosovo war (2004: 719). He explains that although Popa wrote in the 1970s, when 'Serbian atavistic images ... such as the Kosovo myth or the figure of the wolf as tribal totem' could be used positively to explore an author's cultural roots, by the time Jones began to translate Popa's *Collected Works* in the late 1990s rampant nationalism had come to dominate the area. Translating these texts against a backdrop of 'murderous misuse of such imagery by Serbian nationalists' and at a time when 'White Wolves', for instance, stood for an anti-Muslim death squad, could easily lend credibility to the new narratives (Jones 2004: 719). The meaning(s) and interpretive potential of a text or utterance, then, are always decisively shaped by their spatial and temporal location.

A particularly powerful example of temporal and spatial framing involving translation is the staging of 1,029 readings of *Lysistrata* in 59 countries[11] on 3 March 2003 (Figure 15). Aristophanes' *Lysistrata* is an anti-war comedy about a group of Greek women who unite to end the Peloponnesian War by taking over the building where public funds are kept and withholding sex from their partners, until the men finally decide to lay down their arms and negotiate a peaceful resolution to the conflict. Some of the 2003 readings had to take place in secret, for fear of persecution – in Nothern Iraq, Israel and China, among other places.[12] This amazing world-wide expression of protest against the invasion of Iraq was made possible through 'the kind and generous translators and adaptors who ... offered their scripts free of charge for this one time event!'.[13]

In 1971, Dionyses Divares, using the pseudonym Giorgos Vergotes, translated a collection of Brecht's political essays into Greek under the title *Politika Keimena*. Greece was then under the ruthless rule of the junta, and Divares was in effect 'invit[ing] readers to interpret the text as a metacomment about the situation in Greece' (Asimakoulas, 2005). Brecht's powerful critique of Nazi Germany was 'transformed into a topical commentary of the translator who speaks through Brecht' (Asimakoulas, in progress), indirectly linking the narrative of oppression in Nazi Germany to the oppressive practices of the fascist dictators who ruled his

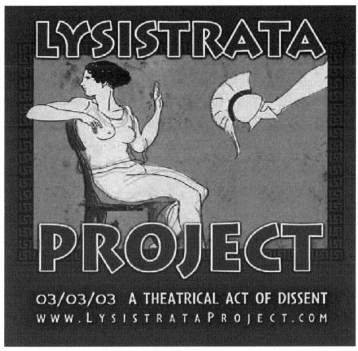

Figure 15 The Lysistrata Project

country. This was again achieved by embedding the source text in a temporal and spatial context that accentuated its narrative and projected it onto a new setting.

In terms of spatial framing, Watts (2000) offers an interesting example which he explains in terms of the 1960s narratives of decolonization in North America being configured more around the notion of origin than of diaspora. The example he discusses concerns the paratextual framing of *Cahier d'un retour au pays natal* by the Francophone Caribbean poet Aimé Césaire. The paratexts of various editions of the poem that appeared around that time, including bilingual editions as well as the 1969 English translation, 'displace' the poem to cater for the narrative viewpoint of a North American audience, either by erasing its Caribbean origins altogether or by relegating them to the margins of the core theme of Africanness. The preface of the 1969 translation 'situates the *Cahier* squarely in the context of African decolonization and cultural renewal' (Watts 2000: 39). In one bilingual edition of the poem published in 1971, the back cover announces that this work 'will inspire those from Africa and *elsewhere*' (Watts 2000: 39; emphasis in original). As Watts explains, this erasure and downplaying of the Caribbean is significant; it means that the 'large thematic part of the poem in which Césaire describes the abjection and possible redemption of the *pays natal*, Martinique, is elided and becomes, implicitly, a prelude to the *Cahier*'s assertions of Africanness' (Watts 2000: 39). Once again, a narrative viewpoint is accentuated or suppressed merely through spatial and/or temporal (re)framing.

The next strategy, selective appropriation of textual material, involves intervening in the text itself, rather than relying on the context to elaborate particular aspects of the narrative(s) it depicts.

6.3 Selective appropriation of textual material

> Selective appropriation of textual material is realized in patterns of omission and addition designed to suppress, accentuate or elaborate particular aspects of a narrative encoded in the source text or utterance, or aspects of the larger narrative(s) in which it is embedded.

In Chapter 4, I discussed selective appropriation broadly as a feature of narrativity and gave examples of texts being selected for translation by organizations such as MEMRI to elaborate a narrative of a specific cultural group as extremist, dangerous or criminal. Here, I want to focus on selective appropriation *within* individual translations, as evident in patterns of omission and addition that are traceable in the text itself. This is not to dismiss the importance of higher-level patterns of selectivity, whether in terms of inclusion or exclusion of specific texts, authors, languages or cultures. The literature abounds with examples that demonstrate how and why these patterns come to be actively pursued. Two examples will suffice here before we move on to examine patterns of selectivity within the text.

In order to filter out Jewish authors, the censorship programme enforced under Nazi rule required that every translation of a work of fiction be submitted for approval, with one of the items of information to be provided being the author's racial background (Sturge 2002: 155). This higher-level pattern of selectivity ensured that the narrative voice of an entire religious group was effectively erased and that German public narratives remained immune to its influence. In a very different context and for very different reasons, Stecconi and Torres Reyes (1997) describe a similar pattern of *deselecting* a particular group of authors in three anthologies of translations published in the Philippines in 1971 and 1975. The background to this particular pattern of selectivity is a national resistance movement that decried, among other things, an 'educational system set up by the American colonizers' to ensure that Filipinos remain 'estranged from themselves and their values' (1997: 71). In this context, it is obvious why none of the three anthologies featured a single Anglo-American author. Prioritizing translations of literary texts from Asia, Africa and Latin America, as well as indigenous texts written in the different languages of the Philippines, these anthologies challenged Anglo-American literary hegemony and simultaneously participated in elaborating a narrative in which local Filipino resistance could be framed as part of a wider international movement of self-determination.[14]

6.3.1 Selective appropriation in literature

In terms of selective appropriation *within* the text, scholars of literary translation in particular have long been interested in patterns of omission that result from the exercise of censorship, including self-censorship, though they do not normally approach this issue from a narrative perspective. The discussion of censorship in children's literature in López (2000) is particularly interesting. While confirming many of the now familiar patterns of censorship under Franco, including suppression of sexual and religious elements that would have undermined the official narratives of the regime, López also offers numerous examples of a less known type of selectivity. She demonstrates how aspects of a narrative may be repeatedly censored in the source text but *retained* in its translations.

While later editions of English source texts such as Roald Dahl's and Enid Blyton's are 'purified' of elements branded racist or xenophobic in our current public narratives, Spanish translations of these texts continue to retain the original ingredients of the narrative intact, and even accentuate them. The 1986 'modified' edition of Enid Blyton's *Five Fall into Adventure* reads 'The girl stared at him', but the 1990 Spanish edition still states 'La niña que parecía un gitano le contempló con fijeza' ('The girl, who looked like a Gypsy, stared at him intently') (López 2000: 33). Similarly, 'It had nasty gleaming eyes – oh, I was frightened!' in the current source edition appears in the Spanish translation as 'Sus ojos eran crueles y relucían. Todo lo demás estaba demasiado oscuro. ¡Quizás era el rostro de un negro! ¡Oh, qué miedo he pasado!' ('Its eyes were cruel and gleaming. It was too dark to see anything else. Perhaps it was the face of a black man. Oh, how afraid I was!') (López 2000: 34). And whereas all references to the ethnic origin of the workers in Willy Wonka's factory in Roald Dahl's *Charlie and the Chocolate Factory* have long been removed from the English edition, the Spanish translations continue to link their colour to the colour of chocolate (López 2000: 34). López concludes that 'a society's patterns of behavior and its moral values are not only reflected in the textual modifications introduced in translations of foreign works, ... in the case of Spain they are also reflected in the fidelity to the first editions of texts that have been modified in their countries of origin' (2000: 30). This 'fidelity' gives the uncensored narratives a new life in a different setting and allows them to remain in circulation and hence continue to participate in shaping the narrative perspectives of the target audience.

Tymoczko (1999) offers very interesting examples of framing by selective appropriation of textual material in the context of the Irish movement of independence in the nineteenth and twentieth centuries. She explains that in order for Cú Culainn, the medieval hero whose statue still stands in Dublin's General Post Office, to serve as an exemplar of Irish struggle, 'his story – or, more properly, stories – had to be rewritten and retold in ways that were different from those found in the early Irish texts' (1999: 80). Originally an independent tale, an episode describing a fight between Cú Culainn and his foster brother Fer Diad was at one point integrated into *Táin Bó Cúailnge*, the centrepiece of Irish heritage, and thereafter 'became emblematic and metonymic in English translations of TBC as a whole' – even though it 'was not even originally part of the tale' (1999: 80). As Tymoczko goes on to explain, the importance of incorporating this episode into the most important text of Irish nation-alism lies in its moral, namely that 'violence toward one's friend and brother is sad but necessary if one is to fulfil one's group loyalties (and patriotic duties)' (1999: 81). Eventually, given this motivation and bearing in mind that most Irish readers by that stage could only access their heritage through the medium of English, 'in English translation the Fer Diad episode became the epitome of TBC [*Táin Bó Cúailnge*], the tail that wagged the dog' (Tymoczko 1999: 82). At the same time, there were elements in the Irish literary heritage that reinforced current English stereotypes; these stereotypes 'attributed to the Irish a love of violence, a readiness to fight, a tendency to be easily angered, a love of battle, and violent passions that lead to unprovoked attacks' (Tymoczko 1999: 23). Against this background, undignified descriptions of Cú Culainn's 'transformation when he is in his battle fury' were suppressed in Standish O'Grady's translations, which included no more than a passing reference to the passage in a footnote, and a heavily negotiated one at that – the footnote in ques-tion referring to 'an idea that in battle his stature *increased*' (Tymoczko 1999: 22, emphasis added), when in fact the transformation made Cú Culainn 'into a monstrous thing, hideous and shapeless, unheard of' (Kinsella 1969: 152; cited in Tymoczko 1999: 22). Given that current English stereotypes of the Irish were used to elaborate a colonial narrative in which the Irish could not be trusted to govern themselves because of their violent tempers and emotionalism, any translation that reproduced these stereotypes could not but bolster the colonial agenda of Britain.

Bongie (2005) shows how *The Slave-King*, the first English translation of Victor Hugo's novel about slavery, *Bug-Jargal*, applies the same strategy – framing by selective appropriation – to modify the narrative into one that unequivocally portrays slavery as 'a "dastardly" institution in need of eradication' (2005: 6). Published in 1833, when the legislation for abolishing slavery was being debated in the British Parliament and only one year before it became law, the translation[15] 'takes every opportunity to … adapt the novel to the requirements of abolitionist discourse' (Bongie 2005: 6). The story of *Bug-Jargal* revolves around Captain Leopold d'Auverney, a white French officer who befriends a black slave by the name of Pierrot.[16] Pierrot turns out to be Bug-Jargal, leader of the slave revolt that in real life (rather than Hugo's novel) would eventually lead to the creation of the independent black republic of Haiti. In the course of the narrative, Pierrot rescues D'Auverney twice from the clutches of a wicked mulatto rebel by the name of Habibrah. The second time Pierrot rescues D'Auverney, he asks his white friend whether he is pleased by the way things turned out. In the original novel, Hugo simply has d'Auverney embrace Bug-Jargal in response and entreat him 'never to leave me again, to remain with me among the whites; I promised him a commission in the colonial army' (Hugo 2004: 192; cited in Bongie 2005: 9). In *The Slave-King*, d'Auverney's response is expanded considerably into the following stretch:

> 'Satisfied!' cried I – 'shall I not be satisfied with the purest and most exalted friendship the world ever saw? Yes, my brother, the friendship of Bug-Jargal, his deeds of disinterested benevolence, will remain engraven on my heart as long as it continues to beat; and, though his complexion be different from

mine, and another country have given him birth, my brother he shall be. Are we not children of the same great Being, to whom colour and clime are distinctions unknown? I entreat you to leave me no more – remain with me among the whites, and I shall obtain for you a commission in the colonial army.'

(Hugo 1833: 253–4; cited in Bongie 2005: 9–10)

At the same time, the translator of *The Slave-King* omits stretches of text that undermine the narrative position he wishes to elaborate. Here is one example:

Sans doute pour se délasser des travaux auxquels ils avaient été condamnés toute leur vie, les nègres restaient dans une inaction inconnue à nos soldats, même retirés sous la tente. Quelques-uns dormaient au grand soleil, la tête près d'un feu ardent; d'autres, l'oeil tour à tour terne et furieux, chantaient un air monotone, accroupis sur le seuil de leurs *ajoupas*, espèces de huttes couvertes de feuilles de bananier ou de palmier, dont la forme conique ressemble à nos tentes canonnières.

(Hugo 2004: 115)

[No doubt seeking relaxation from the labours to which they had all their lives been condemned, the negroes were in a state of inactivity that you do not find among our soldiers, even when they are back under their tents. Some were sleeping out in the sun, their heads next to a scorching fire; others, with a look in their eyes that was by turns lacklustre and full of fury, were singing a monotonous tune as they squatted down on the threshold of their *ajoupas* – a sort of hut covered with banana or palm leaves and having a conical form similar to that of our bell-tents.]

(Bongie 2005: 10–11, emphasis added)

In *The Slave-King* this passage is rendered as follows:

Many a poor negro (on whose body the marks of the stripes, so lately inflicted by a cruel, perhaps a now deceased master, were not yet obliterated) lay stretched fast asleep, in conscious security, upon the scorched ground; and not many feet distant from a hot fire. Whilst others, who in slavery had forgotten to sing, now fearless of the voice of an oppressor, lay singing their monotonous airs upon the threshold of their little *ajoupas*, or open huts, covered with banana or palm trees, and resembling, in their conical form, our military tents.

(Hugo 1833: 101; in Bongie 2005: 10–11)

There are several instances of framing by selective appropriation in the above stretch, including the obvious omission of an unflattering comparison between the black slaves' 'inactivity' and the white soldiers' energetic disposition, as well as the foregrounding of the issue of oppression. Through the cumulative interventions of the translator, especially the numerous instances of addition and omission, *The Slave-King* then becomes 'a novel in which both protagonist and reader are educated into a new, more human(e) way of understanding their intercultural world' (Bongie

2005: 10). The original narrative, *Bug-Jargal*, adopts a much more ambivalent attitude to the issue of slavery, but this frame ambiguity is resolved in translation.

6.3.2 Selective appropriation in the media

A more recent example of framing by selective appropriation is discussed in Munday (2002). One of the stories that dominated the media in late 1999 and well into 2000 was that of Elián González, a six-year-old Cuban who was rescued by the US navy after the small boat in which he and his parents had attempted to flee Cuba capsized. As the boy's mother was lost when the boat capsized, his remaining relatives in Miami and his father in Havana became embroiled in a long fight over custody. Munday analyses three English translations of a two-page column on this story by Gabriel García Márquez, which first appeared in the Cuban Communist magazine *Juventud Rebelde*. One of the English translations, by Edith Grossman, was published in the *New York Times* on 29 March 2000. The cuts discussed by Munday in this version include details such as 'at the order of a frantic nun, a police officer snatched their mobile phones' (2002: 90), referring to the boy's grandmothers during their trip to Miami to visit their grandson. The cuts are generally of material that portrays the US authorities in a negative light (Munday 2002). In this particular case, the suppressed material reinforces a narrative of American policemen and policewomen as aggressive, rough, and inclined to treat the public with disrespect; this narrative has some currency both in the USA and abroad and is elaborated in many Hollywood films. Munday also highlights the omission of 800 words towards the end of the article; this section discusses the history of relations between the USA and Cuba and analyses potential repercussions for one of the candidates (Al Gore) in the American presidential campaign later in the year (2002). García Márquez, it should be noted, is an outspoken supporter of Fidel Castro and critic of US foreign policy; his narrative position on these issues inevitably undermines the official US narrative of the conflict. The *New York Times* is arguably more closely aligned to the mainstream official narratives circulating in the US than, say, *The Nation*.

Claims of narrative manipulation through omission and/or addition in translation are frequently made in the media in relation to statements by 'rogue' personalities such as Saddam Hussein and Osama Bin Laden. An article published by BBC News on 10 November 2001 points out that the mass-circulation Pakistani newspaper *Dawn* wrongly quoted Bin Laden as saying that al-Qaeda possesses chemical and nuclear weapons and intends to use them against America (emphasis added):

> while the English-language newspaper carries a clear message from Bin Laden that he has access to such weapons, he makes no such claim in an Urdu-language version of the interview.
>
>   ... Dawn's English version quotes Bin Laden as saying: 'If America used chemical and nuclear weapons against us, then **we may retort with chemical and nuclear weapons. We have the weapons as a deterrent**.'
>
>   Mr Mir then asks Bin Laden where he got the weapons, which the al-Qaeda leader declines to answer.

But in the Urdu version of the article, Bin Laden does not threaten to use nuclear or chemical weapons.

'The US is using chemical weapons against us and it has also decided to use nuclear weapons. But our war will continue,' he says, according to the BBC's own translation of the Ausaf article.

The two versions are otherwise very similar, says the BBC Monitoring unit.[17]

The tabloid press in most countries generally tends to exaggerate sensational aspects of public narratives in a bid to improve the newspaper's circulation. It also tends to regurgitate official narratives, especially in less democratic systems, in order to ingratiate itself to the regime or at least avoid confrontation with it. In this case, putting the threat of nuclear and chemical weapons in Bin Laden's mouth seems to serve both purposes very well. Pakistan's government publicly bought into the meta-narrative of the War on Terror very early on, arguably to stay on the right side of the US war machine and to strengthen its hold on its own population. The *Dawn* translation embellishes this narrative with supporting detail and strengthens its hold on public consciousness.

Selective appropriation within the text is not always easy to explain in the case of web-based translations, as in any translation whose provenance is not clear. Without knowing who is behind the www.welfarestate.com site that featured the following translation, and without information about the person who carried out the translation, it is difficult to explain the obvious omission of important detail below (highlighted in the back-translation). Here, first, is the English translation published on the site:[18]

Translation of Funeral Article in Egyptian Paper:
al-Wafd, Wednesday, December 26, 2001 Vol 15 No 4633
News of Bin Laden's Death and Funeral 10 days ago
Islamabad

A prominent official in the Afghan Taleban movement announced yesterday the death of Osama bin Laden, the chief of al-Qa'da organization, stating that binLaden [*sic*] suffered serious complications in the lungs and died a natural and quiet death. The official, who asked to remain anonymous, stated to The Observer of Pakistan that he had himself attended the funeral of bin Laden and saw his face prior to burial in Tora Bora 10 days ago. He mentioned that 30 of al-Qa'da fighters attended the burial as well as members of his family and some friends from the Taleban. In the farewell ceremony to his final rest guns were fired in the air. The official stated that it is difficult to pinpoint the burial location of bin Laden because according to the Wahhabi tradition no mark is left by the grave. He stressed that it is unlikely that the American forces would ever uncover any traces of bin Laden.

It is not clear why reference to continued American bombardment of the Tora Bora region is suppressed here (see original and backtranslation overleaf). One might speculate that the site owners are deliberately playing down American aggression, but this does not seem to fit with other material on the site, which suggests a critical and unsympathetic attitude to American domestic and foreign policies.

إسلام أباد – أ. ش. أ:

أعلن مسؤول بارز في حركة طالبان الأفغانية
أمس عن وفاة أسامة بن لادن زعيم تنظيم
القاعدة وأشار الى أن «بن لادن» كان يعاني من
مضاعفات خطيرة بالرئة ومات بشكل طبيعي
وهادئ. أكد المسؤول الذي رفض ذكر اسمه في
تصريحات لصحيفة «أبزورفر» الباكستانية
انه حضر جنازة بن لادن بنفسه ورأى وجه بن
لادن قبل الدفن في تورا بورا منذ ١٠ أيام.
وأشار الى أن الجنازة حضرها ٣٠ من مقاتلي
القاعدة وأفراد الأسرة وبعض الأصدقاء من
طالبان. وتم اطلاق وابل من الأعيرة النارية
لتوديعه الى مثواه الأخير. وأكد المسؤول
صعوبة تحديد المكان الذي دفن فيه «بن لادن»
لأن قبره سوي بالأرض طبقاً للمذهب الوهابي
الذي ينتمي اليه. وأكد احتمال طمس مكان
الدفن بسبب القصف الجوي المستمر منذ
أسبوعين لمنطقة تورا بورا. واستبعد أن تنجح
القوات الأمريكية في العثور على أثر «بن لادن».

Back-translation:
News of Bin Laden's Death and Funeral 10 Days Ago
Islamabad

A prominent official in the Taliban Afghan movement yesterday announced the death of Bin Laden, the leader of Al-Qaeda organization,[*] and indicated that Bin Laden had suffered from serious complications in the lung and died naturally and calmly. The official, who refused to reveal his name, asserted in a statement to the Pakistani 'Observer' newspaper that he attended Bin Laden's funeral himself and saw Bin Laden's face before the burial in Tora Bora ten days ago. He mentioned that the funeral was attended by 30 Al-Qaeda fighters, members of the family, and some friends from the Taliban. A hail of bullets were fired to bid him farewell on the way to his final resting place. The official confirmed the difficulty of specifying the place where Bin Laden was buried because his grave was flattened according to the [tradition of the] Wahabi sect to which he belongs. **He confirmed that the burial site might have been obliterated because of the continued aerial bombardment of the Tora Bora region for the past two weeks.** He thought it unlikely that American forces would be able to find any trace of 'Bin Laden'.

[*] The word used is *tanzeem*, which does mean organization, but generally one that lies outside the mainstream institutions of society. It tends to be used of illegal, militant, or terrorist groups.

6.3.3 Selective appropriation in interpreting

Framing by selective appropriation also features in interpreting, though perhaps to a lesser extent. Jacquemet (2005) offers several examples in the context of processing Kosovar refugees through the United Nations High Commission on Refugees' office in Tirana, Albania, in 2000. The situation in Albania had become extremely dire by that stage, with the result that many Albanians who had never set foot in Kosovo were claiming to be Kosovars in order to get out of the country. UN officials then turned the interview procedure into a judicial process designed to establish the true identity of every would-be refugee. They developed a strict routine to be followed by case workers and interpreters, which involved suppressing the claimants' narratives and focusing instead on their accents, clothes, and their knowledge of the Kosovo region and its customs. In the following example, a young female would-be refugee (R) claims to have been attacked by Serbian soldiers. The interpreter (I) questions her on the colour of their uniforms and renders what he deems relevant into English for the benefit of the case worker (C):

01	I	çfarë uniforme kanë pasë?
		(What was their uniform?)
02	R	kur na-
		(when we-)
03	I	çfarë ngjyre kanë pasë?
		(What color?)
04	R	ngjyrë- unë kur jam ardhë vetëm për shqipni kam pa ma së
		shumti serb-
		(color- while coming to Albania I saw mostly Serbians-)
05		ata ishin me ngjyrën- qashù ngjyrë ushtarake-
		(they had the color- a military color, like this)
06	I	çfarë?
		(which?)
07	R	sikur ajo ngjyra [points to green sweater]
		(like that color)
08	I	kjo? [points to green sweater]
		(this one?)
09	R	e si ajo-
		(yes like that-)
10	I (to C)	this kind of color [points to green sweater]
11		the uniform- uniform
12	C	uh uh- serbian force/
13	I	serbian police
14	C	uh uh
15	R	edhe me maska në kry-
		(and with masks on their heads)
16	I (to C)	and with some masks=
17	R	=ne na kanë vjedh- kur kemi ardhè këndej na kanë
		vjedhé=
		(they robbed us- when we came here they robbed us=)
18	I (to C)	=but is not true

(Jacquemet 2005: 212)

The interpreter knows that Serbian police wear black uniforms. Once the young woman identifies the colour of her attackers' uniforms as green (which could be due to a lapse of memory following a traumatic experience), he decides that her claim is false and simply disregards her contribution in line 17. Her ontological narrative is then dismissed, and her case becomes another episode in the evolving narrative of

Albanians cheating UN officials in order to gain entry to a relatively more prosperous country. Compare this with the more charitable attitude adopted towards witnesses and defendants in other contexts. In the trial of John Demjanjuk, for instance, interpreters and other participants repeatedly corrected slips of the tongue in relation to both dates and places without dismissing the relevant narratives as false, as can be seen in the following examples:

> Prosecutor (in Hebrew): When did the Russo-German War break out?
> Witness (in Hebrew): 22.6.1921.
> Bench (in Hebrew): '41.
> English interpreter (late rendering, after bench): Witness says 1921; Bench corrects: 1941.
>
> (Morris 1995: 34)

> Witness (in German): Some said they would not travel to Israel.
> Interpreter: ... to Germany; witness says Israel, but it must be Germany.
>
> (Morris 1995: 35)

Selection of material to highlight, add or suppress aspects of the immediate narrative is then a question of the larger narrative in which the interpreting or translation is embedded, and each decision taken by the interpreter or translator contributes to the elaboration or modification of this larger narrative.

6.4 Framing by labelling

By *labelling* I refer to any discursive process that involves using a lexical item, term or phrase to identify a person, place, group, event or any other key element in a narrative. It could make a big difference whether we call the opposition party in the US *The Democrats* or *The Democratic Party*, as Silverstein explains:

> 'Democratic' or 'Democrat?' Republican Party operatives these days teach their politicians to avoid the first, older and official name that ends with '-ic' and to use the second form, without it. For political partisans, remember, there is real danger that the '-ic' form would simultaneously convey the meaning of the lower-case d-word, *democratic*, as what those other guys are about.
>
> (2003: 9–10; emphasis in original)

Any type of label used for pointing to or identifying a key element or participant in a narrative, then, provides an interpretive frame that guides and constrains our response to the narrative in question. This explains the motivation for the use of euphemisms in many contexts. Speaking of the Monsanto GM advertising campaign, Reynolds says:

> It is interesting that the terms 'genetically modified' and its acronym 'GM' do not appear in the ads, although this is the most commonly-used way of

referring to the phenomenon. Bartle Bogle Hegarty explained that 'The client asked for this term to be used minimally, since it was deemed emotive and off-putting in the consumer climate – and therefore would not allow the reader to move beyond that to read the viewpoint'. ... 'Food biotechnology' is the more euphemistic term used throughout the campaign.

(2004: 350, fn 3)

Such euphemisms abound in the political and commercial sphere. The euphemism 'comfort women' was coined by imperial Japan to refer to young women who were forced to offer sexual services to the Japanese troops before and during the Second World War. Today, 'civilian contractors' in the context of Afghanistan and Iraq is often a euphemism for 'hired guns' or 'mercenaries', 'neighbourhoods' in Occupied Palestine is a euphemism for 'colonial settlements', and 'rationalization' really means getting rid of a lot of employees. Similarly, the labelling by UK newspaper *The Sun* of the 1991 massive bombardment of Iraq as *blitz on Baghdad* (18 January 1991) is a euphemism that 'reduces the slaughter to a game of alliteration' (Keeble 2005: 43). Translators and interpreters tend to pride themselves on their creativity in dealing with such challenging linguistic features, sometimes without considering the political and social setting in which they are used.

Counter-naming is an interesting strategy worth researching in the context of translation and interpreting, especially in activist venues. See Baker (in press, a) for a discussion of the work of groups such as *Babels* and *Translators for Peace*.

Examples of counter-naming include

- FBI (Federal Bureau of **Intimidation**)
- IOF (Israeli **Offence** Forces) instead of IDF (Israeli Defence Forces)

Counter-naming is the activist's response to the systematic use of euphemisms in the political sphere – a deliberate attempt to demystify and undermine Nukespeak (Chilton 1982), Massacrespeak (Keeble 2005) and Marketspeak (Herman 2005).

Names[19] and titles are particularly powerful means of framing in the sense elaborated here. This section will focus on rival systems of naming and titles of texts as examples of the way in which labelling devices constrain the interpretation of narratives.

6.4.1 Rival systems of naming

Rival systems of naming[20] are especially problematic in translation. MacIntyre explains the difficulty as follows:

there may be rival systems of naming, where there are rival communities and traditions, so that to use a name is at once to make a claim about political and social legitimacy and to deny a rival claim. Consider as an example the two rival place names 'Doire Columcille' in Irish and 'Londonderry' in English. ... To use either name is to deny the legitimacy of the other. Consequently there is no way to translate 'Doire Columcille' into English, except by using 'Doire Columcille' and appending an explanation. 'Londonderry' does not translate 'Doire Columcille'; nor does 'St. Columba's oak grove', for in English there is no such name.

What this brings out is that in such communities the naming of persons and places is not only naming as; it is also naming for. Names are used *as* identification *for* those who share the same beliefs, the same justifications of legitimate authority, and so on. The institutions of naming embody and express the shared standpoint of the community and characteristically its shared traditions of belief and enquiry.

(1988: 378; emphasis in original)

What's in a name?

Derry's original name was Daire Calgaigh, meaning 'oak grove of Calgach'. In the 10th century it was renamed Doire Colmcille, or 'the oak grove of St Columbia', in remembrance of the 6th century saint who had established the first monastic settlement on the site. However, in 1609 when the English government decided to 'plant' Derry properly, it signed an agreement with the Corporation of London to provide the necessary settlers. To commemorate this fact the new city's name was lengthened to Londonderry.

Until the Troubles, people readily abbreviated the town's name to 'Derry'. At that point, however, what anyone called it suddenly became a touchstone for their political views, with Protestant Unionists dogmatically asserting the full Londonderry and Catholic Republicans equally firmly shortening it to Derry. Although the city is still officially called Londonderry, in 1984 the city council was renamed Derry City Council.

The naming controversy persists today, turning the normally straightforward business of buying a bus ticket into a political minefield; you can easily judge someone's position on the conflict by noting whether they react to your Derry with an emphatic *Londonderry* or vice versa. All over the country, but especially in the border areas, you'll see the word 'London' scratched off offending signposts.

On the radio, to avoid offending anyone, you may hear announcers say both names together – 'DerrystrokeLondonderry' – almost as one word.

Luckily, not everyone takes the Derry/Londonderry controversy too seriously. In Belfast, for example, wags have dropped both possibilities, opting instead for the simple 'Stroke City'!

(Smallman *et al.* 1998: 687)

MacIntyre's brief comment does not do justice to the complexity of the Irish situation.[21] The relevant city and county in the North of Ireland are now known as either *Derry* or *Londonderry*, depending on the speaker's narrative location. Also depending on the speaker's narrative location, *Derry* derives either from the Irish *Doire*, or *Doire Columcille*, the original name of that area, or is a shortened form of *Londonderry*. Continued rivalry over these place names reflects a violent history and heavily contested narratives of that history. The Lonely Planet's guide to the area offers one version of this narrative, which starts as follows:

County Derry

The chief attraction of the county is the town of Derry (Doire) itself, nestled poetically by the wide sweep of the River Foyle. There's a terrible sadness in the contrast between the cosy feel of the town itself and its recent past, scarred by injustice and bitterness. After the defeat of Hugh O'Neill in 1603, the part of the county inland from Derry was systematically planted with English and Scottish settlers. The dour, staunchly Protestant towns continue to evoke and live out the history of sectarian apartheid ...

(Smallman *et al.* 1998: 685)

The Lonely Planet guide cites only *Derry* in the title of its entry on the area and does not feature *Londonderry* as an entry in the index, which signals the narrative location of its authors quite clearly.

Still in the context of Irish history, Sinn Fein refuses to accept as legitimate the partition of Ireland under the Anglo-Irish treaty of 1921. It signals this refusal through the consistent use of *Six Counties* to refer to what is more widely known as the *North of Ireland*, *Ulster* or *Northern Ireland*. These choices are not interchangeable, and none of them is 'neutral'. The choice of *Six Counties* clearly signals a specific narrative position, one that views the six counties of Ulster – namely, Fermanagh, Armagh, Tyrone, Derry/Londonderry, Antrim and Down – as temporarily and illegally held under British rule. A translator or interpreter who disregards the implications of this choice and simply translates *Six Counties* as *Northern Ireland*, *Ulster* or *North of Ireland* would inevitably undermine the narrative position of the author or speaker. At the same time, translators and interpreters have narrative positions of their own and are responsible for their share of elaborating and circulating public narratives. They must therefore make informed and careful decisions in this as in other aspects of their professional and social life.

The choice of *West Bank* vs. *Judea and Samaria* offers a further example of rival place names in the context of the Middle East conflict. *Judea* and *Samaria* are biblical names for the southern and central areas of Palestine, currently under Israeli occupation. These place names are embedded in a Zionist narrative in which the entire West Bank and Gaza Strip, in addition to pre-1967 Israel, are regarded as the natural homeland of the Jews. Uncritical use of *Judea and Samaria* immediately signals the narrative location of the speaker or writer; it embeds them within a Zionist narrative whether or not they consciously subscribe to it. Translators and editors working for the BBC Monitoring Unit adopt an interesting strategy in dealing with this problem. When quoting

Israeli politicians or reproducing extracts from Israeli papers, they tend to leave the original place reference intact and gloss it as *West Bank* following the first mention only, as in the following examples (relevant stretches highlighted):

> The presentation of plans for construction in **Judea and Samaria [West Bank]** constitute another manoeuvre by Prime Minister Ariel Sharon. What a strange coincidence, exactly on the eve of the Likud conference, that the prime minister suddenly emerges as 'the biggest builder of **Judea and Samaria**'. Time after time the prime minister initiates futile manoeuvres and he thinks that there are still those who believe him. Mr Prime Minister, there is no longer anyone who believes you.[22]

> 'In the future, there will be a need to evacuate more settlements in **Judea and Samaria [the West Bank]** – not because it's just, but because there is no choice if we want to remain a Jewish and democratic state,' Mr Olmert's office quoted him as saying to settler leaders.[23]

The first extract is from the Israeli paper *Hatzofe*; it is one of several extracts translated from news sources and embedded in a BBC article reporting on responses in the Middle East to Israel's plans to expand the settlements. The first mention of *Judea and Samaria* is glossed as *West Bank* within square brackets. The second mention, within the quote, is left unglossed. The second example is from one of BBC's own items of news, which quotes Ehud Olmert, Israel's Deputy Prime Minister, expressing his opposition to the settlements. *Judea and Samaria* is again glossed within explicit brackets as *West Bank*. Although Olmert opposes the settlements, he does so not because he does not subscribe to the Zionist narrative, 'not because it's just' (in his words), but for pragmatic reasons. His use of *Judea and Samaria* is therefore entirely consistent with his narrative perspective.

> When the Israeli army occupied Deir Ghassaneh and the whole eastern part of Palestine in 1967, the news bulletins began to speak of the Israeli Defence Force's occupation of the West Bank. The pollution of language can get no more blatant than in the term West Bank. West of what? Bank of what? The reference here is to the west bank of the River Jordan, not to eastern Palestine. The west bank of a river is a geographical location – not a country, not a homeland.
>
> (Barghouti 2003)

The title of the first BBC article, to which the extract from *Hatzofe* is appended, is 'Press anger over **West Bank** home plans' (emphasis added). The first paragraph of the article reads as follows (relevant items highlighted): 'Newspapers in the Middle East have condemned plans announced by the Israeli government to build 1,000 new homes in Jewish settlements in **the West Bank**.'

What seems to be happening here is that BBC translators and editors have devised a way of signalling their disassociation from the Zionist narrative while staying within their prescribed frame space as journalists and translators.[24] First, the square brackets around the gloss alert the reader to the fact that this is an addition by the translator, thus signalling the translator's intention to stay within their prescribed frame space; the contentious term *Judea and Samaria* is after all reproduced rather than suppressed, and the translator has therefore discharged his or her duty to be faithful to the source text. However, the use of *Judea and Samaria* is not left uncontested, and both the title and actual text of the article in which one of the translations is embedded uses *West Bank* without glossing it as *Judea and Samaria*.[25] This unequivocally signals the BBC's (and BBC translators') commitment to this aspect of the Palestinian narrative, which treats the relevant areas as part of Occupied Palestine. This aspect of the Palestinian narrative is of course also officially recognized by international law and UN resolutions relating to the conflict. As an official institution, the BBC – irrespective of the position(s) of its individual editors and translators on this issue – cannot afford to undermine a legally sanctioned aspect of any narrative it reports on. BBC Monitoring selects and translates information from over 3,000 radio, television, press, Internet and news agency sources from 150 countries in some 100 languages. The way it renders rival place names is very important, since its framing of various conflicts feeds into official, media and expert narratives of the regions in question. Its subscribers include government departments, journalists and academics, as well as multinational businesses.

Stronger signals of dissociation from the narrative location elaborated in the source text are often used in translations by activist groups. Just as the choice between *West Bank* and *Judea and Samaria*, or *settlements* and *neighbourhoods*, immediately signals the narrative location of the speaker or writer in the context of the Middle East conflict, the choice of *wall, fence* or *barrier* (and various other options such as *Apartheid Wall* and *security fence*) to refer to the structure erected by Israel and condemned by the International Court of Justice in July 2004 gives a very clear indication of the narrative being evoked. Writing for the *Electronic Intifada* on 9 July 2004, El Fassed (2005) quotes a ruling by the Israeli Cabinet thus (relevant items highlighted):

> One year after the ruling of the International Court of Justice (ICJ), in which it made clear that the construction of the Wall and the settlements were illegal, the Israeli cabinet called for 'the immediate completion of the **security fence** [**sic**] in the Jerusalem area'.

The use of *[sic]* here leaves the reader with no doubt as to the narrative location of the writer/translator, especially given the author's own use of *the Wall* and *settlements*.

Translators and interpreters, then, may want to consider the larger narratives in which a text or utterance is embedded in order to make an informed decision about how to handle names, especially rival names of places. The alternative, to simply repeat whatever name the writer or speaker uses without comment, means participating in uncritical circulation of a narrative they may well find ethically reprehensible if they stopped to ponder its implications. Where frame space allows them more latitude, translators, and to a lesser extent interpreters, can insert their own critical comments and glosses at various points. This will not necessarily be welcomed by all readers or listeners, nor indeed even be understood by some, but it does allow the translator or interpreter to signal their position in relation to the narrative in question. As with every choice a human being makes, this one has its limitations. One such limitation is that because in this type of situation 'adequacy of explanation is relative to the beliefs of those to whom something is being explained' and because 'each scheme of belief involves the rejection of the other' (MacIntyre 1988: 381), any comments by the translator or interpreter may simply fail to hit their mark. Ultimately, in this type of situation we cannot apply 'one standard test of translation and translatabily' (MacIntyre 1988: 380) nor develop an ethically and professionally foolproof strategy for all translators and interpreters to adopt. We each make our own decisions on the ground and have to live with the consequences. The main thing to stress here is that neutrality is an illusion, and thus uncritical fidelity to the source text or utterance also has consequences that an informed translator or interpreter may not wish to be party to.

It is also important for us as scholars of translation and interpreting to realize that we too are firmly embedded within specific narratives. Ben-Ari (2000) unwittingly offers a very interesting example of this in the context of translating rival place names. In an article entitled 'Ideological Manipulation of Translated Texts', she starts by expressing surprise and distaste at the practice of Egyptian translators of Israeli literature, who 'admitted' to her that

> in literary texts translated from Hebrew to Arabic, the name of the country, Israel, must be converted to Palestine. The name of the capital, Jerusalem, must be converted into its Moslem [*sic*] name 'Al Kuds' [*sic*], etc.
>
> (Ben-Ari 2000: 40; [*sic*] added)

Writing from a very different narrative location, Ibrahim Muhawi points out a number of ideological manipulations in Ben-Ari's own analysis of ideological manipulations in this stretch alone. First, in relation to her comment on Jerusalem, he argues:

> The international community does not acknowledge Jerusalem as the capital of Israel (the American embassy, as well as that of the overwhelming majority of UN members, is in Tel Aviv). Secondly, the name of the city that is the Capital of Palestine/Israel is al-Quds (not al-Kuds). And thirdly, that is its Arabic name, not its Muslim name. I'm Christian, and that's what I, and the entire Christian community of Palestine, call the city. Fourthly, even assuming that the international community does acknowledge Jerusalem as the capital of Israel, by not willing to contemplate an Arabic name for the city, the author denies the existence of the majority of the population in East Jerusalem, and a minority in West Jerusalem. Granted, the name 'Jerusalem' is more commonly known than al-Quds, but the usage as a name does not make it any the less ideological. There are at least 250 million Arabs for whom that is the name of the place.
>
> (personal communication, December 2002)

I should add that the Egyptian translators whose practice Ben-Ari finds surprising were of course translating *into Arabic*. Their use of *Al-Quds*, which is the standard Arabic equivalent of *Jerusalem*, is therefore hardly surprising. The confusion of Arab and Muslim designations and narratives, on the other hand, is itself an effect of the narrative location of Ben-Ari.

> The ethical systems by which we judge cultural narratives are themselves cultural narratives.
>
> (Angela Ryan, personal communication, December 2003)

Secondly, Ben-Ari's distaste for the Egyptian translators' 'admission' that they find it necessary to use *Palestine* rather than *Israel* as the name of the country does not preclude her from resorting to the same strategy in her own writing. In discussing translations of German Jewish historical novels in Eastern Europe during the nineteenth century, she says:

> And since these historical novels were later a basis for a new literature written in Israel up to the establishment of the state, adapted in countless school readers and magazines, their translations into Hebrew done in Israel are in a way their third ideological metamorphosis.
>
> (Ben-Ari 2000: 49)

As Muhawi points out (personal communication), 'here Israel predates itself. It's Israel when it was Palestine, and it's Israel before it came into being as a state'. In spite of her distaste for what she calls 'ideological manipulation', then, Ben-Ari turns out to be as firmly – but perhaps less consciously or critically – embedded in her own narratives as the translators whose practices she finds surprising. What narrative theory alerts us to is that our own pieces of research are also narratives, mini narratives which are part of larger, master narratives of different types (some political, some social, some academic). As with any narrative, there is no way that the story can be told from a privileged position of absolute neutrality. The narrator cannot stand outside the narrative.

Rival place names are among the most challenging and interesting discursive features to study in the context of translation and conflict. Both as professionals and as researchers we would do well to approach them, and our own narratives of the history in which they are embedded, in a critical, reflexive and responsible manner.

6.4.2 Titles

Titles of textual and visual products such as novels, films and academic books are not normally part of a rival system in which they compete with each other, but they too can be used very effectively to (re)frame narratives in translation.[26] *The Slave-King*, title of the 1833 translation of Hugo's *Bug-Jargal*, foregrounds the issue of slavery and frames the narrative as part of the abolitionist discourse, explicitly situating it on the anti-slavery side of the debate. Similarly, Aphra Behn's choice of *A Discovery of New Worlds* as a title for Fontenelle's *Entretiens sur la pluralité des mondes habités* 'suppresses both the conversational quality of the text and its uncomfortably provocative idea about the possible existence of many other worlds' (Knellwolf 2001: 104), both of which challenged Behn's own narratives of science and the world in general. And as we saw in the discussion of *relationality* in Chapter 4 (section 4.2 on p. 61), Margot Badran's choice of *Harem Years: Memoirs of an Egyptian Feminist* as a title for her English translation of Huda Sha'rawi's *Mudhakkirati* (My Memoirs) reframed this ontological narrative of a rich and complex personal experience as an episode in a Western public narrative about the seclusion of Arab and Muslim women.

Here's a more interesting example from recent history, as narrated in the first part of a three-part documentary entitled *The Power of Nightmares* (BBC2, 20 October 2004). In 1972, Henry Kissinger negotiated a treaty with the Soviet Union to limit nuclear arms. This was the beginning of a détente that alarmed neo-conservatives such as Dick Cheney and Donald Rumsfeld, who were (even then) committed to a politics of fear. Over the following few years, they began to develop a now familiar argument of an invisible but overwhelming threat from the enemy. Richard Pipes, a historian of the Soviet Union interviewed in the documentary, insisted that 'whatever the Soviets said publicly, secretly they still intended to attack and conquer America. This was their hidden mindset' *(ibid.)*. Then, as in the build up to the 2003 invasion of Iraq, the CIA repeatedly argued there was no evidence to support claims of an imminent threat to the USA. One of the things the neo-conservatives did to sustain their narrative in the face of this lack of cooperation from the CIA was to translate a Russian military intelligence manual originally entitled 'The Art of Winning' under the title *The Art of Conquest* (Anne Cahn, Arms Control and Disarmament Agency, 1977–80, interviewed in *The Power of Nightmares*). 'Conquest', unlike 'winning', framed the Soviet position as one of calculated aggression, in line with the narrative of fear favoured by the neo-conservatives.

The use of titles to reframe narratives in translation is often accompanied by subtle shifts in the texts themselves, in line with the narrative position signalled in the new title. For example, Sturge (2002) explains that under Nazi rule the relationship between the sexes formed part of a broader narrative in which sanctioned gender hierarchies assigned specific roles for men and women, as for every other group in society. In this context, it is not surprising to see a detective novel originally entitled *Mystery in Kensington* being reframed under the German title *Gore/Hilf mir, Peter!* (Help me, Peter!), Peter being the male hero in the novel. This choice of title is then reinforced by a series of subtle shifts in the text itself, including a 'switch of gender in the description of the heroine's hair, when tousled "like a boy's," [which] becomes "*wie bei einem kleinen Mädchen*" (like a little girl's ...)', and 'the insertion of "*sie knickte zusammen*" (she collapsed, ...), introducing a note of female frailty' (Sturge 2002: 164). These subtle changes reinforce the narrative of a world in which women are frail and passive and men are masterful and heroic, as already signalled in the new title.

In 1996, Joseph Finklestone, a journalist then working for the Tel Aviv daily *Maariv* and the *Jewish Chronicle* in London, wrote a book entitled *Anwar Sadat:*

Visionary Who Dared. The Arabic translation, by Adel Abdel Sabour, came out in 1999 under the title *Al-Sadat: Wahm Al-Tahaddi* (*Sadat: The Illusion of Challenge*). The Arabic title signals a very different narrative of Sadat and his role in initiating what came to be known as the Peace Process. In the original version, Finklestone strives to present Sadat in a positive light, as a visionary who dared to challenge reactionary forces in the region. Those who opposed him are portrayed as either petty-minded or extremist, which fits well with a broader narrative of the Middle East that is particularly dominant in the USA and Britain. The Arabic title on the other hand evokes a narrative that is very familiar to the Arab reader: Sadat was an American stooge who operated under the illusion that he could force his people to make peace with Israel at the expense of 'selling' the Palestinians. The Egyptian people, however, continually frustrated his plans by refusing to cooperate with Israel in any arena, whether cultural or economic. Indeed, the movement against 'normalization', which started in 1979, remains extremely strong to this day, with the vast majority of writers, artists, academics and entrepreneurs refusing to work with institutions and individuals in Israel. Thus, *The Illusion of Challenge* evokes a narrative that has considerable currency among the target audience of the translation. Sadat, this version of the narrative goes, was under the illusion that he could force a peace without dignity on his people. He was not a visionary but rather another deluded politician.

This interpretation, clearly signalled by the new title, is further supported by a series of subtle shifts throughout the translation. Here is one example from the first page of the introduction, with relevant shifts highlighted in the back translation:

English original

After centuries of living under the shadow of great powers, often humiliated and derided, Egypt, under Sadat, was grappling with tremendous, almost insoluble problems – inadequate resources, insufficient fertile land and a burgeoning population which was increasing at the rate of over one million every year.

(Finklestone 1996: xiii)

والحادث تاريخياً، أن مصر بعد أن ظلت قروناً طويلة في ذل ومهانة تحت قسوة القوى العظمى،خضعت لحكم السادات، ومع حكم السادات شهدت مصر العديد من المشاكل الضخمة والمعقدة، والتي جاء في مقدمتها، نقص الموارد، ومحدودية الأراضى الزراعية، والتكدس السكانى الذى يزداد بمعدل يفوق المليون نسمة سنوياً . .

Back translation of Arabic

Historically, after Egypt had remained for long centuries humiliated and oppressed by the cruelty of the Great Powers, it **submitted/surrendered** to Sadat's rule. And **with Sadat's rule** Egypt witnessed numerous large and complex problems, foremost of which were the lack of resources, the limited availability of agricultural land, and the growth of population at a rate of over one million every year.

(Abdel Sabour 1999: 11)

Unlike the English original, the Arabic text suggests through the choice of *khada'at* (submitted/surrendered) that Egypt did not willingly accept Sadat as its ruler. Secondly, whereas the English original implies that Sadat's performance as President was admirable given that he inherited such insurmountable problems from the previous regime, the Arabic version makes very subtle use of a preposition (*ma'a*/with) to indicate that these problems were *created* rather than inherited by Sadat's regime. These relatively subtle changes in the body of the text sustain and reinforce the reframed narrative already signalled in the title of the translation.

Like rival place names then, titles of books, films and other types of material are among the numerous devices available to the translator for (re)framing narratives. Given that interpreters deal with spoken material in the context of events that either have no title as such (a doctor–patient interview) or have titles over which the interpreter has no control (a United Nations meeting, a scientific conference), this feature is of much less relevance for them.

6.5 Repositioning of participants

One aspect of relationality, a feature of narrativity discussed in Chapter 4, concerns the way in which participants in any interaction are positioned, or position themselves, in relation to each other and to those outside the immediate event. Any change in the configuration of these positions inevitably alters the dynamics of the immediate as well as wider narratives in which they are woven.

> West Germans represent themselves in the stories they tell as centrally 'here' or 'there', as close to the West or to the East, as looking back or forward, or as 'in between' through linguistic choices involving verbs, adverbs and temporal expressions. They also use, and negotiate with their interlocutors, linguistic configurations of time and place and referential expressions to place themselves in certain ideological positions with respect to shared stereotypical notions about Eastern and Western Germany.
>
> (Baynham and De Fina 2005: 12)

In translation and interpreting, participants can be repositioned in relation to each other and to the reader or hearer through the linguistic management of time, space, deixis, dialect, register, use of epithets, and various means of self- and other identification. Cumulative, often very subtle choices in the expression of any of these parameters allow the translator or interpreter to reconfigure the relationship between *here* and *there*, *now* and *then*, *them* and *us*, *reader* and *narrator*, *reader* and *translator*, *hearer* and *interpreter*. Whether in the form of paratextual commentary or shifts in the expression of any of these parameters within the text itself, translators and interpreters can actively reframe the immediate narrative as well as the larger narratives in which it is embedded by careful realignment of participants in time and social/political space.

6.5.1 Repositioning in paratextual commentary

Introductions, prefaces, footnotes, glossaries and – to a lesser extent, since translators do not normally control these – cover design and blurbs are among the numerous sites available to translators for repositioning themselves, their readers and other participants in time and space.

Hong Kong Collage: Contemporary Stories and Writing (Cheung 1998) is a collection of 23 short stories, essays and excerpts from novels by Hong Kong writers in English translation. The collection is edited by Martha Cheung, who is also the translator of several pieces in the volume. In her introduction, the editor/translator weaves a narrative that is itself partly dedicated to repositioning the main players in the Hong Kong/Other interface. This narrative depicts 'Western writers as well as those from the Mainland' as outsiders who have continually imposed and superimposed 'a plethora of images on Hong Kong', images that 'have hardened into stereotypes' (Cheung 1998: x). The new rulers of Hong Kong, the Chinese, are thus positioned alongside its old rulers, the West/British, in the same socio-political space. This positioning of the two main political players together is also evident in the question 'Which version of Hong Kong history is one to take as "true" – that produced by the British? by the Chinese? by Hong Kong historians? by supposedly apolitical and objective scholars?' (1998: xi). Cheung, on the other hand, describes herself as a 'long-time inhabitant of the city' (1998: x) and is clearly positioned in the same space as the writers represented in the volume, whose writing 'illuminates Hong Kong *from the inside*' (1998: xii; my emphasis).

The editor/translator's response to what she describes as 'living in an echo chamber reverberating with voices claiming to be speaking on one's behalf' (1998: xii) is to put together a collage of Hong Kong life that is 'unashamedly subjective' and 'defiantly idiosyncratic' (1998: ix), in an attempt to resist and undermine the grand, reductive narratives of Hong Kong promoted by outsiders (relevant items highlighted):

> this book registers my own personal response to the many voices that have claimed to represent Hong Kong, or have been proclaimed as representative of Hong Kong over the last decade. It registers my own personal response too, to the many **new** voices that are **now** claiming to represent Hong Kong. The collection also marks this individual's attempt to counter the grand narratives, the master images, and the controlling identities – imposed on Hong Kong **from the outside** – with narratives, images, and identities chosen by the people of Hong Kong for themselves.
>
> (1998: xii)

Cheung's choice of pronouns and deictic expressions in this extract and throughout the five-page introduction participates in elaborating a narrative in which she and the people of Hong Kong are positioned together, and on the opposite side of others who would represent them in ways with which they do not identify. These 'others' are politically configured: they are the longstanding, established voice of the Western colonial powers as well as the *new* voices *now* claiming to represent Hong Kong. Read in the context of the then very recent 1997 handover, that 'momentous event of Hong Kong's return to Chinese sovereignty' (1998: ix), *new* and *now* clearly signal the incoming political power, namely China. The introduction thus sets the scene for reading every piece in the collection from the perspective of this positioning. It also encourages the reader to interpret each piece as evidence of the diversity and richness of Hong Kong life, as an episode in the editor/translator's ontological-cum-public narrative designed to contest and undermine the 'grand narratives' promoted by the political and social other, the outside repeatedly encroaching on and appropriating the inside.

Short introductions written by the editor/translator also preface individual pieces in the collection and participate in elaborating the narrative outlined in the main introduction and in positioning the main players either outside or inside the Hong Kong space (relevant items highlighted):

> Xiao Si's writings, noted for the fineness of their observations, often make **those of us who have lived in this city for a long time** feel that **we** have never really got to know the place. For Hongkongers over the age of thirty, the bronze lions referred to in this piece will almost certainly play a part in **our** memories of **our** growing up experience.
> But how many of **us** have looked at the lions the way she does?
>
> (1998: 81)

This short introduction prefaces a piece entitled 'The Bronze Lions' by Xiao Si, translated by Jane C.C. Lai. Like the prefaces to other pieces in the collection, it picks up on the matrix of relationships set up in the main introduction and explicitly situates the players, including the translators, on the inside or outside of the 'real', diverse, rich tapestry of Hong Kong life, as 'us' or 'them'. In this particular preface, 'those of us who have lived in the city for a long time' are set off from both Westerners and those described in the preface to another piece as 'immigrants from the Mainland' (1998: 122).[27] The 'us/we' of the translators and editor is the 'us/we' of those with inside knowledge and real empathy, contesting the narratives of outsiders looking for easy stereotypes and shallow explanations.

Translators can also intervene in paratexts to guide the way in which 'we' the readers are positioned vis-à-vis the community depicted in the source narrative. St André (forthcoming) explains that it was a feature of sinological translation in the nineteenth century to signal a split between what the text said in Chinese and the reality of Chinese life – in other words to question the veracity of the source narrative. The assumption was not only that a certain split existed between text and reality, but also that it was the translator's duty 'to reveal to the British reader the "truth" behind the fictive text'. This duty was discharged in the form of direct and indirect commentary 'which shaped and guided the readers' understanding of the nature of Chineseness as being inferior' (St André, forthcoming). St André gives as an example Robert Morrison's 1815 translation of some Chinese edicts:

After translating an edict in which the emperor lashes out against abuses committed by his army while putting down a rebellion (they had kidnapped children to sell as slaves), Morrison adds a commentary: 'The tenor of the Imperial Edicts, unquestionably shews [*sic*] the reigning Emperor to be a humane man. This is also the character which his People give him; *but they complain, that he keeps in the Government a bad set.*' ... The translation shows the emperor to be a good man, but the commentary warns the reader that this one good man is surrounded by many evil ones. Slightly earlier, Morrison also warns the reader of the profound discrepancy between what the Chinese say and how they act: 'there is no nation in the world in which professions and practice are more at variance than in China'.

(forthcoming; emphasis in original)

This type of commentary by nineteenth-century translators of Chinese official documents intervened in configuring the immediate relationship between the reader and the community depicted in the source narrative. It also actively contributed to elaborating the larger colonial narratives of the time.

6.5.2 Repositioning within the text or utterance

Much repositioning in translation, and almost all repositioning in interpreting, is realized within the text or utterance. The range of devices available for effecting this reconfiguration of positions is open-ended in principle. Almost any textual feature can be renegotiated at the local or global level to reconfigure the relationship between participants within and around the source narrative. Mason and Şerban (2003) offer a detailed analysis of systematic shifts in deixis in English translations of Romanian literature which result in reconfiguring the relationship between readers and the events and participants depicted in the source narratives; in Mason and Şerban's terms, these shifts 'continuously reshape the relationship between translator/text', allowing translators 'to create distance or, on the contrary, closeness between translations and readers' and 'position themselves toward the text they work on' (2003: 290).

The well-documented move from *wenyan* (classical literary Chinese) to *baihua* (Mandarin vernacular) in the translation of both literature and scriptures in early twentieth-century China[28] participated in reconfiguring social relations as part of the larger narrative of modern, egalitarian, democratic society, as well as the relationship between the Christian God and His subjects. The use of the vernacular in theatre translation in Quebec since the staging of Michel Tremblay's *Les Belles-Soeurs* in 1968 fulfils a similar function of repositioning participants, including readers and audience, in social and political space. Brisset (1989) explains that Québécois theatre translations 'are almost always marked by a proletarization of language' (1989: 17). This proletarization is realized by the choice of joual as the language of translation, as opposed to continental French. In Robert Lalonde's translation of Checkhov's *Three Sisters*, the choice of joual, the language of the working class, is accompanied by a series of shifts that contribute to 'proletarizing' the setting and participants within the play:

The house of Brigadier General Prozorov becomes that of a village physician. The 'drawing-room with columns beyond which a ballroom can be seen' (Hingley 1964: 73) becomes a 'salon modeste' (a humble living-room) where reigns 'une atmosphère très "familiale" et ordinaire' (a typical and ordinary family atmosphere). The theatrical representation of Québec-ness often relies on the social degrading of the protagonists in the original work. This social degrading is directly related to the language since it allows the protagonists to use modes of expression in which phonetic, lexical and syntactic Québécois markers can be found.

(Brisset 1989: 17)

The 'proletarization' of source texts and the participants they depict in the Québécois context influences the positioning of participants in the larger narrative of Quebec. It serves to carve out a distinct position for the Québécois people, one that is separate from both the English and the French. This is because joual, a language heavily influenced by English, 'symbolizes the condition of a colonized Quebec' (Brisset 1989: 10). At the same time, joual 'is also what gives the Québécois a distinctively North American feature and differentiates him from his French-speaking European counterpart' (1989: 10).

Interestingly, Brisset notes that whereas joual is used in the translation of plays, stage directions – which 'reflect the playwright's own speech and, as such, bear no specific Québécois mark' (1989: 17) – are translated into 'educated French' (1989: 17). This stratification of language/dialect choice further participates in delimiting the positions occupied by different participants in the reading/theatrical experience. Those positioned within the Quebec space, whether as readers or characters within the play, are associated with joual. The playwright, on the other hand, is linguistically and politically positioned outside that space. But in Mustapha Safouan's 1998 Arabic translation of *Othello*, where *'amiyya* (the Egyptian vernacular) is used throughout, even the translator's introduction is written in the vernacular. This is consistent with the positioning of translator and audience within the same social and political space:

> The objective of the translation into the vernacular is clear: that one day Muhammad Ali Abdel Mula, and millions like him, would be able to read established writers in ours and other cultures in the language they were fed by their mothers, the language in and through which they live, and which they speak to their last breath.
>
> (Safouan 1998: 5; translated and quoted in Hanna 2005: 119)

As Hanna explains, Safouan's choice of the Egyptian vernacular as a vehicle for both his translation of *Othello* and his own meta-discourse on the translation is an explicit attempt to undermine the claim of a homogeneous collective Arab identity, a claim consistently made by numerous intellectuals and other translators of Shakespeare into Arabic, including earlier translators of *Othello*. Safouan thus positions himself in opposition to all these intellectuals and translators, and positions the

Egyptian reader outside what he sees as the oppressive and debilitating homogeneity of the Arab World. Safouan further sees the choice of the vernacular as serving another important political purpose:

> it bridges [the] ... artificial gap between the masses and the intellectuals; this gap, Safouan asserts, has always been in the interest of political power, since it helps disempower both the masses and the intellectuals and makes them both susceptible to manipulation.
>
> (Hanna 2005: 119)

By narrowing the gap between the masses and intellectuals, the choice of the Egyptian vernacular increases the proximity of the two groups in social and political terms.

Like the choice of language and/or dialect, selective use of register identifies a participant with a particular social category and sets him or her apart from other participants in a narrative.[29] Hale (1997) reports a tendency among court interpreters to raise the level of formality when interpreting into the official language of the court and lower it when interpreting in the direction of witnesses and defendants, as in the following examples:

Raising the level of formality, in the direction of court officials (Spanish into English):
Witness: .... me me **agarró aquí** el dedo. (lit: he he *got me here*, on the finger)
Interpreter: ... he **injured** my hand.

(Hale 1997: 46)

Witness: Ahora, si yo no tomé ningún acto de **echarla**, porque yo le prometí que no la iba a **echar**. (lit: Now, if I didn't take any act to *throw her out*, because I promised her that I wouldn't *throw her out*)
Interpreter: And also I had promised her that I wouldn't **evict** her.

(Hale 1997: 47)

Lowering the level of formality, in the direction of defendants and witnesses (English into Spanish):
Magistrate: So, you would say that your relationship with Mrs X has been at least **acrimonious**?
Interpreter: Sería, usted diría entonces que su relaxión con la señora X has sido bastante, **en un situación bastante mala**? (It would, you would say then that your relationship with Mrs X has been rather, *in a bad situation?*)

(Hale 1997: 49)

Solicitor: And you are the **defendant** before the court?
Interpreter: Y usted es **el que está aquí** en le corte? (And you are *the one who* is here in court?)

(Hale 1997: 49)

Hale explains this tendency as a form of '"empathy" with one's audience' (1997: 52), a natural communicative need to accommodate our listeners by adjusting our speech to match what we deem to be their expectations. This may well be true, but it is also clear from these examples and other strategies reported in the same article that interpreters are simultaneously positioning themselves in relation to the court (projecting themselves as part of its professional apparatus and aligning themselves with its function) and in relation to those who are positioned on a lower social scale (projecting themselves as their superiors by virtue of 'talking down' to them). In each case, interpreters employ a register that reflects their own assumptions about where each type of participant fits into the social and educational hierarchy, and their very use of this register participates in locating each participant in social space.

Variation in register also allows interpreters to position themselves emotionally vis-à-vis the witness or defendant. Hale reports, for instance, that one interpreter in her study never interpreted the diminutives used by the witness in Spanish, but she herself used the diminutive 'to express familiarity and sympathy towards the witness', as in the following examples:

> Sergeant: With your wife and daughter.
> Interpreter: Estaba con su esposa y su **hijita**. (You were with your wife and your *little daughter*)

> Magistrate: When you had gone back to look after your child.
> Interpreter: cuando cuando usted fue a ver a su **niñita**, as su **hijita**. (when when you went to see your *little girl*, your *little daughter*)
>
> (Hale 1997: 50)

Finally, repositioning in translation can also influence the interplay between ontological and public narratives, resulting in a different level of visibility of the personal in the context of shared, collective experience. Polezzi (1998, 2001) describes the cumulative effect of shifts in tense and pronoun use in *To Lhasa and Beyond*, the 1956 English translation of Giuseppe Tucci's *A Lhasa e Oltre*, and explains the effect of these shifts:

> The continuity between narration and description guaranteed by the generalized use of the present tense, and the identification of traveller and reader encouraged by such devices as the use of personal pronouns, give the whole of the source text the status of an objective and timeless account, one which the reader can still access as if through his or her own eyes but also accept as an authoritative expert account of the 'reality' of Tibet. The English translation, on the other hand, clearly defines the boundaries of personal experience through the use of different tenses (the present for the initial, general introduction and the past for the account of travel experiences), and discourages personal identification with the narrator, transforming 'the scientist' Tuci into just one of the many travel writers whose personal accounts the reader can draw upon to obtain an interesting and learned, but only partial and definitely historicised, vision of Tibet.
>
> (2001: 128)

May (1994: 76–7) discusses similar tense shifts in English translations of Russian literature which result in suppressing the narrator's voice. Like the downplaying of personal, anecdotal aspects of a text or utterance, erasing the voice of the author/narrator also contributes to reconfiguring the balance between personal and public narratives.

The purpose of this chapter was to highlight and exemplify the framing function of translation and some of the wide array of devices available for fulfilling this function. Whatever local strategies a translator or interpreter opts for, their cumulative choices always have an effect beyond the immediate text or event. Individual textual narratives do not exist in isolation of the larger narratives circulating in any society, nor indeed of the meta-narratives circulating globally. As social actors, translators and interpreters are responsible for the narratives they help circulate, and for the real-life consequences of giving these narratives currency and legitimacy.

Core references

Benford, Robert (1993) 'Frame Disputes within the Nuclear Disarmament Movement', *Social Forces* 71: 677–701.

Benford, Robert and David Snow (2000) 'Framing Processes and Social Movements: An Overview and Assessment', *Annual Review of Sociology* 26: 611–39.

Blum-Kulka, Shoshana and Tamar Liebes (1993) 'Frame Ambiguities: *Intifada* Narrativization of the Experience by Israeli Soldiers', in Akiba Cohen and Gadi Wolfsfeld (eds) *Framing the Intifada: People & Media*, Norwood NJ: Ablex, 27–52.

Davies, Bronwyn and Rom Harré (1990) 'Positioning: The Discursive Production of Selves', *Journal for the Theory of Social Behaviour* 20(1): 43–63.

Goffman, Erving (1986 [1974]) *Frame Analysis: An Essay on the Organization of Experience*, Boston: Northeastern University Press.

Goffman, Erving (1981) *Forms of Talk*, Philadelphia: University of Pennsylvania Press.

Tannen, Deborah (ed.) (1993) *Framing in Discourse*, New York: Oxford University Press.

Further reading

Bongie, Chris (2005) 'Victor Hugo and "The Cause of Humanity": Translating *Bug-Jargal* (1826) into *The Slave-King* (1833)', *The Translator* 11(1): 1–24.

Brisset, Annie (1989) 'In Search of a Target Language: The Politics of Theatre Translation in Quebec', *Target* 1(1): 9–27.

Cunningham, David and Barb Browning (2004) 'The Emergence of Worthy Targets: Official Frames and Deviance Narratives Within the FBI', *Sociological Forum* 19(3): 347–69.

Harvey, Keith (2003b) '"Events" and "Horizons": Reading Ideology in the "Bindings" of Translations', in María Calzada Pérez (ed.) *Apropos of Ideology – Translation Studies on Ideology – Ideologies in Translation Studies*, Manchester: St Jerome Publishing, 43–69.

Jones, Francis R. (2004) 'Ethics, Aesthetics and Décision: Literary Translating in the Wars of the Yugoslav Succession', *Meta* 49(4): 711–28.

Kovala, Urpo (1996) 'Translations, Paratextual Mediation, and Ideological Closure', *Target* 8(1): 119–47.

Kuhiwczak, Piotr (1990) 'Translation as Appropriation: The Case of Milan Kundera's *The Joke*', in Susan Bassnett and Andre Lefevere (eds) *Translation, History & Culture*, London and New York: Pinter Publishers, 118–30.

López, Marísa Fernández (2000) 'Translation Studies in Contemporary Children's Literature: A Comparison of Intercultural Ideological Factors', *Children's Literature Association Quarterly* 25(1): 29–37.

Noakes, John (2000) 'Official Frames in Social Movement Theory: The FBI, HUAC, and the Communist Threat in Hollywood', *The Sociological Quarterly* 41(4): 657–80.

Nord, Christiane (1995) 'Text-Functions in Translation: Titles and Headings as a Case in Point', *Target* 7(2): 261–84.

Pettersson, Bo (2001) 'The Finnish National Anthem in Translation: Deixis and National Sentiment', in Pirjo Kukkonen and Ritva Hartama-Heinonen (eds) *Mission, Vision, Strategies, and Values: A Celebration of Translator Training and Translation Studies in Kouvola*, Helsinki: Helsinki University Press, 187–94.

Watts, Richard (2000) 'Translating Culture: Reading the Paratexts of Aimé Césaire's *Cahier d'un retour au pays natal*', *TTR* XIII(2): 29–46.

7   Assessing narratives

The narrative paradigm

Writing about the way in which scientific narratives are elaborated, and acknowledging the threat that the notion of narrativity presents in relation to our traditional conception of science, Landau poses the following question:

> Does working within a narrative form negate the conscious goals and rationales of doing science? This question can be rephrased as: Are narratives testable?
>
> (1997: 116)

Given that the version of narrative theory elaborated in this book and adopted in Landau (1997) assumes that narrative constitutes reality rather than merely representing it, and hence that none of us is in a position to stand outside any narrative in order to observe it 'objectively', we might conclude that there can be no criteria for assessing narratives – in any genre – and no sensible means for us to establish whether we should subscribe to or challenge any specific narrative. But our embeddedness in narratives clearly cannot preclude our ability to reason about individual narratives. If it did we would never be able to connect with other individuals who share at least some of the narratives we subscribe to in order to form communities of various types – from a scientific association to a political party.

In order to address the issue of how we assess narratives to decide whether we should subscribe to them, dissociate ourselves from those who subscribe to them, or even actively set out to challenge them, this final chapter will focus on Walter Fisher's influential narrative paradigm (1984, 1985, 1987, 1997), which provides one method of analysing the effectiveness of individual narratives – not in absolute terms, but from the variable perspectives of individuals with different sets of values and priorities. I will also attempt to demonstrate how we assess narratives in practice by applying Fisher's system of analysis to two separate narratives from the field of language mediation. Needless to say, the analysis is inevitably conducted from my specific narrative location, which means that others applying the same system may come up with a different analysis of the same narrative, and where my analysis might dissuade me from subscribing to a version of the narrative in question theirs could well encourage them to support it. The value of Fisher's paradigm lies in enabling us to retrace our steps and articulate our reasons for supporting or opposing any given narrative. It is meant 'to ensure that people are conscious of the values they adhere to and would promote in rhetorical transactions, and to inform their consciousness *without dictating what they should believe*' (Fisher 1987: 113; emphasis in original). In other words, it is not a mechanistic method of applying a rigid set of 'universal' values in any specific context, nor across different contexts.

7.1 The narrative paradigm: basic tenets

Fisher's narrative paradigm challenges the traditional paradigm of rationality which assumes that we make decisions purely on the basis of rational arguments. Instead, Fisher explains that we communicate in the form of stories, and in order to relate stories to each other. We are thus all storytellers who 'creatively read and evaluate the texts of life and literature' (1985: 86). This does not mean that we are irrational beings who make decisions randomly. Rather, the narrative paradigm assumes that

> No matter how strictly a case is argued – scientifically, philosophically, or legally – it will always be a story, an interpretation of some aspect of the world that is historically and culturally grounded and shaped by human personality.
>
> (Fisher 1987: 49)

As both storytellers and audience, we make decisions on the basis of what Fisher calls *good reasons*, but what we consider good reasons is determined by our history, culture, experience of the world, and ultimately the stories we come to believe about the world(s) in which we live. The notion of good reasons represents the core of Fisher's paradigm. Fisher (1987: 48) defines good reasons as '*elements that provide warrants for accepting or adhering to the advice fostered by any form of communication that can be considered rhetorical*' (emphasis in original). By 'warrant', he means 'that which authorizes, sanctions, or justifies belief, attitude, or action – these being the usual forms of rhetorical advice' (1987: 107). I will return to the notion of good reasons to discuss its components in more detail in section 7.3 on p. 152 (Fidelity).

> Evaluation inherently involves tautology. ... my concern is not to avoid circularity; it is to increase the diameter of the circle that contains good reasons. The circle can be expanded by broadening the concept of good reasons to allow more instances of reasons and values to find their place within it.
>
> (Fisher 1987: 106)

The notion of good reasons is not meant to suggest that any 'good reason' is as good as another, nor that anything that 'warrants' a belief or action is good in and of itself. It 'only signifies that whatever is taken as a basis for adopting a rhetorical message is inextricably bound to a value – to a conception of the good' (Fisher 1987: 107). This suggests that assessing narratives in order to position ourselves in relation to them does not just depend on how well they fit with our experience of the world in factual terms. The notion of *reason* used here is value-laden:

> All forms of human communication function to influence the hearts and minds of others – their beliefs, values, attitudes, and/or actions. The concept of good reasons coincides with the assumption that human beings are as much valuing as they are reasoning beings. The fact is that values may serve as reasons, and what we usually call reasons are value-laden.
>
> (Fisher 1997: 314)

The narrative paradigm thus acknowledges that 'values may be reasons and that reasons affirm values in and of themselves' (Fisher 1987: 107).

The narrative paradigm does not reject rationality as such; it merely subsumes it under the notion of narrativity. It does not deny the usefulness of technical logic but stresses that 'the values of technical precision are not as important as the values of coherence, truthfulness, wisdom, and humane action, which are necessary for transforming technical logic and empirical knowledge into a force for civilized existence' (Fisher 1987: 48). For Fisher, narrative rationality 'does not exclude the long tradition of rhetorical logic; it is a rhetorical logic itself' (1987: 48). Fisher further argues that

> The concept of narrative rationality asserts that it is not the *individual form* of argument that is ultimately persuasive in discourse. That is important, but *values* are more persuasive, and they may be expressed in a variety of modes, of which argument is only one.
>
> (Fisher 1987: 48; emphasis in original)

Fisher's narrative paradigm ultimately attempts to explain what features of a narrative induce us to believe in and act upon it. It offers us an explanation of the type of features and qualities we look for and scrutinize in a narrative or set of narratives in order to decide 'whether or not they are deserving of our adherence' (1997: 315).

The two principles that define narrative rationality and embody the concept of good reasons in Fisher's paradigm are coherence (section 7.2 below) and, more specifically, fidelity (section 7.3, on p. 152).

7.2 Coherence (probability)

Fisher's principle of narrative coherence concerns the internal consistency and integrity of a narrative – how well it hangs together as a story. This involves assessing a narrative with reference to (a) its structural make-up, the way it is organized internally (structural or argumentative coherence); (b) its external consistency and completeness in terms of how it differs from or tallies with other stories on the same issue (material coherence); and (c) 'how it is told' – its believability in terms of the consistency and reliability of the characters involved (characterological coherence).

7.2.1 Structural (or argumentative) coherence

Structural coherence concerns the internal consistency of a narrative – whether or not it reveals contradictions within itself 'in form or reasoning' (Fisher 1997: 315). This is a straightforward application of the kind of traditional logic that focuses on flaws within the argument itself.

In an article in *The Independent* newspaper published on 15 July 2004, Robin Cook, a former member of the British Cabinet who resigned over the 2003 invasion of Iraq,[1] criticized the outcome of an inquiry headed by Lord Butler into the events that led up to the war for what we might describe as a lack of structural coherence in Fisher's terms:

> Yesterday Lord Butler calmly pronounced the intelligence on which the war was launched as hopelessly overheated. His conclusions on this point are so irrefutable that even Tony Blair had to admit that Saddam did not have any WMD [weapons of mass destruction] ready for use.
> ...
> This must be the most embarrassing failure in the history of British intelligence. Yet according to Lord Butler, no one is to blame. Everyone behaved perfectly properly and nobody made a mistake. Poor things, they were let down by the system and institutional weaknesses.
>
> (Cook 2004)

What Robin Cook was pointing out here are inconsistencies within Lord Butler's own report; admitting that the intelligence on which the war was launched was highly exaggerated, the argument goes, is inconsistent with concluding that no one is to blame for this state of affairs. This critique says: we cannot subscribe to Lord Butler's narrative because its own logic is seriously flawed.

Barsky (1993: 142) argues that in the context of refugee hearings in Canada 'failed interpretation can lead to contradictions in the testimony, which in turn can be grounds for rejection of the claimant as refugee'. He cites statements by the Refugee Appeal Board that demonstrate how the issue of consistency is key in this context. Here is one example:

> The various events of the applicant's odyssey as related by him in the record, as well as during the course of the hearing, are full of inconsistencies and contradictions which lead the Board to question the credibility of the applicant.
>
> (1993: 143)

Barsky goes on to explain that there are many cases where it is obvious that 'officials clearly misunderstood the cultural context of the claim and therefore found contradictions where there were none, or uncovered so-called "lies" when a simple explanation from a learned advisor would have sufficed' (1993: 153). One example he gives is officials' failure to understand that 'brother' in Ghanian means member of the same tribe, not necessarily member of the same family. Pérez González (in press) quotes another example, this time from court interpreting in Spain, which demonstrates how an impression of structural incoherence may also be created through syntactic choices:

[Participants: (S1) lawyer; (S2) defendant; (I) interpreter; > = interrupted utterances]

75 S1 La vez anterior ya le había dicho dónde estaba la llave de la puerta del> e: : : h del garaje de Las Matas, ¿no?
[The previous time [she] had already told you where the key of the door of the garage in Las Matas was, right?]

76 I But she had already told you in your last visit where the key of the garage in Las Matas was, didn´t she?

77 S2 She had told the three of us.

78 I Nos lo había dicho a las tres.
[She had told us three.]

79 S1 **La cual seguramente sería demasiado pesada** para abrirla con una mano en caso de necesidad.
[**Which would probably be too heavy** to open with one hand if it were necessary for you to do so.]

80 I And do you think you would manage to open it with only one hand, if you had to?

81 S2 I shouldn't think so.

82 I No creo.
[I don't think so.]

83 S1 Ah> Así que ya la había abierto antes, ¿no?
[Oh> so you had opened it before, right?]

(Pérez González, in press)

In the above example, the lawyer's question is framed as a non-restrictive relative clause: 'La cual seguramente sería demasiado pesada para abrirla con una mano en caso de necesidad' (Which would probably be too heavy to open with one hand if it were necessary for you to do so). The interpreter renders this as a polar interrogative that calls for a yes/no answer: 'And do you think you would manage to open it with only one hand, if you had to?'. This choice of formulation on the interpreter's part breaks the connection between the lawyer's *which*-clause and his previous question in line 75: 'La vez anterior ya le había dicho dónde estaba la llave de la puerta del> e: : : h del garaje de Las Matas, ¿no?' (The previous time [she] had already told you where the key of the door of the garage in Las Matas was, right?). It hence invites what appears to be an incoherent or at least unexpected response from the defendant.

Over and beyond local equivalence, then, individual choices made by translators and interpreters can give an impression of inconsistency in the context of other choices they have made or go on to make in the translation or interpreting event. This impression of inconsistency inevitably has an impact on the way readers and hearers assess the structural coherence of the narrative(s) elaborated in the text or utterance.

7.2.2 Material coherence

Material coherence is a question of how a narrative relates to other narratives that have a bearing on the same issue and with which we are familiar. More specifically, what 'facts' might it downplay or ignore, what counter-arguments does it choose not to engage with, what relevant information or issues does it overlook? No story exists in a vacuum, and because all narratives are embedded in other narratives they must be assessed within this broader context. 'The meaning and merit of a story', Fisher writes, 'are always a matter of how it stands with or against other stories' (1997: 316).

A straightforward invocation of the principle of material coherence in assessing a narrative can be seen in this extract from an article published by the UK newspaper *The Independent* on 17 June 2005, entitled 'US Lied to Britain Over Use of Napalm in Iraq War':

> Yesterday's disclosure led to calls by MPs for a full statement to the Commons and opened ministers to allegations that they held back the facts until after the general election.
>
> Despite persistent rumours of injuries among Iraqis consistent with the use of incendiary weapons such as napalm, Adam Ingram, the Defence minister, assured Labour MPs in January that US forces had not used a new generation of incendiary weapons, codenamed MK77, in Iraq.
>
> But Mr Ingram admitted to the Labour MP Harry Cohen in a private letter obtained by The Independent that he had inadvertently misled Parliament because he had been misinformed by the US. 'The US confirmed to my officials that they had not used MK77s in Iraq at any time and this was the basis of my response to you,' he told Mr Cohen. 'I regret to say that I have since discovered that this is not the case and must now correct the position.'
>
> ....
>
> Mr Ingram did not explain why the US officials had misled him, but the US and British governments were accused of a cover-up. The Iraq Analysis Group, which campaigned against the war, said the US authorities only admitted the use of the weapons after the evidence from reporters had become irrefutable.
>
> (Brown 2005)

In this example, it is fairly easy to draw a line between two opposing narratives: one narrative (the official US and earlier British account) denies that napalm and similar weapons were used in Iraq. The second narrative (Iraq Analysis Group and others who believe the Parliament and country were misled) suggests that they have, and quotes as evidence of the material incoherence of the first narrative 'persistent rumours of injuries among Iraqis consistent with the use of incendiary weapons such as napalm', the contents of 'a private letter' from the British Defence Minister to a

Labour Member of Parliament, and 'evidence from reporters [that] had become irrefutable'. As long as the opposing narratives can be clearly delineated, applying the principle of material coherence – separately from the principle of structural coherence – seems intuitively satisfying and straightforward enough. But distinguishing between material and structural coherence is not always easy, as I hope the next example demonstrates.

Erik Saar, an Arabic translator who volunteered to translate for guards and interrogators at Guantanamo Bay in 2002, believed he was helping to defend his country against terrorism. He later co-authored a book with Viveca Novak in which he described the extensive abuse and sexual torture of prisoners that he witnessed at Camp Delta (Saar and Novak 2005). One of the issues he repeatedly raised in relation to the Guantanamo experience related to what we might call the material (or structural?) incoherence it highlighted in the American narrative of spreading democracy abroad:

> It's difficult to see how the United States, in good conscience, can hold other nations to standards we're not meeting ourselves. In a head-snapping move in February 2005, the State Department issued its annual human rights report, criticizing countries for a range of practices it called torture – including sleep deprivation, threatening prisoners with dogs, stripping them – methods we've used in our own detention camps. The report attacked treatment of prisoners in countries like Syria and Egypt, two of the nations which the OGA[2] has used for renditions, shipping terrorism suspects there for questioning precisely because their interrogators are known for taking the gloves off.
>
> (Saar and Novak 2005: 249–50)

> 'We are trying to promote democracy worldwide. I don't see how you can do that and run a place like Guantanamo Bay. This is now a rallying cry to the Muslim world,' he [Erik Saar] said.
>
> (Harris 2005)

> I don't know how, as [sic] country, we can say we're going to promote democracy and human dignity and justice throughout the Arab and Muslim world and at the same time defy some of those very same principles at Guantanamo Bay.
>
> (Interview with Onnesha Roychoudhuri, 24 May 2005)[3]

Saar's critique of Guantanamo casts doubt on the veracity and consistency of the American narrative of spreading democracy and human dignity abroad. It is possible to see it as an example of material (in)coherence if we assume that the American narrative of exporting democracy is separate from the narrative of Guantanamo as he elaborates it in his book, interviews and articles. But it is also possible to see this same example as one of structural rather than material incoherence: as an example of inconsistencies within the same narrative. One could argue that one difference between Robin Cook's (p. 144) and Eric Saar's critiques is that whereas Robin Cook's is based on a single report – a bounded textual entity, however long – Saar's rejection of the Guantanamo model is based on a diffuse set of statements, speeches, press releases, and other types of material that together elaborate a narrative of America spreading democracy and human dignity abroad, with the Guantanamo story conceivably being a sub-set of that same narrative; Guantanamo in this case is a necessary evil, an important element in ensuring the spread of democracy by protecting us against terrorism. Treated as a self-contained narrative, and seen from the perspective of structural coherence, the point Saar would be making in the above quotes and elsewhere is that this narrative is inconsistent within its own bounds given the Guantanamo abuses of human rights that he witnessed firsthand.

The overlap between structural and material coherence is a by-product of two assumptions that underpin narrative theory as I have tried to elaborate it in this book. First, narratives construct reality for us; they do not represent it. This means that any boundaries assumed to exist between separate narratives are constructed by us in the course of elaborating the narratives in question; they are not stable, solid boundaries that we simply have to 'discover' and can easily agree on. Second, narratives are not tied to individual, concrete texts but are usually diffuse and have to be pieced together from a variety of sources. Our assessment of the integrity of a diffuse narrative – such as 'America spreading democracy and dignity abroad' – may invoke structural or material coherence, depending on how we piece the narrative together and what we construct as lying within or outside its boundaries.

7.2.3 Characterological coherence

Characterological coherence assumes that the reliability of any narrative depends to a significant extent on the credibility of its main characters, whether narrators or actors within the narrative. A 'character' is 'an organized set of actional tendencies' (Fisher 1997: 316). If these tendencies seem to contradict each other significantly, we tend to judge the person in question as untrustworthy. Elsewhere (1987: 148), Fisher defines character as 'a generalized perception of a person's fundamental value orientation', on the basis of which one infers how the character is likely to behave and how their behaviour and action might relate to one's own values and perspective on the world. Fisher also confirms that his concept of character overlaps with the contemporary notion of source credibility and the traditional concept of ethos (1997: 316), but it differs from them in terms of emphasis on features such as expertise and intelligence. Nuances of definition aside, the ultimate question here 'is not only do we understand the story, do we like it, but do we trust the storyteller?' (Whitebrook 2001: 135). Assessing a narrative in terms of characterological coherence 'is an inquiry into motivation ... Determining a character's motives is prerequisite to trust, and trust is the foundation of belief' (Fisher 1987: 47).

We judge the trustworthiness of a character on the basis of 'interpretations of a person's decisions and actions that reflect values' (Fisher 1997: 316). If the decisions and actions associated with a character change significantly 'in strange ways' (1997: 316) or contradict each other, we inevitably question the credibility of the character and hence the narrative in question. By contrast, once we decide that a given person is trustworthy, honourable, courageous, and so on, we are prepared to 'overlook and forgive many things: factual errors if not too dramatic, lapses in reasoning, and occasional discrepancies' (1997: 316). Fisher (1987, 1997) argues that President Reagan was widely considered to be such a credible figure even though it was also widely noted that he made many factual errors, inconsistent statements, and clearly attempted to divert attention from relevant issues on many occasions (Fisher 1987: 145). By the standards of the rational-world paradigm, Reagan should unequivocally be regarded as a poor rhetor. And yet, he was extremely popular in America and thought to be a great communicator; so much so, in fact, that 'Reagan's critics, like those who would criticize any heroic figure, discover that *their* characters rather than his come under attack' (Fisher 1987: 148; emphasis in original).

Fisher attributes Reagan's success to the 'coherence and fidelity of his character' (1987: 147). But he also stresses that Reagan's story was effective because it was consistent with the story of America, that it was 'easy to identify him with mythic qualities and forces that are often referred to collectively as "the American Dream"' (1987: 148). More specifically, Fisher offers three reasons for Reagan's success:

> First, Reagan's story is grounded in American history and it is informed by central values of the American Dream. Second, his perceived character is constituted by this background and renders him virtually immune to 'rational' criticism. Third, the implied audience of heroes in his rhetoric is as efficacious as just about any that one might conceive, given our troubled times.
>
> (Fisher 1987: 146)

This means that characterological coherence, as conceived within the narrative paradigm, cannot be achieved in a vacuum; it is heavily dependent on the nature of the narratives that a character draws on to elaborate their own story, *and* on the resonance of these narratives within a specific historical and cultural context.

We repeatedly invoke characterological coherence as a principle in the course of assessing narratives in everyday life. Where it overlaps with the concept of source credibility, characterological coherence can be seen to be invoked explicitly in statements such as 'Nor do I know of a single reputable living biologist who supports straightforward vitalism' (from Ernst Mayr's *This is Biology: The Science of the Living World*, quoted in Booth 2004: 57), and is also signalled by the very practice of citation and references in academic and scientific writing. Perhaps more obviously, and much more in line with the notion of characterological cohrence as defined by Fisher, corporate business regularly relies on branding to present itself as human, benevolent and trustworthy (Bakan 2004: 26). One form that this branding takes involves associating a corporation with a specific person or a number of different people who each bestows a particular quality on the corporation. When British Telecom (BT) in Britain decided to rebrand and redefine its corporate image, it ran adverts with key public figures who are perceived to have considerable characterological coherence in Fisher's terms. In a particularly memorable set of adverts, BT attempted to rebrand its image by associating itself with Stephen Hawking, the well-known theoretical physicist and holder of the chair once held by Isaac Newton in Cambridge. Hawking suffers from a form of motor neurone disease that has left him dependent on a voice synthesizer to communicate with the outside world. Internationally acclaimed and admired for his scientific achievements and active involvement in public life despite his severe disability (in other words, for his determination and strength of character), his characterological coherence conferred considerable credibility on British Telecom as audiences across Britain repeatedly watched the adverts on their TV screen and listened to him speak through his synthesizer:

Stephen Hawking:
For millions of years mankind lived just like the animals. Then something happened which unleashed the power of our imagination.
We learned to talk, we learned to listen. Speech has allowed the communication of ideas enabling people to work together ... to build the impossible.
Mankind's greatest achievements have come about by talking ... and its greatest failures by not talking.
It doesn't have to be like this.
Our greatest hopes could become reality in the future with the technology at our disposal – the possibilities are unbounded.
All we need to do is make sure we keep talking.

Because characterological coherence has become a commodity in the modern world, another product with a price tag attached to it, individuals who allow themselves – or are perceived as allowing themselves – to be used to lend legitimacy and credibility to corporate business or dominant narratives can be severely criticized and often end up losing credibility with specific groups of audience. Thus, what is perceived as characterological coherence by one constituency may be seen as evidence of untrustworthy or incoherent 'value orientations' by another. The 2005 G8 summit was arguably a major attempt by the British Labour Party to rebrand itself as humane and caring following its controversial involvement in the Iraq War, which cost the party dearly in the 2005 general election. Blair and his Chancellor Gordon Brown seized the opportunity to adopt the slogan 'Make Poverty History' and sell the idea that corporate Britain and corporate America were responding to pressure from media stars such as Bob Geldof and Bono and committing to rescuing Africa from its misery. Writing in *The New Statesman*, John Pilger, a well-known journalist and activist, cast doubt on the characterological coherence of both politicians and media stars involved in this show:

The front page of the London Observer on 12 June announced, '55 billion Africa debt deal "a victory for millions".' The 'victory for millions' is a quotation of Bob Geldof, who said, 'Tomorrow 280 million Africans will wake up for the first time in their lives without owing you or me a penny ... '. The nonsense of this would be breathtaking if the reader's breath had not already been extracted by the unrelenting sophistry of Geldof, Bono, Blair, the Observer et al. Africa's imperial plunder and tragedy have been turned into a circus for the benefit of the so-called G8 leaders due in Scotland next month and those of us willing to be distracted by the barkers of the circus: the establishment media and its 'celebrities'. The illusion of an anti establishment crusade led by pop stars – a cultivated, controlling image of rebellion – serves to dilute a great political movement of anger.

(Pilger 2005a)

For activists sharing this narrative with John Pilger, the entire 'Make Poverty History' campaign 'is an important facade, held up by the famous and the naive and the inane' (Pilger 2005a), including celebrities such as Geldof and Bono. For them, Bob Geldof's characterological coherence is not enhanced by the fact that he described George W. Bush as 'passionate and sincere' about ending poverty (Pilger 2005a), nor by his being featured on the front page of *The Guardian* 'resting his smiling face on smiling Blair's shoulder' (Pilger 2005b). Bono's credibility is similarly tarnished by the fact that he called Blair and Brown 'the John and Paul of the global development stage' (Pilger 2005a) and 'laud[ed] "compassionate" George Bush's "war on terror" as one of his generation's greatest achievements' (Pilger 2005b). An important part of the critique of the 'Make Poverty History' narrative then says: we cannot trust Bob Geldof and Bono because their actions and values are inconsistent: on the one hand they claim commitment to a better, more equitable world, and on the other they participate in conferring legitimacy and respectability on two politicians considered by many to be among the worst offenders of human rights in the world.[4]

One interesting issue that Fisher does not discuss but that invites us to treat the notion of characterological coherence with some caution concerns what is known as the 'sleeper effect'. The 'sleeper effect' refers to the findings of research in psychology which confirm that although we may be suspicious of the motives of a communicator and initially decide not to subscribe to the narratives he or she presents to us, with time we tend to 'remember and accept *what* was communicated but not remember *who* communicated it' and are then 'more inclined to agree with the position which had been presented by the communicator' (Hovland and Weiss 1951: 636; emphasis in original). More interestingly, Hovland and Weiss's research established that with the passage of time 'there is a *decrease* in the extent of agreement with the high credibility source, but an *increase* in the case of the low credibility source' (1951: 645; emphasis in original). They conclude that 'the passage of time serves to remove recall of the source as a mediating cue that leads to rejection [of a position or opinion]' (1951: 648). In other words, the key to the phenomenon of the 'sleeper effect' is that with time the message gets separated from its source, which means that characterological coherence influences our initial reaction to a narrative but its effect *decreases* with time in the case of characters we perceive as coherent and *increases* in the case of characters we perceive as incoherent. This has at least two implications. First, the narrative is more important than its source, and hence those who wish to promote a given narrative must spend more time embellishing it and improving its appeal and less time associating it with someone who may exhibit characterological coherence for a specific audience. And second, the more critical among us ought to make a point of remembering the sources of information that come our way and continue to question narratives elaborated by individuals or groups whose motives and values we have reason to question.

To sum up this section, it is worth stressing that the coherence of a narrative ultimately lies not within the narrative itself but within the minds of those who believe in it. Moreover, a narrative can be consciously and deviously constructed and presented as coherent purely in the service of self-interest or a political or military objective. Nelson (2002: 8) reminds us that '[w]aging war to make the world more democratic in order to have less war may strike more than a few as a grand paradox. Yet, within such a looking glass, we construct our discourses on peace and war'. Indeed, for many the neo-conservative narrative of 'waging war to make the world more democratic in order to have less war' will be perceived as perfectly coherent – structurally, materially and characterologically. For others, myself included, it is as incoherent as any narrative can be.

7.3 Fidelity

The principle of coherence, as discussed above, focuses on the consistency and integrity of the narrative as a whole. Fidelity, on the other hand, is assessed by applying the logic of good reasons, which requires a narrative to be examined with reference to 'the soundness of its reasoning and the value of its values' (Fisher 1987: 88). Reasons are assessed using the logic of reasons; values are assessed with reference to the logic of good reasons.

7.3.1 Reasons (the logic of reasons)

By assessing a narrative in terms of 'the soundness of its reasoning', Fisher means examining it largely from the perspective of traditional logic: its representation of the facts, patterns of inference and implicature, the relevance of justification to the nature of the problem; in other words, the types of reason discussed in textbooks of argumentation, which teach us how to reason in public discourse.

The logic of reasons has five components (Fisher 1987: 108–9):

- First, we attempt to ascertain 'whether the statements in a message that purport to be "facts" are indeed "facts"; that is, are confirmed by consensus or reliable, competent witnesses'.[5]
- Second, we attempt to establish whether any relevant facts have been omitted, and whether those that are offered in the narrative are distorted or presented out of context.
- Third, we recognize and assess 'the various patterns of reasoning, using mainly standards from informal logic'; these relate mostly to patterns of inference and implicature.
- Fourth, we assess the arguments – rather than facts – presented, in terms of whether these arguments are sound and relevant to the decision that has to be taken and whether other arguments should be considered in this case.
- Fifth, on the basis of the above we judge whether the narrative addresses the

'real' issues – those that are relevant in a particular context and on which our decision(s) should be based.

Fisher stresses that the logic of reasons is only invoked 'when relevant' (1987: 88). He thus clearly regards it as secondary to the assessment of values, based on the logic of good reasons. It is the logic of good reasons – rather than the logic of reasons – that embodies the notion of fidelity.

7.3.2 Values (the logic of good reasons)

The notion of value ultimately concerns the real world effects of accepting a given narrative: 'a value is valuable not because it is tied to a reason or is expressed by a reasonable person per se, but because *it makes a pragmatic difference in one's life and in one's community*' (Fisher 1987: 111; emphasis in original). Fisher's incorporation of the notion of values in the principle of fidelity attempts to complement and transform the logic of reasons into the logic of good reasons – the key concept in his paradigm. Like the logic of reasons, the logic of good reasons, which relates specifically to values, has five components (Fisher 1987: 109):

- *Fact.* We begin our assessment of fidelity by asking what implicit and explicit values are embedded in a narrative. This criterion assumes that the narrative itself is a story of values, and that we can trace and identify these values in the narrative.
- *Relevance.* Like the second component of the logic of reasons, this criterion concerns the relevance of what is presented in the narrative; but the focus here is on values rather than arguments and facts: 'Are the values appropriate to the nature of the decision that the message bears upon? Included in this question must be concern for omitted, distorted, and misrepresented values'.
- *Consequence.* This criterion focuses on the real world consequences of accepting the values elaborated in the narrative. Here, we ask '[w]hat would be the effects of adhering to the values – for one's concept of oneself, for one's behavior, for one's relationships with others and society, and to the process of rhetorical transaction?'.
- *Consistency.* 'Are the values confirmed or validated in one's personal experi- ence, in the lives or statements of others whom one admires and respects, and in a conception of the best audience that one can conceive?'. This is a question of whether the values expressed in the narrative are consistent with one's own experience of the world.
- *Transcendent issue or values.* This is the most important component of the logic of good reasons and hence the most important criterion in assessing any narrative. Under this heading, Fisher invites us to ask whether 'the values the message offers … constitute the ideal basis for human conduct', irrespective of the facts and '[e]ven if a prima-facie case exists or a burden of proof has been established' in relation to a specific narrative. Fisher stresses that identifying and assessing the transcendent value in a narrative 'is clearly the paramount issue that

confronts those responsible for decisions that impinge on the nature, the quality, and the continued existence of human life, especially in such fields as biology and weapons technology and employment'. Transcendent values are the 'ultimate values' we live by and can override any other consideration in assessing a narrative.

> I am convinced that value judgments are inevitable, that they are not irrational, that consensus about them will never be fully realized, and that no analytically grounded hierarchy of values will ever claim universal adherence.
>
> (Fisher 1987: 105)

The most important element in the principle of fidelity, and indeed in the entire logic of good reasons, then, is transcendent values, which 'reveal one's most fundamental commitments' (Fisher 1987: 109). Fisher readily concedes that the critic's own assessment of a narrative, especially in relation to *consequence, consistency* and *transcendent values*, itself expresses values and is inevitably subjective. But he does not see this 'intrusion of subjectivity' as undermining the logic of good reasons. Subjectivity, he argues, is inherent in human communication. What the narrative paradigm and the logic of good reasons allow us to do is to be conscious of and examine this subjectivity:

> By making the considerations of values a systematic and self-conscious process, the logic of good reasons fills the space left open by technical logic with its primary concern with formal relationships and certitude. ... In other words, the logic of good reasons is important because it renders open and intelligible the grounds and valuing of interpreter-critics. And by doing so it acknowledges and encourages awareness of the contingent character of rhetorical communication and provides information that enhances discourse on truly fundamental matters.
>
> (Fisher 1987: 110)

Assessing a narrative according to the principle of fidelity means asking what effects adhering to it would have on the world, on our sense of self- respect, on our relationship to others, and on our ability to uphold our most fundamental commitments.

In a brief contribution to the BBC Radio Four programme *Thought for the Day*, broadcast on 16 September 2004, Dr Giles Fraser argued in favour of the Countryside and Rights of Way Act that was to come into effect a few days later. The Act gave the public the right to roam over four million hectares of uncultivated country in England and Wales, and was warmly welcomed by the Ramblers' Association in Britain. Owners of land falling within the boundaries of these four million hectares, however, did not necessarily see the Act as just since it meant that anyone could walk freely across their land at any time. The question to be debated, then, was who the land belonged to and whether the notion of property was just. Dr Fraser argued that 'the creation narratives in the book of Genesis are essentially political, proclaiming the land as "a common treasury" for all', and concluded his argument thus:

> we have to choose between two very different ideas of creation: Darwin's story tells of the survival of the fittest, the Genesis story of the earth as a common treasury for all. Darwin's story may be better science, but the Genesis story is far better politics.
>
> (Fraser 2004)

Applying the principle of fidelity, Dr Fraser's point is that irrespective of issues of 'fact', including 'scientific fact', the real world effects of adhering to the Christian narrative are far more preferable to those of adhering to Darwin's story. We have to accept that the land belongs to God and hence all people – rather than only those people who have acquired and own the land – in order to avoid disaster. How else, he asks, 'are we to tackle issues of global warming and climate change, if not by first acknowledging that we all share the same planet, and that a selfish regard for our own consumption may turn out to defeat us all?'.

7.4 Assessing narratives: applying the model

Fisher's narrative paradigm can help us assess a narrative elaborated in a single text as well as diffuse narratives that have to be pieced together from a variety of sources and media. It can also be used to assess any narrative: ontological, public or conceptual, whether elaborated by an individual or an institution. In this section, I start with a brief assessment of a narrative elaborated by one individual within a single text, mainly to demonstrate how different sets of transcendent values determine the course and outcome of our assessments (7.4.1, The MLA narrative, below). I then offer a revised and extended assessment of the narrative of a group of volunteer translators, first presented in Baker (in press, a). This is a diffuse *and* institutional narrative: it is elaborated by an organization, rather than an individual,[6] across different texts and media (7.4.2, the Translators Without Borders narrative, on p. 157). It goes without saying that the assessment in both cases is not – and cannot be – 'objective'. It is inevitably shaped by the transcendent values and narrative location of the assessor.

7.4.1 The MLA narrative

Fisher (1987: 111–13) demonstrates how the principle of fidelity works and where values enter an argument, and determine its outcome, with reference to two opposing narratives of serving in the Vietnam War: one based on the duty-to-country value and one on the moral-conscience value. He stresses that these values are context-specific, and that

> [i]t is not unreasonable that a person – not necessarily a militarist – who was convinced by national-administration arguments that national pride was at

stake in Vietnam should take a position ultimately based on the duty to country value. Nor would it be unreasonable for a person – not necessarily a pacifist – who was persuaded by the war's opponents that America's professed reverence for life was at stake should take a position grounded on the moral-conscience value.

(Fisher 1987: 111, 113)

Using a narrative that is directly relevant to us as translators and interpreters, I now want to adapt a visual representation of the two opposing arguments of serving in the Vietnam War presented in Fisher (1987: 112) to the specific arguments embedded in this new narrative. But first we need to look at the text that elaborates one of the opposing narratives.

Andrew Rubin is a Professor of English at Georgetown University. His open letter to the Executive Council of the Modern Languages Association is reproduced in full below, with his kind permission.

February 8, 2005
An Open letter to the Executive Council of the MLA,

From 1996 to 2002, I was a doctoral student in the Department of English and Comparative Literature at Columbia University where I completed my dissertation under the supervision of the late Professor Edward W. Said, who, as you know, was the president of the MLA in 1999. As a close friend and colleague of Edward's, I am sure that he would share the surprise that I encountered when I learned recently that the Modern Language Association allowed the Central Intelligence Agency to advertise for and recruit prospective language instructors at the MLA's last annual convention in Philadelphia. The CIA was seeking qualified individuals to teach languages such as Arabic, Chinese, Dari/Pashtu, French, Greek, Indonesian, Japanese, Korean, Persian (Farsi), Russian, Serbo-Croatian, Spanish, Thai and Turkish.

The CIA, as you well know, has a long and well-documented history – over 50 years in the making – of contravening countless international laws including numerous articles of the Geneva Convention as well as the Charter of the United Nations. It has committed crimes of war and crimes against humanity. It has tortured and taught the instruction of torture in both Asia, the Americas, and Africa. It has assassinated many human beings, overthrown democratically elected governments, sown discontent throughout the world by arming mercenaries and turning human beings into outright murderers and professional butchers.

That the Modern Languages Association would allow an organization – whose annual budget remains classified and whose activities remain concealed from the world – to exploit its membership is both shameful and unconscionable. That an organization whose activities are classified as a state secret is afforded the privilege to exploit the MLA's 30,000 members in over 100 countries goes against the very charter and mission of the MLA: to establish the conditions whereby scholars of languages and literatures may freely and openly share their findings with one another in a situation that flourishes not under the duress of coercion, repression, and unfreedom. I hope it need not be said that the CIA undermines the open and free dissemination of knowledge (see for example Judge Denise Cotes' opinion in Rubin v. CIA, Federal District Court, New York, 2001).

Language instruction is indispensable to understanding the relationship between cultures. The more languages we as scholars and students as human beings openly (and not covertly) study and know, the better the peoples of this world are able to communicate with one another; the better the world is able to turn conflict into reconciliation, hatred into understanding.

In the future, I hope the Executive Council of the MLA would be more circumspect for the sake of the principles of the open dissemination of knowledge for which the MLA has putatively stood for the past 122 years.

Professor Rubin's letter argues for a position of non-cooperation with organizations such as the CIA on the basis of a transcendent value that we might informally label 'duty to humanity'. One can easily imagine the MLA Executive and many MLA members defending MLA cooperation with the CIA by invoking a transcendent value of 'duty-to-profession'. After all, the MLA Constitution clearly states that '[t]he object of the association shall be to promote study, criticism, and research in the more and less commonly taught modern languages and their literatures and *to further the common interests of teachers of these subjects*'[7] (emphasis added). The two values are not mutually exclusive, but they can come into conflict in some contexts. Following Fisher (1987: 112), we might present the opposing set of values as shown in Figure 16.

Rubin's narrative may seem idealistic to those whose fundamental commitment is to values such as professionalism, success and political acumen. But Fisher (1987: 188) argues that there is – and probably always will be – a universal community that believes in higher ideals of truth and justice. Idealistic narratives tend to generate adherence 'because they are coherent and "ring true" to life *as we would like to live it*'; their appeal lies in 'evoking the best in people and activating it' (1987: 187). If Fisher is right about the existence of stable communities stimulated by higher ideals of justice and truth rather than success and professionalism, the narrative elaborated in Rubin's letter to the MLA will be readily accepted by many readers. For them, the narrative will be coherent in terms of the logic of good reasons: '*relevant* to the good life; *consequential* in advancing moral obligation and civilized relations; *consistent* with their highest experiences … ; and satisfying in regard to the *transcendental issue*; the ideal basis for human conduct' (Fisher 1987: 188; emphasis in original).

7.4.2 Translators Without Borders

In Baker (in press, a), I demonstrated how Fisher's narrative paradigm may be used to assess the narrative of a group of volunteer translators who operate under the title Translators Without Borders/Traducteurs sans Frontières[8] and provide free translations to many well-known organizations such as Doctors Without Borders, Amnesty

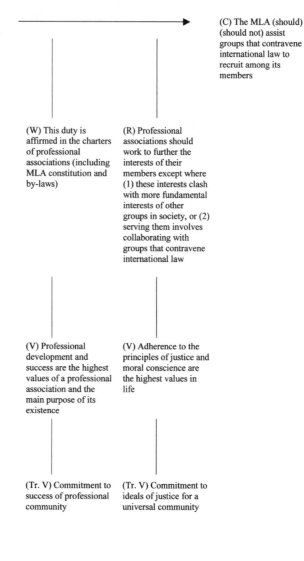

(D) Professional associations have a duty to further the interests of their members

(C) The MLA (should) (should not) assist groups that contravene international law to recruit among its members

(W) This duty is affirmed in the charters of professional associations (including MLA constitution and by-laws)

(R) Professional associations should work to further the interests of their members except where (1) these interests clash with more fundamental interests of other groups in society, or (2) serving them involves collaborating with groups that contravene international law

(V) Professional development and success are the highest values of a professional association and the main purpose of its existence

(V) Adherence to the principles of justice and moral conscience are the highest values in life

(Tr. V) Commitment to success of professional community

(Tr. V) Commitment to ideals of justice for a universal community

B = Backing
C = Claim
D = Data
R = Reservations
Tr. V = Transcendent value
W = Warrant

Figure 16 Where values enter an argument (based on Fisher 1987: 112)

International, and Reporters Without Borders. As the name suggests, Translators Without Borders (TWB) aligns itself with what has come to be known as the 'sans frontièrisme' or 'without borderism' movement (Fox 1995: 1607; DeChaine 2002: 355) and espouses similar ideals to those championed by Médecins sans Frontières (MSF), winners of the 1999 Nobel Peace Prize.[9]

Translators Without Borders is very different from other politically and socially engaged groups in the professional world of translation and interpreting, most notably Babels,[10] Translators for Peace,[11] Translators and Interpreters Peace Network,[12] and ECOS (Traductores e Intérpretes por la Solidaridad).[13] Unlike any of these groups, TWB is an offshoot of a commercial translation agency (the Paris-based Eurotexte) and, as we will see shortly, it features prominently as a selling point in the portfolio of that company. This is a very different set-up from Babels, for example, which is not linked to any commercial enterprise. Babels does invest in promoting its image, as do other politically engaged groups; for instance all Babels volunteers and interpreters wear distinctive Babels T-shirts at the World Social Forum and related events that they service, and Babels also maintains a website that promotes its various activities. But none of this is done in the interest of commercial gain, nor to further the prestige of one or more individuals. Indeed, there is nothing on the Babels site to indicate who set it up, and nothing to appeal to potential supporters to buy or donate anything, other than their time if they happen to have the requisite translation and interpreting skills. No single individual or organization, it seems, benefits commercially or in prestige terms from the existence of Babels.[14] The same seems to apply to the other groups listed above, with the exception of TWB.

Applying the rule of coherence to the narrative elaborated by TWB and its parent company Eurotexte, I argued (Baker, in press, a) that there is a lack of internal consistency within the TWB narrative, largely as a result of a confusion of humanitarian and commercial agendas. For instance, TWB is listed as a 'partner' on the Eurotexte site and explicitly used as a selling point by the Eurotexte Managing Director, who stresses in an undated speech to the Italian Federation of Translation Companies that 'good works not only help the world: they can also be good for business'.[15] A T-shirt available on the Eurotexte/TWB site for 21 Euros is sold in support of Médecins sans Frontières; all proceeds, we are told, go to MSF. The T-shirt itself, however, features not MSF but Translators without Borders, hence indirectly providing free advertising space for Eurotexte.

> A man in Chechnya says, 'A ground-to-ground missile killed my two sons in the market in Grozny. They weren't fighters – they were just there to buy some jeans'. The Palestinian girl who at first is too afraid to talk to the visitors, whispers, 'I don't think we're going to come out of this alive.' On a forced march to the border a mother in Kosovo cries as the soldier takes aim, 'Not him, he's not even 15!'
> Lori Thicke, Speech to the Italian Federation of Translation Companies

There is further evidence of structural and material incoherence in the Translators Without Borders narrative. In the same speech to the Italian Federation of Translation Companies, Eurotexte Managing Director Lori Thicke reminds us that the atrocities committed in Chechnya, Palestine and Kosovo make it imperative for volunteer translators to help the victims in these regions tell their stories. At the same time, however, Eurotexte proudly lists among its top clients several companies that are widely thought to be implicated in the very atrocities that TWB presumes to bring to our attention, including General Electric[16] and L'Oréal[17] (Baker, in press, a). We might compare this with the decision by Médecins sans Frontières, reported in Bakan, to refuse collaboration with Pfizer:

> when Doctors without Borders set up its trachoma treatment program in the African country of Mali, it said 'No, thank you' to Pfizer's offer of free Zithromax. Instead it imported, and paid for, a generic version of the drug.
>
> (2004: 48)

Arguably, then, the attitude and practices of TWB, especially in terms of collaboration with organizations that are implicated in the atrocities TWB and Eurotexte publicly denounce, make the narrative somewhat incoherent within its own bounds as well as in relation to other narratives that touch on similar issues.

And yet, one can see that there is an internal logic to the kind of pragmatism that justifies some level of structural and even material incoherence in order to effect changes in the world. We can easily sympathize with Lori Thicke's assertion, in the same speech to the Italian Federation of Translation Companies, that 'we're in business. We all need to make money'. Excessive idealism does not help a humanitarian organization to function effectively. DeChaine (2002: 360ff.) points to a similar issue in the case of MSF and seems to accept a pragmatic threshold of incoherence which we might also contemplate in the case of TWB. He questions MSF's 'advocacy of mass media exploitation in the name of humanitarian action' and argues that its courting of the media undermines its declared principle of neutrality and demonstrates the politicized nature of the enterprise. At the same time, he reminds us that 'MSF's credibility as a humanitarian agency turns in part on its ability to establish a perception of its volunteers as courageous, ideologically pure, morally committed agents of change' (2002: 360); MSF also needs visibility in order to attract donations and continue doing what it does. In other words, DeChaine offers 'good' reasons (in the narrative paradigm sense) for the apparent structural incoherence of the MSF narrative. The question is whether 'good reasons' can also be found in the case of TWB. If they can, according to my understanding of Fisher's paradigm, they would certainly override issues of both structural and material coherence.

Closer analysis of the TWB/Eurotexte narrative in relation to the principle of fidelity points to a number of factors that are at odds with a set of transcendent values shared by many activists. First, Eurotexte arguably sustains and justifies an ethics of consumerism through the commodification of human grief. It does so by using a humanitarian enterprise as a selling point for its commercial arm and publicly exploiting genuine examples of suffering to enhance its standing and appeal.

Second, Eurotexte practices and pronouncements give credence to the typically 'cosmetic' use of good causes by big business to improve its image and deflect attention from its less savoury practices. Clearly, Eurotexte itself is not 'big business', nor is it likely to be involved in any unsavoury practices. But Eurotexte actively promotes the idea of commercial organizations advertising their involvement in 'good causes' to enhance their image, as can be seen in the following extract from an article by Lori Thicke in *Multilingual Computing & Technology*:

> Early this year, Prem Dan, a Madrid-based translation agency, contacted Eurotexte about starting up Traductores sin fronteras in Spain. As managing director Jorge Cabezas Lopez explains, 'We feel that it's going to add extra value to Prem Dan.' About 500 translators have already offered to collaborate with the Spanish organization. Next on the program is letting clients know about the new foundation with the launch of a hot-air balloon featuring the logo created by Eurotexte for Translators Without Borders, adapted for the new Spanish organization.
>
> Another company that intends to set up a branch of Translators Without Borders is Ireland's leading independent localization company, Eurotext Translations (no connection with Eurotexte in Paris).
>
> 'Every business and its staff and associates are open to helping those in need in society by sharing a little of their skills and expertise. For a translation company, Translators Without Borders is a brilliant idea, and my colleagues here in Eurotext Translations are very enthusiastic about it,' says managing director John Shine.
>
> Good works, as it turns out, is good business. Says Lopez, 'We believe we will get an advantage from informing our clients that we are supporting Traductores sin fronteras.'
>
> That's the sort of win-win situation all translation companies should be thinking about.
>
> (Thicke 2003)

It seems clear from the above extract that translation companies are being encouraged to provide some free translations to worthy organizations because this will enhance their public image and help them attract more clients. It is also obvious that this is the main motivation for the companies that decided to follow the example of Eurotexte. However well-intentioned, the model being promoted in the professional world of translation by companies such as Eurotexte encourages uncritical acceptance of the cosmetic use of humanitarian themes by corporate business.[18] It further turns potentially revolutionary networks of committed translators and interpreters into 'centres of civic virtue that forestall deeper kinds of change or critiques of longstanding assumptions' (Said 2005: 18).

Finally, the TWB/Eurotexte narrative arguably sustains and exploits cultural narratives of social responsibility that focus more on making the donors feel good about themselves than on addressing the real needs of the recipients. The very language used by the Managing Director of Eurotexte clearly points to underlying motives and a world view that are incompatible with a set of transcendent values shared by at least some committed translators and interpreters:

> Giving away translations for a worthy cause is a win-win scenario. Eurotexte feels good about it. The translators feel good about it, and they see Eurotexte as

an agency that really cares – which we do. And last but not least, our customers consider this to be a point of distinction.

(Thicke 2003)

The choice of phrases such as 'giving away translations' to describe what TWB is engaged in doing betrays a casual and charity-based attitude to 'doing good' that is arguably self-serving and exploitative.

Many readers will no doubt disagree with the above assessment of the Translators Without Borders narrative, and may well find it uncharitable. This does not, however, invalidate the analysis. It merely points to our divergent sets of transcendent values, an issue fully anticipated in Fisher's paradigm.

7.5 Concluding remarks

Fisher's narrative paradigm is not without its weaknesses, nor its critics. For one thing, it fails to explain the power and attraction of evil stories – why we are drawn to narratives such as *The Silence of the Lambs*, for instance. Fisher himself also acknowledges that although the narrative paradigm allows us to assess all genres of discourse, the criteria for assessing a scientific text will necessarily differ from those required for assessing a popular film (1987: 143). To date, however, he has not offered an elaboration of these different criteria.

More seriously, perhaps, McGee and Nelson (1985: 145–6) take Fisher to task for pitting the paradigm of narrativity against that of rationality and hence perpetuating rather than dispelling an unnecessary dichotomy.[19] Fisher, they argue, 'merely privileges public narrativity at the expense of expert rationality', when he should instead be deconstructing this 'perverse opposition' (1985: 146). Interestingly, McGee and Nelson (1985: 146ff) argue that the false dichotomy between narrativity and rationality was created by a mistranslation of *narratio* to fit with our current ideas of truth and the tenets of modern science. Restoring *narratio* to its original meaning, they suggest, would allow us to project a narrative reason in public argument and hence undercut Fisher's contrast of the two paradigms (1985: 151).

To my mind, the most serious critique of Fisher's paradigm comes from Kirkwood (1992), who convincingly argues that the narrative paradigm implies that narratives necessarily reinforce – rather than challenge – the values of the audience. This would suggest that the most appealing narratives are those that sustain and promote the status quo, that effective stories 'cannot and perhaps should not exceed people's values and beliefs, whether or not these are admirable or accurate' (1992: 30). If Fisher is right, Kirkwood argues, 'it would seem that those who "simply cannot imagine" the possibility of unselfish love cannot "hear" a story about it' (1992: 34). To address this weakness in Fisher's model, Kirkwood advocates what he calls a 'rhetoric of possibility', a model of storytelling that involves 'direct[ing] attention to specific possibilities previously unsuspected by audiences' (1992: 33). One way in which a rhetoric of possibility may be put into effect involves calling our interlocutors' attention to their own behaviour, or explicitly drawing their attention to aspects of a narrative that might have otherwise escaped them. Because

Kirkwood disagrees with Fisher's assertion that 'the people' are always able to judge the soundness of narratives for themselves and contends instead that 'sometimes the immanent facts and internal consistency of a story do not allow people to determine *which* possibilities of thought or action it expresses' (1992: 41; emphasis in original), he suggests that commentary can sometimes be added to reveal possibilities that cannot be derived from the simple facts of an account.

Like Kirkwood, Bennett and Edelman (1985: 162) recognize the importance of opening people's minds to 'creative possibilities' by constructing narratives that 'provoke intellectual struggle ... and the creation of a more workable human order'. But they focus on challenging the self-perpetuating, conservative aspect of narrativity by developing a more critical stance towards all narratives, particularly political ones. We need to understand how narratives work, how they socialize us into dominant conceptions of the world by simplifying contested issues and casting them in 'mutually exclusive ideological terms' (Bennett and Edelman 1985: 158). And we must become alert to 'pregnant references' in typically implicit political narratives in order to resist their hold on our minds. 'Evocative references that permeate political and statutory language', they argue, 'serve as Pavlovian cues for people who have been conditioned to use language to reinforce their ideologies rather than to challenge them' (1985: 165–6).

Whatever the limitations of the narrative paradigm, its attraction and strength lie in the fact that it privileges values where other models tend to privilege expertise, intelligence and tradional logic. It is radically democratic where the traditional rational paradigm is arguably elitist. It is also compatible with the overall approach to narrativity adopted in this book. Complementing the narrative paradigm with a critical understanding of how narratives function and how they allow us to contest social reality in spite of their normalizing effect can take us a long way towards a new and hopefully productive way of investigating acts of translation and intepreting in situations of conflict.

Core references

Fisher, Walter R. (1987) *Human Communication as Narration: Toward a Philosophy of Reason, Value, and Action*, Columbia: University of South Carolina Press.

Fisher, Walter R. (1997) 'Narration, Reason, and Community', in Lewis P. Hinchman and Sandra K. Hinchman (eds) *Memory, Identity, Community: The Idea of Narrative in the Human Sciences*, Albany: State University of New York Press, 307–27.

Kirkwood, William G. (1992) 'Narrative and the Rhetoric of Possibility', *Communication Monographs* 59: 30–47.

McGee, Michael Calvin and John S. Nelson (1985) 'Narrative Reason in Public Argument', *Journal of Communication* 35(4): 139–55.

Warnick, Barbara (1987) 'The Narrative Paradigm: Another Story', *The Quarterly Journal of Speech* 73: 172–82.

Further reading

Bakan, Joel (2004) *The Corporation: The Pathological Pursuit of Profit and Power*, London: Constable & Robinson Ltd.

Baker, Mona (in press, a) 'Translation and Activism: Emerging Patterns of Narrative Community', *The Massachusetts Review*.

Bennett, W. Lance and Murray Edelman (1985) 'Toward a New Political Narrative', *Journal of Communication* 35(4): 156–71.

DeChaine, D. Robert (2002) 'Humanitarian Space and the Social Imaginary: Médecins Sans Frontières/Doctors Without Borders and the Rhetoric of Global Community', *Journal of Communication Inquiry* 26(4): 354–69.

Fisher, Walter R. (1984) 'Narration as a Human Communication Paradigm: The Case of Public Moral Agreement', *Communication Monographs* 51: 1–22.

Fisher, Walter R. (1985) 'The Narrative Paradigm: In the Beginning', *Journal of Communication* 35(4): 74–89.

Fox, Renée, C. (1995) 'Medical Humanitarianism and Human Rights: Reflections on Doctors Without Borders and Doctors of the World', *Social Science and Medicine* 41(12): 1607–16.

Greer, J. and K. Bruno (1996) *Greenwash: The Reality behind Corporate Environmentalism*, Penang and New York: Third World Network and The Apex Press.

Klein, Naomi (2000) *No Logo*, London: Flamingo.

Manuel Jerez, Jesús de, Juan López Cortés and María Brander de la Iglesia (2004) 'Traducción e interpretación: Voluntariado y compromiso social' [Translation and Interpreting: Volunteer Work and Social Commitment], *Puentes* 4: 65–72.

Glossary

This glossary does not attempt to offer comprehensive definitions of every term listed. Unless otherwise indicated, the explanations given are restricted to the way each term is used within the framework elaborated in this book. Many of the terms listed have alternative definitions in other theoretical frameworks, and some of these may be considerably different from the ones offered here.

Argumentative coherence (see *structural coherence*)

Biographical narratives According to Pratt (2003), biographical narratives stress continuity by explaining what a collectivity is in terms of its evolution over time; for example, who the Kurds are as a function of what is narrated as their past, present and future. See also *vertical narratives*.

Canonicity and breach One of the features of narrativity in Bruner's model (1991). Bruner argues that for a story to be worth telling, it 'must be about how an implicit canonical script has been breached, violated, or deviated from in a manner to do violence to … the "legitimacy" of the canonical script' (1991: 11). But he acknowledges that both canonical script and breach provide opportunities for innovation. See also *normativeness*.

Causal emplotment One of the core features of narrativity in the model elaborated by Somers (1992, 1997) and Somers and Gibson (1994). Causal emplotment 'gives significance to independent instances, and overrides their chronological or categorical order' (Somers 1997: 82). Emplotment allows us to turn a set of propositions into an intelligible sequence about which we can form an opinion and thus charges the events depicted with moral and ethical significance. See also *temporality*; *relationality*; *selective appropriation*.

Characterological coherence In Fisher's narrative paradigm, one of three types of *coherence* that influence our assessment of a narrative. Characterological coherence assumes that the reliability of any narrative depends to a significant extent on the credibility of its main characters, whether narrators or actors within the narrative. Character is 'a generalized perception of a person's fundamental value orientation' (Fisher 1987: 148), on the basis of which one infers how the character is likely to behave and how their behaviour and action might relate to one's own values and perspective on the world. This concept of character overlaps with the contemporary notion of source credibility and the traditional concept of ethos (Fisher 1987: 148), but it differs from them in that it places more emphasis on values and less on features such as expertise and intelligence. Characterological coherence, as conceived within the narrative paradigm, is heavily dependent on the nature of the narratives that a character draws on to elaborate their own story and on the resonance of these narratives within a specific historical and cultural context. See also *structural coherence*; *material coherence*.

Coherence   In Fisher's (1987) narrative paradigm, coherence (or probability) is one of the two principles by which narratives are assessed, the other being *fidelity*. Coherence concerns the internal consistency and integrity of a narrative – how well it hangs together as a story. This involves assessing a narrative with reference to its *structural coherence, material coherence* and *characterological coherence*.

Conceptual narratives   As social theorists, Somers and Gibson (1994: 62) define conceptual narratives as 'concepts and explanations that we construct as social researchers'. The definition adopted in this book is broader. Conceptual narratives may be understood more generally as disciplinary narratives which consist of the stories and explanations that scholars in any field elaborate for themselves and others about their object of inquiry. See also *ontological narratives*; *public narratives*; *meta-narratives*.

Conflict   A situation in which two or more parties seek to undermine each other because they have incompatible goals, competing interests, or fundamentally different values.

Counter-domestication   A term used by Liu (1999) to refer to attempts by a party to justify its position by adopting its rival's terms of debate. Liu suggests that in this 'peculiar mode of cross-cultural argumentation', 'the two opposing parties ... venture into the other's "territory" and seek to win the "battle" by provoking a "civil war" behind the opponent's line' (1999: 309). This strategy makes it more difficult for an opponent to 'maintain their focus on the target of their criticism or to sustain their argumentative offensive' (1999: 305).

Culture jamming   A radical form of genre-based subversion of dominant narratives. Culture jamming is 'the practice of parodying advertisements and hijacking billboards in order to drastically alter their images' (Klein 2000: 280). Adbusters, those who engage in culture jamming, argue that since most of us are not in a position to buy back these spaces and display our own messages, we are entitled to talk back to the images of corporate culture. They elaborate 'counter-narratives that hack into a corporation's own method of communication to send a message starkly at odds with the one that was intended' (Klein 2000: 281).

Disciplinary narratives   (see *conceptual narratives*)

Emplotment   (see *causal emplotment*)

Fidelity   In Fisher's narrative paradigm, fidelity is one of the two principles by which narratives are assessed, the other being *coherence*. Fidelity is assessed by examining a narrative with reference to 'the soundness of its reasoning and the value of its values' (Fisher 1987: 88). See also *logic of reasons*; *logic of good reasons*.

First-order narratives   First-order narratives (Hinchman and Hinchman 1997a:

xvii) consist of the personal stories we tell ourselves and broadly correspond to *ontological narratives* as defined in this book. See also *second-order narratives*.

Frame, framing In this book, frames are structures of anticipation, strategic moves that are consciously initiated in order to present a narrative in a certain light. Framing is an active process of signification by means of which we consciously participate in the construction of reality.

Frame ambiguity According to Goffman, 'the special doubt that arises over the definition of the situation' (1974: 302). Frame ambiguity is a feature of everyday life and is often experienced by different parties to a conflict as a by-product of competing attempts to legitimize different versions of a given narrative.

Frame space Participants in any interaction play different roles (announcer, author, translator, prosecutor), engage in the interaction in different capacities (speaker, reader, primary addressee, overhearer, eavesdropper), and take different positions in relation to the event and other participants (supportive, critical, disinterested, indifferent, uninformed outsider, committed). The sum total of all these possibilities constitute what Goffman (1981) calls the frame space of a participant. This frame space is 'normatively allocated' (1981: 230) – a contribution is deemed acceptable when it stays within the frame space allocated to the speaker or writer and unacceptable when it falls outside that space.

Genericness A feature of narrativity discussed in Bruner (1991). Individual narratives have to be elaborated within established frameworks of narration in order to be intelligible and effective. These frameworks 'provide both writer and reader with commodious and conventional "models" for limiting the hermeneutic task of making sense of human happenings' (1991: 14). The frameworks in question are *genres*, in the sense of 'recognizable "kinds" of narrative: farce, black comedy, tragedy, the *Bildungsroman*, romance, satire, travel saga, and so on' (*ibid.*).

Genres Conventionalized kinds of narrative that provide established frameworks for narration. Generic identification endows a narrative experience with coherence, cohesiveness, and a sense of boundedness. It allows us to recognize it as an instantiation of a recognizable communicative practice which is meaningful and discrete. It also encourages us to project certain qualities onto the narrative experience. See also *genericness*.

Good reasons The notion that lies at the heart of Walter Fisher's narrative paradigm. Good reasons are 'elements that provide warrants for accepting or adhering to the advice fostered by any form of communication that can be considered rhetorical' (Fisher 1987: 48). Warrant is 'that which authorizes, sanctions, or justifies belief, attitude, or action – these being the usual forms of rhetorical advice' (1987: 107). The concept of good reasons is based on the assumption that 'human beings are as much valuing as they are reasoning beings' (1997: 314). See also *logic of good reasons*.

Hermeneutic composability (see *relationality*)

Labelling One of the strategies discussed under 'Framing narratives in translation' (Chapter 6). Labelling refers to any discursive process that involves using a lexical item, term or phrase to identify a person, place, group, event or any other key element in a narrative. See also *temporal and spatial framing*; *selective appropriation of textual material*; *repositioning*.

Logic of good reasons   In Fisher's narrative paradigm, the more important of two types of logic used in applying the principle of *fidelity*, the other being the *logic of reasons*. The logic of good reasons relates specifically to values – rather than facts or arguments – and requires examining a narrative by establishing what values are embedded in it; assessing the appropriateness and integrity of these values; considering the real world consequences of accepting the values elaborated in the narrative; deciding whether the values expressed in the narrative are consistent with one's own experience of the world; and above all, deciding whether 'the values the message offers … constitute the ideal basis for human conduct' (Fisher 1987: 109).

Logic of reasons   In Fisher's narrative paradigm, one of two types of logic used in applying the principle of *fidelity*, the other being the *logic of good reasons*. The logic of reasons requires examining a narrative largely from the perspective of traditional logic: its representation of the facts, patterns of inference and implicature, and the relevance of justification to the nature of the problem. The logic of reasons has five components (Fisher 1987: 108–9): ascertaining that the statements in a message that purport to be facts are indeed facts; establishing whether any relevant facts have been omitted, distorted or presented out of context; assessing various patterns of reasoning, using standards from informal logic; assessing the soundness and relevance of the arguments presented; and deciding whether the narrative addresses the 'real' issues, those that are relevant in the specific context.

Master narratives   (see *meta-narratives*)

Master plots   As used in this book, master plots are skeletal stories that combine a range of raw elements in different ways. See *particularity*.

Material coherence   In Fisher's narrative paradigm, one of three types of *coherence* that influence our assessment of a narrative. Material coherence concerns the way a narrative relates to other narratives that have a bearing on the same issue and with which we are familiar. More specifically, what 'facts' might it downplay or ignore, what counter-arguments does it choose not to engage with, what relevant information or issues does it overlook? No story exists in a vacuum, and because all narratives are embedded in other narratives they must be assessed within this broader context. See also *structural coherence*; *characterological coherence*.

Meta-narratives   Narratives 'in which we are embedded as contemporary actors in history … Progress, Decadence, Industrialization, Enlightenment, etc.' (Somers and Gibson 1994: 61). For Somers (1992: 605), meta-narratives can also be 'the epic dramas of our time: Capitalism vs. Communism, the Individual vs. Society, Barbarism/Nature vs. Civility'. Although the borderline between public and meta-narratives is fluid, generally speaking a narrative is required to have considerable temporal and geographical spread, as well as a sense of inevitability or inescapability, to qualify as a meta-narrative. *Meta-* and *master narratives* are often used to mean the same thing. See also *ontological narratives*; *public narratives*; *conceptual narratives*.

Motif   Herman *et al.* (2005: 322) define motif as 'a "moveable stock device" that appears in many periods and genres' and explain that its 'content dimension' comprises character, action, objects, temporal phases and dispositions. In folklore studies, motifs are painstakingly indexed to trace their development and different realizations across cultures and languages. A coding 'B', for instance, would indicate the presence of the motif 'animals' in the plot, 'Q' would indicate 'rewards and punishments', and 'X' would indicate 'humour'. Other combinations can then be derived from these headings; for instance 'L' indicates the plot motif of 'reversal', and 'L162' is the motif number for the plot element 'lowly heroine marries prince'. In another indexing system for whole tales known as the Aarne-Thompson Typology, a complete tale is referred to as a 'type' while the term *motif* refers to a single action or narrative procedure. Drawing on one or both systems, folklore scholars are thus able to make an explicit link between a local version of a given story and the 'canon' to which it belongs.

Narrative(s)   Narrative is the principal and inescapable mode by which we experience the world. Narratives are the stories we tell ourselves and other people about the world(s) in which we live. These stories are constructed – not discovered – by us in the course of making sense of reality, and they guide our behaviour and our interaction with others. In this sense, the terms 'narrative' and 'story' can be used interchangeably.

Narrative accrual   One of the features discussed briefly in Bruner (1991). In this book, narrative accrual is understood as the outcome of repeated exposure to a set of related narratives, ultimately leading to the shaping of a culture, tradition, or history. This history may be personal, as in the case of *ontological narratives*. It may also be public, including institutional and corporate narratives, thus ultimately leading to the elaboration of *meta-narratives*. And it may be conceptual, where we might speak of narrative accrual shaping the history of a discipline or of a particular concept that cuts across disciplines.

Narrative diachronicity   (see *temporality*)

Normativeness   One of the features of narrativity discussed in Bruner (1991). Bruner argues that '[b]ecause its "tellability" as a form of discourse rests on a breach of conventional expectation, narrative is necessarily normative. A breach presupposes a norm. This founding condition of narrative has led students of the subject ... to propose that narrative is centrally concerned with cultural legitimacy' (1991: 15). Normativeness is a feature of all narratives, whether dominant or marginalized. Socialization into any narrative order therefore has its repressive side. See also *canonicity and breach*.

Ontological narratives   Personal stories that we tell ourselves about our place in the world and our own personal history. They are interpersonal and social in nature but they remain focused on the self and its immediate world. These narratives of the self are dependent on and in turn feed into the wider narratives in which they are embedded. See also *public narratives*; *conceptual narratives*; *meta-narratives*.

Particularity   In Bruner's model (1991), particularity means that narratives refer to specific events and people but nevertheless do so within a more general framework of 'story types' which give the specific happenings their meaning and import. All our narratives ultimately derive from sets of skeletal storylines with recurrent *motifs*, and these sets may differ in their entirety or in specific details across cultures.

Probability   (see *coherence*)

Progressive narrative   According to Gergen and Gergen (1997), a type of *ontological narrative* that depicts a pattern of change for the better over time. Progressive narratives allow people to see themselves and their surroundings as capable of improvement. See also *regressive narratives*; *stability narratives*.

Public narratives   Stories elaborated by and circulating among social and institutional formations larger than the individual, such as the family, religious or educational institution, the media, and the nation. Somers (1992: 604) gives as examples of public narratives stories about 'American social mobility', the 'free-born Englishman', and 'the emancipatory story of socialism'. See also *ontological narratives*; *conceptual narratives*; *meta-narratives*.

Regressive narrative   A type of *ontological narrative* that stresses a pattern of decline or change for the worse. Gergen and Gergen (1997) attribute an important motivational function to regressive narratives. See also *stability narrative*; *progressive narrative*.

Relationality   A core feature of narrativity in the model elaborated by Somers (1992, 1997) and Somers and Gibson (1994). Relationality ('hermeneutic composability' in Bruner 1991) means that it is impossible for the human mind to make sense of isolated events or of a patchwork of events that are not constituted as a narrative. See also *temporality*; *causal emplotment*; *selective appropriation*.

Repositioning   One of the strategies discussed under 'Framing narratives in translation' (Chapter 6). Translators and intepreters can actively reframe the immediate narrative as well as the larger narratives in which it is embedded by careful realignment of participants in time and social/political space. Participants can be repositioned in relation to each other and to the reader or hearer through the linguistic management of time, space, deixis, dialect, register, use of epithets, and various means of self- and other identification. See also *temporal and spatial framing*; *selective appropriation of textual material*; *labelling*.

Second-order narratives   According to Hinchman and Hinchman (1997a: xvii), second-order narratives are the stories elaborated by historians to reconstruct the past. They 'involve reflections by a (usually) uninvolved spectator upon the doings and stories of participants in the events themselves'. This category does not correspond directly to any of Somers and Gibson's, but it overlaps to some extent with *conceptual narratives*. See also *first-order narratives*.

Selective appropriation   One of the core features of narrativity in Somers (1992, 1997) and Somers and Gibson (1994). To elaborate a coherent narrative, it is inevitable that some elements of experience are excluded and others privileged. Narratives are constructed according to evaluative criteria which enable and guide selective appropriation of a set of events or elements from the vast array of open-ended and overlapping events that constitute experience. See also *temporality*; *relationality*; *causal emplotment*.

Selective appropriation of textual material   One of the strategies discussed under 'Framing narratives in translation' (Chapter 6). Selective appropriation is realized in patterns of omission and addition designed to suppress, accentuate or elaborate particular aspects of a narrative encoded in the source text or utterance, or aspects of the larger narrative(s) in which it is embedded. See also *temporal and spatial framing*; *labelling*; *repositioning*.

Sleeper effect   Based on the findings of research in psychology, the sleeper effect predicts that with time the message gets separated from its source. More specifically, Hovland and Weiss (1951) established that with the passage of time 'there is a *decrease* in the extent of agreement with the high credibility source, but an *increase* in the case of the low credibility source' (1951: 645; emphasis in original). This means that *characterological coherence* influences our initial reaction to a narrative but its effect decreases with time in the case of characters we perceive as coherent and increases in the case of characters we perceive as incoherent.

Stability narrative   According to Gergen and Gergen (1997), a type of *ontological narrative* that portrays the individual's situation as stable, with little or no change over time. Stability narratives reflect the need for the world to appear orderly and predictable. See also *progressive narrative*; *regressive narrative*.

Story   (see *narrative*)

Structural coherence   In Fisher's narrative paradigm, one of three types of *coherence* that influence our assessment of a narrative. Structural – or argumentative – coherence concerns the internal consistency and integrity of a narrative – whether or not it reveals contradictions within itself 'in form or reasoning' (Fisher 1997: 315). See also *material coherence*; *characterological coherence*.

Temporal and spatial framing   One of the strategies discussed under 'Framing narratives in translation' (Chapter 6). It involves selecting a particular text and embedding it in a temporal and spatial context that accentuates the narrative it depicts and encourages us to establish links between it and current narratives that touch our lives, even though the events of the source narrative may be set within a very different temporal and spatial framework. This obviates the need for further intervention in the text itself, although it does not necessarily rule out such intervention. See also *selective appropriation of textual material*; *labelling*; *repositioning*.

Temporality   One of the core features of narrativity as elaborated in the work of Somers (1992, 1997) and Somers and Gibson (1994). Temporality refers to the embeddedness of narrative in time and space and is understood as constitutive of narrativity rather than as an additional or separable layer of a story. Bruner (1991) uses the term 'narrative diachronicity' to refer to the same feature. See also *relationality*; *causal emplotment*; *selective appropriation*.

Transcendent issue/values   In Fisher's (1987) narrative paradigm, one of the components of the *logic of good reasons* and the most important element of the principle of *fidelity*. Transcendent values are the 'ultimate values' we live by and can override any other consideration in assessing a narrative.

Vertical narratives   According to Pratt (2003), vertical narratives function through opposition. For example, they explain who the Kurds are in terms of how they differ from a specific 'other', such as Iraqis or Turks. See also *biographical narratives*.

Notes

1 Introduction

1 Foucault's approach to power similarly downplays the issue of observable conflict, acknowledges that power takes many forms, and further locates the exercise of power in the way the social and political order structures reality for us. But Foucault, unlike Lukes, sees a positive and productive side to power, asserting, for instance, that '"Sexuality" is far more of a positive product of power than power was ever repression of sexuality' (1984: 62).

2 A great deal of literature in translation studies engages with attributes such as the translator's gender or sexuality as static and single determiners of behaviour.

3 Hermans (2002: 20) acknowledges 'the need to create within the discourse about translation a certain self-critical distance' and goes on to explicitly propose a shift towards narrativity as one of the means of developing a self-reflexive stance in translation studies (2002: 21). But he does not discuss what form this potential shift might take.

2 Introducing narrative theory

1 Not all social and communication theorists adopt this view, however. Novitz (1997: 156), for example, argues that 'there is no good reason for denying the existence of so-called prenarrative facts, or for insisting ... that all experience and knowledge must be mediated by or derived from, narrative. Not all explanations are narratives, nor are all theories, descriptions, lists, annals, or chronicles. ... To inform someone of a causal sequence (that food nourishes or that people deprived of water must die of dehydration) is not to tell a *story* in anything but the most extended sense of this word' (emphasis in original).

2 He also demonstrates that there are various strategies of evasion that can undermine the usefulness of such efforts. Children, for instance, were concealed from officials in the Ottoman census of Palestine to avoid future conscription in the army.

3 David Kelly, a nominee for the Nobel Peace Prize, was a weapons expert who worked in Iraq between 1991 and 1998 and a senior adviser on biological warfare for the UN in Iraq from 1994 to 1999. In 2003, following the American- and British-led invasion of Iraq, he was thrust into the media spotlight after being identified as the source of leaks that undermined the British government's credibility: he claimed that the government 'sexed up' a dossier on Iraq's weapons capability and used that to win support in parliament for the invasion. Two days after facing a gruelling interrogation by a parliamentary committee, he was found dead, presumably having taken his own life.

4 See www.geocities.com/ru00ru00/racismhistory/19thcent.html (accessed 11 July 2005).

5 After she died, Saartjie Baartman's sexual organs and brain were displayed at the Musée de l'Homme in Paris. Almost 200 years after she left Cape Town for London, she was returned to be buried at home, in the Eastern Cape, on Women's Day, 9 August 2002.

6 This article is no longer archived on *The Guardian* site, where it first appeared. It is however available on numerous other websites. Apart from the site quoted in the Bibliography at the end of this book, it can also be found at www.monabaker.com/pMachine/more.php?id=2011_0_1_120_M6 (accessed 11 July 2005).

7 Joseph Massad, Statement to the Ad Hoc Committee: http;//www.censoringthought.org/ massadstatementtocommittee.html (accessed 3 April 2005).

8 Reproduced in the *Toronto Star*: http://www.thestar.com/NASApp/cs/ContentServer?pagename= thestar/Layout Article_Type1&c=Article&cid=1113342617962&call_pageid=968256290204&col= 968350116795 (accessed 24 July 2005).

9 The relationship between narrative and reality is a different issue from that of narrative as either the only or major mode by which we experience the world, or as one among several such modes. In his earlier work, Bruner (1985) distinguished between paradigmatic cognition and narrative cognition as two modes of cognitive functioning, thus leaning on the side of seeing narrative as one rather than the only or main mode by which we make sense of the world. Paradigmatic cognition works by categories and taxonomies, and by traditional rational argumentation. Narrative cognition consists of storied descriptions of events and actions.

10 Zhang is clearly concerned about the implications of this debate for issues of moral judgement: 'If there is no way to know what the facts are, or the question of facts becomes totally irrelevant, and if competing histories are nothing but different discursive constructions trying 'to sanction one mode of explaining them rather than another', then how can we make a judgement of their relative values and credibility? Without ways of assessing the degree of truth or truth-claims, on what legitimate ground can we uphold truth and condemn its falsification, and strive for social justice against injustice and deception in past history as well as in our own time?' (2004: 397).

11 Scholars working within the field of narratology will not necessarily recognize the view of narrative adopted here, depending on the degree to which they have engaged with other disciplinary discussions of narrative.

12 Liu concludes that '[b]y strategically allying themselves with some Western positions and perspectives against others, they would be able to blur the line between Self and Other, or between the protagonist and the antagonist in a cross-communal debate, making it more complicated and difficult for their opponents to maintain their focus on the target of their criticism or to sustain their argumentative offensive' (1999: 305).

13 Inghilleri (2005) similarly suggests that asylum seekers are sometimes aware of the value of certain 'signs' – and perhaps narrative detail – in the host culture and exploit this awareness for their own benefit.

14 The USA has been singularly unsuccessful in this attempt. Booth (2004: 113) explains its failure as follows: 'President Bush has occasionally attempted to avert full hatred of all Muslims, as if working to achieve worldwide peace and full democracy everywhere. But most of his words referring to those "out there," the opponents and potential opponents, have been words of threat or hate, employing the military revolution as if the media revolution had not occurred. Whatever the conscious goal inspiring the rhetoric might have been, the effect was generally to increase rather than diminish the number of enemies. When asked about the rise in protest bombings in Iraq, his response was "Bring 'em on".'

3 A typology of narrative

1 'Ontological' is Somers and Gibson's term, by which they strictly mean narratives of the self. Hinchman and Hinchman (1997a: xvii) distinguish between first-order narratives and second-order narratives. First-order narratives consist of the personal stories we tell ourselves and broadly correspond to Somers and Gibson's category of ontological narratives. Second-order narratives are the stories elaborated by historians to reconstruct the past. They 'involve reflections by a (usually) uninvolved spectator upon the doings and stories of participants in the events themselves'. This category does not correspond directly to any of Somers and Gibson's, but it overlaps to some extent with *conceptual narratives* (see section 3.3 on p. 39).

2 Reeves-Ellington (1999: 109), following Paul Thompson (1988), suggests that practitioners of oral history, whose work involves a great deal of translation and interpreting, have three options for publishing oral – in our terms, ontological – narratives. First, the life story of an individual may be published on its own, with a very brief introduction by the researcher. Second, full or extensive extracts from individual narratives may be grouped together on the basis of a theme, event, or social group and published as a collection, with extensive commentary. And finally, brief extracts from

individual narratives may be used together with archival material to build an argument. From our current perspective, all three options ultimately draw on ontological narratives to elaborate larger public and conceptual narratives, as defined in sections 3.2 and 3.3 on pp. 33–44.

3 It would be interesting to explore the way in which ontological narratives are made to dovetail with the collective narratives of the target setting in translations of autobiographical writings, eyewitness accounts and various types of testimony.

4 See www.news24.com/Content_Display/TRC_Report/1chap1.htm (accessed 11 July 2005).

5 Somers (1992: 604) initially used the longer designation 'public, cultural and institutional narratives' and equated this category with Charles Taylor's (1989) 'webs of interlocution' and Alasdair MacIntyre's 'traditions' (1981).

6 For a good example of how a family narrative of political events and alignments is discursively elaborated, see Gordon (2004), who describes the way in which one family in the USA interactionally constructs and socializes its members into a political narrative that guides their electoral decision making.

7 Religious narratives such as those of Christianity, Islam and Judaism may be considered meta- rather than public narratives, according to Somers' and Gibson's typology, though the borderline between the two is not easy to draw.

8 www.gush-shalom.org/actions/action19-9-2004.html (accessed 25 March 2005).

9 www.chechnya-mfa.info/paper/en_text.pdf (accessed 25 March 2005).

10 www.prima-news.ru/eng/news/articles/2005/2/21/31249.html (accessed 25 March 2005).

11 As with any narrative, the categories we construct for ourselves are a product of our own narrative location. The decision to privilege conceptual (or disciplinary) narratives and propose them as a distinct category in this case is clearly influenced by the academic settings in which the theorists operate. There is no reason to suggest that professional narratives, for example, are less important or less worthy of a category of their own. I am grateful to Andrew Read for drawing my attention to this point.

12 'Western, Confucian, Japanese, Islamic, Hindu, Slavic-Orthodox, Latin American and possibly African civilization' (Huntington 1993: 25).

13 Huntington's 1996 book and his earlier article in *Foreign Affairs* (1993) have been extensively reviewed. For a particularly interesting analysis of the limitations of Huntington's narrative, see Said (2001), who concludes that '"The Clash of Civilizations" thesis is a gimmick like "The War of the Worlds," better for reinforcing defensive self-pride than for critical understanding of the bewildering interdependence of our time'.

14 http://www.foreignaffairs.org/19930601faessay5188/samuel-p-huntington/the-clash-of-civilizations.html (accessed 11 July 2005).

15 From the book of Abstracts of the 4th International Maastricht-Lodz Duo Colloquium on Translation and Meaning, Maastricht, The Netherlands, 18-21 May 2005; p. 50.

16 http://wsupress.wayne.edu/judaica/folklore/pataiafpi.htm (accessed 11 July 2005).

17 For an interesting rebuttal by Patai's daughters, 'Misreading the Arab Mind', see http://mailman.lbo-talk.org/pipermail/lbo-talk/Week-of-Mon-20040531/011965.html (accessed 25 March 2005). They argue that 'Scholarly research can be used or misused in ways the author never intended and would never have condoned'. This is true of all narratives, but particularly of conceptual narratives.

18 From a postmodernist perspective, Hutcheon (1988: 13) argues that 'no narrative can be a natural "master" narrative: there are no natural hierarchies; there are only those we construct'. This view is totally compatible with the definition of meta- or master narratives adopted here. Hutcheon (1988: 13) goes on to suggest that '[i]t is this kind of self-implicating questioning that should allow postmodernist theorizing to challenge narratives that do presume to "master" status, without necessarily assuming that status for itself'. Somers and Gibson's perspective on narratives, including meta-narratives, also encourages us to reflect on and question the narratives that touch our lives, even as we remain firmly embedded in them.

19 I am grateful to Maria Pavesi of the University of Pavia in Italy for alerting me to this distinction.

20 Nossek (1994) offers an interesting analysis of the use of the Holocaust as a frame of reference in reporting terrorist attacks in Israel and an explanation of 'the possible role of the press in reinforcing that master narrative' (1994: 131).

4 Understanding how narratives work I

1 These are: narrative diachronicity; particularity; intentional state entailment; hermeneutic composability; canonicity and breach; referentiality; genericness; normativeness; context sensitivity and negotiability; and narrative accrual.

2 Ricoeur (1981b: 167) criticizes 'the theory of history and the theory of fictional narratives' because they 'seem to take it for granted that whenever there is time, it is always a time laid out chronologically, a linear time, defined by a succession of instants'.

3 This is evident from the examples Bolden provides, but it is not one of the issues she discusses explicitly.

4 I have relied here on Bolden's back-translations of the Russian. For the original utterances, refer to Bolden (2000: 396–7).

5 www.epic.org/privacy/terrorism/hr3162.html (accessed 12 July 2005).

6 The notion of historicity used here overlaps with what MacIntyre refers to as 'embedding', as when he states: 'the narrative phenomenon of embedding is crucial: the history of a practice in our time is generally and characteristically embedded in and made intelligible in terms of the larger and longer history of the tradition through which the practice in its present form was conveyed to us; the history of each of our own lives is generally and characteristically embedded in and made intelligible in terms of the larger and longer histories of a number of traditions' (1981: 207). MacIntyre argues that 'an adequate sense of tradition manifests itself in a grasp of those future possibilities which the past has made available to the present' (1981: 207).

7 Nor could they be divorced from the events of the fifteenth and sixteenth century in Spain, including the expulsion and forced conversion of Jews and Muslims.

8 www.geocities.com/CollegePark/Classroom/9912/blackholocaust.html (accessed 12 July 2005).

9 http://stopthewall.org/photos/899.shtml (accessed 12 July 2005).

10 Bruner also discusses a very similar feature under the heading 'referentiality' (1991: 13–14), focusing on the sense-reference relationship. I have subsumed this issue within the broader category of relationality.

11 Maurice Leenhardt (1878–1954) was a French Protestant missionary and anthropologist who did fieldwork among the New Caledonian Kanak in Melanesia from 1902 to 1926 and engaged in a passionate defence of their rights.

12 In spite of the loaded vocabulary, which was part of the narrative of anthropology at the time, Lienhardt actually argues that 'any historical sense of proportion … reminds us that it is some of our own habits of thought which are newly-formed and uncommon' and that 'a satisfying representation of reality may be sought in more than one way, that reasoning is not the only way of thinking, that there is a place for meditative and imaginative thought' (1967: 95).

13 Pratt (1987: 62) makes the same point, summarizing the argument in Rafael (1984): 'On the one hand, supplying Tagalog analogues for Christian terms like "obligation" or "sin" inevitably meant incorporating indigenous ideologies that conflicted with Christianity; on the other hand, simply introducing the Spanish terms into Tagalog texts as "untranslatable" items meant that key concepts existed as floating signifiers to which Tagalog speakers could attribute their own meanings'.

14 The film was subtitled into English, Hebrew, French, Spanish and Italian.

15 See Baker (in press, b) for a discussion of some of these examples from a slightly different angle.

16 There is one instance in the documentary where *shaheed* is translated as 'martyr'. This occurs in a complex and extended metaphor drawn by a young Palestinian girl, who likens the camp to a 'tall, tall, proud/towering' tree, with each leaf representing a martyr. The only other instance in which the word martyr is used is in the credits at the end of the film, where the Executive Producer is described as 'The martyr Iyad Samoudi'. The documentary itself starts with a dedication to Samoudi, 'who was murdered at Alyamoun' at the end of filming. The interplay between dominance and resistance here, as in many other contexts, is subtle; it is also characteristic of the taut relationship between the West and the Arab World.

17 In Classical and Qur'anic Arabic, *shaheed* also means 'witness'.

18 This is not to say that a delegitimized term such as 'martyr' cannot be reclaimed by a resistance movement and flaunted in the face of aggressive dominant narratives.

19 Sami Al-Arian is a Palestinian American and former Professor at the University of South Florida. He was chosen as best professor in the Faculty of Engineering in 1993, and as best professor in the entire university in 1994. Al-Arian is a prominent activist who played an important role in establishing various Arab and Islamic institutions during the 1980s and 1990s. In February 2004, the FBI accused him and seven others of assisting a criminal organization linked to the Palestinian 'jihad movement'. See http://en.wikipedia.org/wiki/Sami_Al-Arian (accessed 18 July 2005).

20 Longinovic goes on to say: 'I would like to invoke the horizon of a different translation, presenting the multiplicity of Balkan identities as an effect of unceasing foreign interference to reward or punish the long historical procession of a complex tapestry of ethnic subjects engaged in their own local struggles. This horizon, screened out by the mediated gaze in search of new forms of local violence yields an uncanny shift: from the politics of translation to the translation of politics'.

21 El Oifi (2005: 12) suggests that MEMRI was set up because the growth of Arab satellite television channels meant that Israel no longer had a monopoly on the news, and more specifically that MEMRI was established as a response to the launch of Al-Jazeera, an extremely popular television channel in the Arab World and worldwide. While Miles' study of Al-Jazeera (Miles 2005) does not mention MEMRI, it confirms the worldwide impact of the channel and the vital role it has played in publicizing the suffering of Palestinians under Israeli occupation.

22 For very interesting textual examples of how this is achieved, and a rebuttal by MEMRI, see the email debate between Brian Whitaker and Yigal Carmon on the *Guardian* website: www.guardian.co.uk/israel/comment/0,,884156,00.html (accessed 25 September 2005). See also 'Repressive MEMRI', by Juan Cole: www.antiwar.com/cole/?articleid=4047 (accessed 25 September 2005).

5 Understanding how narratives work II

1 This does not apply so much to folktales, which are highly formulaic, both in terms of character types and settings.

2 Interestingly, Fisher similarly argues that the 1980 election in which Ronald Reagan (Republican) won against Jimmy Carter (Democrat) 'was a contest between argument and narrative as individuated forms of address'. More specifically, he explains, 'Carter's rhetoric was conventional: argumentative, instrumental, and adapted to every segment of the citizenry. Reagan's rhetoric was that of the true storyteller: it was laced with narratives; it was not instrumental in the usual way for it invited participation in a story orally presented. It assumed an audience of poetic auditors rather than argumentative judges' (1987: 147) .

3 See www.imdb.com/title/tt0126029/taglines (accessed 18 April 2005).

4 www.visit4info.com/details.cfm?adid=17769 (accessed 18 April 2005).

5 This applies to the genre of petition as used today, not historically. I have in mind in particular web-based petitions such as the 'Stop ID cards and the database state' petition (www.no2id-petition.net), which requests the British Prime Minister and government to 'immediately cease all further development of, and legislation for, national identity cards and the National Identity Register' on the basis that they 'will lead to an increase in state control and surveillance over the individual, and … create an unacceptable imposition on every citizen'.

6 This journal does not have a dedicated website.

7 www.jir.com (accessed 16 July 2005).

8 www.improb.com (accessed 16 July 2005).

9 www.preparingforemergencies.co.uk/index.htm (accessed 16 July 2005).

10 www.ieee.org/portal/cms_docs/about/dept_treasury.pdf (accessed 18 July 2005).

11 *Ibid.*

12 Tymoczko (1999: 214) attributes the extensive interference in the translation of Irish heroic literature in the twentieth century to the fact that 'Irish hero tale as a genre was in the public sphere and therefore very highly politicized'.

13 This may well be what Bruner meant anyway; the brevity of his treatment of this and other features of narrativity makes it difficult to attribute this position to him with any certainty.

14 The term 'incursion' was and continues to be heavily contested in the media and by numerous pro-Palestinian groups.
15 The badges are given for free or sold in numerous marches and activist events across the world.

6 Framing narratives in translation

1 There are of course also instances where individuals (whether professionally trained or not) are forced to produce a translation or perform as interpreters. When Mulla Abdul-Qadir Badayuni was ordered by Emperor Akbar to translate the *Ramayana*, which he completed in 1580, he regarded this commission as 'a veritable spiritual punishment' (Behl 2002: 93), but he was in no position to refuse an order from the Emperor. Behl (2002: 93) quotes him commenting thus on his predicament: 'I seek God's protection from the cursed writing which is as wretched as the parchment of my life. The reproduction of infidelity (kufr) does not mean infidelity. I utter words in refutation of infidelity, for I fear lest this book written at the order of the Emperor entirely might bear the print of hatred'. People are also sometimes forced to engage in acts of translation and interpreting because they have no other means of providing for their families in situations of extreme poverty and/or unrest, as in the aftermath of the 2003 invasion of Iraq.
2 Prince Dara Shikoh translated fifty Upanishads into Persian and compiled them into the anthology *Sirr-i-Akbar* (*The Greatest Secret*).
3 In addition to *translation*, these include '*insinuation*, in which the words spoken are to be interpreted as having a covert and indirect relation to the meaning of the utterance'; '*joking*, in which the words spoken are to be interpreted as not seriously meaning what they might otherwise mean'; '*imitation*, in which the manner of speaking is to be interpreted as being modeled after that of another person or persona'; and '*quotation*, in which the words spoken are to be interpreted as the words of someone other than the speaker' (Bauman 2001: 168).
4 Or to constrain the interpretation of and response to a given narrative in line with the values and agendas of a particular constituency. For instance, it is interesting that the Republicans' 'theatrically professed moral outrage' over the Clinton sex scandal in the run-up to the 2000 presidential elections presented Clinton's 'bimbo eruptions' as 'offenses against traditional marriage' rather than 'matters of abuse of power' (Silverstein 2003: 19).
5 Similarly, when an Israeli gunman shot dead four Arab Israelis on 4 August 2005 because he was opposed to the closure of the Gaza strip settlements, Israel's Ministry of Defence ruled that the four Arabs were not victims of 'terror', arguing that Israeli law only recognizes as terrorism acts committed by organizations hostile to the state. Refusal to frame the event as one of terrorist attack meant that the families of the four Arabs were not entitled to any compensation. See McGreal (2005), 'Jewish gunman was no terrorist, Israel rules'.
6 http://english.aljazeera.net/NR/exeres/79C6AF22-98FB-4A1C-B21F-2BC36E87F61F.htm (accessed 20 July 2005).
7 http://memri.org/bin/articles.cgi?Page=archives&Area=sd&ID=SP81104 (accessed 20 July 2005).
8 www.worldnetdaily.com/news/article.asp?ARTICLE_ID=41211 (accessed 20 July 2005).
9 www.juancole.com/2004/11/bin-ladens-audio-threat-to-states.html (accessed 20 July 2005).
10 Goffman does not actually spell out the dimensions of frame space in these terms, but they can be reasonably inferred from the discussion.
11 Including every US state. See www.lysistrataproject.com/about.html (accessed 4 May 2005).
12 www.lysistrataproject.com/about.html (accessed 4 May 2005).
13 www.lysistrataproject.com/script.html (accessed 4 May 2005).
14 Venuti (1998: 184) discusses a similar example in the Chinese context. Lu Xun and Zhou Zuoren published a pioneering anthology of translated short stories in 1909 which prioritized Russian and Eastern European writers. Venuti explains this choice in terms of Lu Xun's and Zhou Zuoren's recognition of the importance of literary translation 'as a means of altering China's subordinate position in geopolitical relations', suggesting that 'they gravitated toward foreign countries that occupied a similar position, but whose literatures threw off their minority status to achieve international recognition' (1998: 184). For further examples of higher-level patterns of selectivity in translation, see Said (1994) and Jacquemond (1992).

15 Bongie suggests that the translator is almost certainly Leitch Ritchie, a Scottish novelist and editor of the series in which *The Slave-King* appeared (2005: 6).

16 This is a very crude summary of only those aspects of the narrative that concern us here. For a fuller summary, see Bongie (2005: 6–7, n. 3).

17 http://news.bbc.co.uk/1/hi/world/south_asia/1648572.stm (accessed 13 May 2005).

18 www.welfarestate.com/binladen/funeral (accessed 20 July 2005).

19 Tymoczko (1999, Chapter 8, 'The Names of the Hound') offers a good discussion of issues pertaining to the translation of names more broadly. See also Embelton (1991), Bantaş (1994), Manini (1996) and Farrell (1998).

20 See also Bourdieu (1991: 239–43) on the power of naming.

21 I am grateful to Dorothy Kenny, Dublin City University, for advice and help with locating material on rival place names in the Irish context.

22 'Press anger over West Bank homes plans', *BBC News*, 18 August 2004: http://news.bbc.co.uk/1/hi/world/middle_east/3575836.stm (accessed 21 May 2005).

23 'More Jewish settlements "must go"', *BBC News*, 12 August 2004: http://news.bbc.co.uk/1/hi/world/middle_east/3559844.stm (accessed 21 May 2005).

24 It would be interesting to explore how interpreters in the United Nations, the European Union and similar venues deal with rival place names.

25 Clearly, there is no need to do so since the purpose of the gloss here is not to help readers identify the place in question but to signal the narrative position of the institution and its editors and translators.

26 Titles of sections and chapters within a publication are also often changed to reframe narratives in translation. See Polezzi (1998: 335; 2001: 127) for examples.

27 'Uncle Che' by Lok Siu Ping, translated by Janice Wickeri.

28 See, for instance, Wickeri (1995), Gunn (1991).

29 Another interesting area worth exploring is how the repositioning of participants is effected in the translation of advertising text, given the range of linguistic and visual resources available in this genre.

7 Assessing narratives

1 Robin Cook died in September 2005.

2 Other Government Agency – this could mean CIA, FBI, etc. See Saar's interview with Onnesha Roychoudhuri, 24 May 2005: www.motherjones.com/news/qa/2005/05/saar.html (accessed 25 September 2005).

3 www.motherjones.com/news/qa/2005/05/saar.html (accessed 25 September 2005).

4 Pilger (2005a, 2005b) criticizes the narrative on other grounds, including – most importantly – its lack of material coherence, as in the following extract: 'The G8 communique announcing the "victory for millions" is unequivocal. Under a section headed "G8 proposals for HIPC debt cancellation", it says that debt relief to poor countries will be granted only if they are shown "adjusting their gross assistance flows by the amount given": in other words, their aid will be reduced by the same amount as the debt relief. So they gain nothing. Paragraph Two states that "it is essential" that poor countries "boost private sector development" and ensure "the elimination of impediments to private investment, both domestic and foreign".'

5 See the discussion of 'facts' in Chapter 2, section 2.1.4, on p. 17.

6 Organizational narratives are ultimately of course also elaborated by individuals, but they are presented and perceived as institutional narratives.

7 www.mla.org/mla_constitution (accessed 29 July 2005).

8 www.tsf-twb.org (accessed 29 July 2005).

9 Fox (1995: 1610) explains that '[t]he "without borders" concept is now so appreciated that a plethora of professional and voluntary associations have made it a part of their mission statements, and of their names'. In addition to Reporters Without Borders, these include Teachers Without Borders, Lawyers Without Borders, Engineers Without Borders, and Builders Without Borders, among others. Closer to our own concerns, Words Without Borders is an online magazine of international literature (www.wordswithoutborders.org). DeChaine (2002: 367) suggests that what this 'fairly

disparate movement of groups' has in common is an ethos which 'adheres in a willingness to transcend sanctioned geographical and social boundaries'.

10 www.babels.org (accessed 29 July 2005).

11 www.traduttoriperlapace.org (accessed 29 July 2005).

12 www.saltana.com.ar/pax/paxbabelica.htm (accessed 29 July 2005).

13 www.ecosfti.tk (accessed 29 July 2005).

14 Babels' is also not a humanitarian but rather an openly political agenda. Involvement with Babels constitutes an explicit and relatively risky claim to a stake in global politics; risky in the sense of participants having to defend their political position. This is not the case for humanitarian agendas, which generally go unchallenged and are widely accepted as valid by the vast majority of people around the world, whatever their political or ideological position.

15 www.eurotexte.fr/downloads/TSFspeechRiminiEurotexte.pdf (accessed 29 July 2005).

16 General Electric was the subject of an intense boycott campaign by various peace groups between 1986 and 1993 because of its involvement in the production and sale of nuclear weapons. As a major US defence contractor, it is now back on the boycott lists of several anti-war groups.

17 L'Oréal is on the boycott list of groups such as Naturewatch because of its dismal record on animal testing. In addition, L'Oréal established Israel as its commercial centre in the Middle East in 1995, and in 1998 received Israel's Jubilee Award, the highest tribute ever awarded by the State of Israel to individuals and organizations who have done most to strengthen the Israeli economy. The company, and its subsidiary Lancôme, are on the boycott lists of numerous solidarity groups working to end Israel's oppression of Palestinians.

18 Greer and Bruno (1996) designate one type of this practice in the world of corporate environmental advertising as 'Greenwash'. Greenwash allows large corporations to maintain and expand their markets 'by posing as friends of the environment and leaders in the struggle to eradicate poverty' (1996: 11). A sobering example of the dangers of accepting big-business narratives of doing good uncritically is a story recounted in Williams (1991) and summarized in Ewick and Silbey (1995: 219–20). An African American woman, Williams tells her story of being locked out of Benetton one Saturday afternoon by a salesperson who refuses to buzz her in. This is the same Benetton 'whose advertising campaign appropriates images of racial and ethnic diversity to sell the sweaters they wouldn't give Williams the chance to purchase' (Ewick and Silbey 1995: 219).

19 Warnick (1987: 175) accepts McGee and Nelson's assessment of the narrative paradigm in this respect and similarly criticizes Fisher for overstating his case against traditional rationality.

Bibliography

Abbott, H. Porter (2002) *The Cambridge Introduction to Narrative*, Cambridge: Cambridge University Press.

Alexander, Jeffrey C. (2002) 'On the Social Construction of Moral Universals: The "Holocaust" from War Crime to Trauma Drama', *European Journal of Social Theory* 5(1): 5–85.

Asimakoulas, Dimitris (2005) *Translations as Acts of Resistance: Brecht's Works in the Censorship Context of the Greek Junta (1967–1974)*, PhD Thesis, Centre for Translation and Intercultural Studies: University of Manchester.

Bachrach, Peter and Morton S. Baratz (1962) 'The Two Faces of Power', *American Political Science Review* 56: 947–52.

Bachrach, Peter and Morton S. Baratz (1970) *Power and Poverty. Theory and Practice*, New York: Oxford University Press.

Bakan, Joel (2004) *The Corporation: The Pathological Pursuit of Profit and Power*, London: Constable & Robinson Ltd.

Baker, Mona (1992) *In Other Words: A Coursebook on Translation*, London and New York: Routledge.

Baker, Mona (2005) 'Narratives *in* and *of* Translation', *SKASE Journal of Translation and Interpretation* 1(1): 4–13. Online: www.skase.sk.

Baker, Mona (in press, a) 'Translation and Activism: Emerging Patterns of Narrative Community', *The Massachusetts Review*.

Baker, Mona (in press, b) 'Contextualization in Translator- and Interpreter-mediated Events', *Journal of Pragmatics*.

Bantaş, Andrei (1994) 'Names, Nicknames and Titles in Translation', *Perspectives: Studies in Translatology* 2(1): 79–88.

Baquedano-López, Patricia (2001 [1997]) 'Creating Social Identities through *Doctrina* Narratives', *Issues in Applied Linguistics* 8(1): 27–45; reprinted in Alessandro Duranti (ed.) *Linguistic Anthropology: A Reader*, Malden MA and Oxford: Blackwell, 343–58.

Barghouti, Mourid (2003) 'Verbicide', *New Internationalist* 359 (August). Available online at www.newint.org/issue359/essay.htm (accessed 28 July 2005).

Barsky, Robert (1993) 'The Interpreter and the Canadian Convention Refugee Hearing: Crossing the Potentially Life-threatening Boundaries between "coccode-e-eh," "cluck-cluck," and "cot-cot-cot",' *TTR: Traduction, Terminologie, Rédaction* 6(2): 131–56.

Barsky, Robert (1996) 'The Interpreter as Intercultural Agent in Convention Refugee Hearings', *The Translator* 2(1): 45–63.

Barsky, Robert (2005) 'Stories from the Court of Appeal in Literature and Law', in Mike Baynham and Ana De Fina (eds) *Dislocations/Relocations: Narratives of Displacement*, Manchester: St Jerome Publishing, 221–41.

Barthes, Roland (1972) *Mythologies*, trans. Annette Lavers, London: Jonathan Cape.

Bauman, Richard (2001 [1975]) 'Verbal Art as Performance', *American Anthropologist* 77: 290–311; reprinted in Alessandro Duranti (ed.) *Linguistic Anthropology: A Reader*, Malden MA and Oxford: Blackwell, 165–88.

Baynham, Mike and Ana De Fina (eds) (2005) *Dislocations/Relocations: Narratives of Displacement*, Manchester: St Jerome Publishing.

Behl, Aditya (2002) 'Premodern Negotiations: Translating between Persian and Hindavi', in Rukmini Bhaya Nair (ed.) *Translation, Text and Theory: The Paradigm of India*, New Delhi: Sage Publications, 89–100.

Ben-Ari, Nitsa (2000) 'Ideological Manipulation of Translated Text', *Translation Quarterly* 16–17: 40–52.

Benford, Robert (1993) 'Frame Disputes within the Nuclear Disarmament Movement', *Social Forces* 71: 677–701.

Benford, Robert and David Snow (2000) 'Framing Processes and Social Movements: An Overview and Assessment', *Annual Review of Sociology* 26: 611–39.

Benjamin, Walter (1999 [1968]) 'Theses on the Philosophy of History', in *Illuminations*, trans. Harry Zohn, London: Pimlico, 245–55.

Bennett, Alan (1997 [1994]) *Writing Home*, London & Boston: Faber & Faber.

Bennett, W. Lance and Murray Edelman (1985) 'Toward a New Political Narrative', *Journal of Communication* 35(4): 156–71.

Bilgrami, Akeel (1992) 'What is a Muslim? Fundamental Commitment and Cultural Identity', *Critical Inquiry* 18(4): 821–42.

Blommaert, Jan (2005) *Discourse: A Critical Introduction*, Cambridge: Cambridge University Press.

Blum-Kulka, Shoshana and Tamar Liebes (1993) 'Frame Ambiguities: *Intifada* Narrativization of the Experience by Israeli Soldiers', in Akiba Cohen and Gadi Wolfsfeld (eds) *Framing the Intifada: People & Media*, Norwood NJ: Ablex, 27–52.

Boje, D. M. (1991) 'The Storytelling Organization. A Study of Story Performance in an Office-supply Firm', *Administrative Science Quarterly* 36: 106–26.

Bokor, Gabe (2001) 'Translation and International Politics', Editorial, *Translation Journal* 5(4). Available online at http://accurapid.com/journal/18editor.htm (accessed 25 July 2005).

Bokor, Gabe (2003) 'War and Peace', Editorial, *Translation Journal* 7(2). Available online at http://accurapid.com/journal/24editor.htm (accessed 25 July 2005).

Bolden, Galina (2000) 'Toward Understanding Practices of Medical Interpreting: Interpreters' Involvement in History Taking', *Discourse Studies* 2(4): 387–419.

Bongie, Chris (2005) 'Victor Hugo and "The Cause of Humanity": Translating *Bug-Jargal* (1826) into *The Slave-King* (1833)', *The Translator* 11(1): 1–24.

Booth, Wayne C. (2004) *The Rhetoric of Rhetoric: The Quest for Effective Communication*, Malden MA and Oxford: Blackwell Publishing.

Bourdieu, Pierre (1991) *Language and Symbolic Power*, ed. and introduced by John B. Thompson, translated by Gino Raymond and Matthew Adamson, Cambridge: Polity Press.

Bourdieu, Pierre (1998) *Acts of Resistance: Against the New Myths of Our Time*, trans. Richard Nice, Cambridge: Polity Press.

Bourdieu, Pierre (2000 [1986]) 'L'Illusion biographique', *Actes de la recherche en sciences sociales* 62(3): 69–72; trans. Yves Winkin and Wendy Leeds-Hurwitz as 'The Biographical Illusion', in R. J. Parmentier and G. Urban (eds) *Working Papers and Proceedings of the Centre for Psychosocial Studies*, pp. 1–7. Reprinted in Paul du Gay, Jessica Evans and Peter Redman (eds) *Identity: A Reader*, London: Sage Publications, 297–303.

Brennan, Mary and Richard Brown (1997) *Equality Before the Law: Deaf People's Access to Justice*, Durham: Deaf Studies Research Unit, University of Durham.

Briggs, Charles (ed.) (1996) *Disorderly Discourse: Narrative, Conflict, and Social Inequality*, Oxford: Oxford University Press.

Brisset, Annie (1989) 'In Search of a Target Language: The Politics of Theatre Translation in Quebec', *Target* 1(1): 9–27.

Brown, Colin (2005) 'US Lied to Britain Over Use of Napalm in Iraq War', *The Independent*, 17 June.

Bruner, Edward M. (1997) 'Ethnography as Narrative', in Lewis P. Hinchman and Sandra K. Hinchman (eds) *Memory, Identity, Community: The Idea of Narrative in the Human Sciences*, Albany: State University of New York Press, 264–80.

Bruner, Jerome (1985) *Actual Minds, Possible Worlds*, Cambridge MA: Harvard University Press.

Bruner, Jerome (1991) 'The Narrative Construction of Reality', *Critical Inquiry* 18(1): 1–21.

Burman, Erica (2003) 'Narratives of Challenging Research: Stirring Tales of Politics and Practice', *International Journal of Social Research Methodology* 6(2): 101–19.

CBS News (2004) 'The Holy Warrior', 15 September. Available online at www.cbsnews.com/stories/2004/09/15/60II/main643650.shtml (accessed 11 July 2005).

Cheung, Martha P. Y. (ed.) (1998) *Hong Kong Collage: Contemporary Stories and Writing*, Oxford and New York: Oxford University Press.

Chilton, Paul (1982) 'Nukespeak: Nuclear Language, Culture and Propaganda', in C. Aubrey (ed.) *Nukespeak: The Media and the Bomb*, London: Comedia Publishing Group, 94–112.

Chilton, Paul (1997) 'The Role of Language in Human Conflict: Prolegomena to the Investigation of Language as a Factor in Conflict Causation and Resolution', *Current Issues in Language & Society* 4(3): 174–89.

Clegg, Stewart R. (1993) 'Narrative, Power, and Social Theory', in Dennis K. Mumby (ed.) *Narrative and Social Control: Critical Perspectives*, Newbury Park CA: Sage, 15–45.

Clifford, James (1998) 'The Translation of Cultures: Maurice Leenhardt's Evangelism, New Caledonia 1902–26', in Robert Con Davis and Ronald Schleifer (eds) *Contemporary Literary Criticism: Literary and Cultural Studies*, New York: Longman, 680–94.

Cook, Robin (2004) 'Britain's Worst Intelligence Failure, and Lord Butler Says no one is to Blame', *The Independent*, 15 July. Available online at http://comment.independent.co.uk/columnists_a_l/robin_cook/article47377.ece (accessed 28 July 2005).

Cortazzi, Martin (1993) *Narrative Analysis*, London and New York: RoutledgeFalmer.

Cunningham, David and Barb Browning (2004) 'The Emergence of Worthy Targets: Official Frames and Deviance Narratives Within the FBI', *Sociological Forum* 19(3): 347–69.

Damrosch, David (2005) 'Death in Translation', in Sandra Bermann and Michael Wood (eds) *Nation, Language, and the Ethics of Translation*, Princeton NJ and Oxford: Princeton University Press, 380–98.

Davies, Bronwyn and Rom Harré (1990) 'Positioning: The Discursive Production of Selves', *Journal for the Theory of Social Behaviour* 20(1): 43–63.

DeChaine, D. Robert (2002) 'Humanitarian Space and the Social Imaginary: Médecins Sans Frontières/Doctors Without Borders and the Rhetoric of Global Community', *Journal of Communication Inquiry* 26(4): 354–69.

Dennett, Jane (2002) 'Foreign Literature in Fascist Italy: Circulation and Censorship', *TTR* 15(2): 97–123.

Diriker, Ebru (2005) 'Presenting Simultaneous Interpreting: Discourse of the Turkish Media, 1988–2003', *AIIC Webzine*, March–April. Available online at www.aiic.net/ViewPage.cfm/page1742.htm (accessed 25 September 2005).

Draper, Jack (2002) 'Breaking the Imperial Mold: Fragmented Translations'. Paper presented at the Colloquium *Problems of Translation: Violence as Language Within Global Capital*, 26 January 2002. Available online at www.duke.edu/~jad2/draper.htm (accessed 28 June 2005).

Ehrenhaus, Peter (1993) 'Cultural Narratives and the Therapeutic Motif: The Political Containment of Vietnam Veterans', in Dennis K. Mumby (ed.) *Narrative and Social Control: Critical Perspectives*, Newbury Park CA: Sage, 77–118.

El Fassed, Arjan (2005) 'One Year after ICJ Ruling, Israel OKs Wall in Jerusalem', *Electronic Intifada*, 10 July. Available online at http://electronicintifada.net/v2/article3986.shtml (accessed 12 July 2005).

El Oifi, Mohammed (2005) 'Gained in Translation: Why the Middle East Media Research Institute is a Source of English Versions of Arabic Texts that are Designed to Mislead and Disinform', *Le Monde diplomatique* (English edition), October, 12–13.

Embleton, Sheila (1991) 'Names and Their Substitutes. Onomastic Observations on Astérix and Its Translations', *Target* 3(2): 175–206.

Ewick, Patricia and Susan S. Silbey (1995) 'Subversive Stories and Hegemonic Tales: Toward a Sociology of Narrative', *Law & Society Review* 29(2): 197–226.

Fadhil, Ali (2005) 'City of Ghosts', *The Guardian*, 11 January. Available online at www.guardian.co.uk/Iraq/Story/0,2763,1387460,00.html (accessed 11 July 2005).

Farrands, Alice (2003) 'It's just politics in a lab coat', *The Times Higher Education Supplement*, 22 August, p. 14.

Farrell, Tim (1998) 'Christos – Mr Christ or the Anointed One of God', *Notes on Translation* 12(4): 46–55.

Finklestone, Joseph (1996) *Anwar Sadat: Visionary Who Dared*, London and Portland OR: Frank Cass; translated 1999 by Adel Abdel Sabour as *Al Sadat: Wahm Al-Tahaddi* (Al-Sadat: The Illusion of Challenge), Al-Dar Al-'Alamiyya Lilkutub Walnashr.

Fisher, Walter R. (1984) 'Narration as a Human Communication Paradigm: The Case of Public Moral Agreement', *Communication Monographs* 51: 1–22.

Fisher, Walter R. (1985) 'The Narrative Paradigm: In the Beginning', *Journal of Communication* 35(4): 74–89.

Fisher, Walter R. (1987) *Human Communication as Narration: Toward a Philosophy of Reason, Value, and Action*, Columbia: University of South Carolina Press.

Fisher, Walter R. (1997) 'Narration, Reason, and Community', in Lewis P. Hinchman and Sandra K. Hinchman (eds) *Memory, Identity, Community: The Idea of Narrative in the Human Sciences*, Albany: State University of New York Press, 307–27.

Fleming, Peter (2004) 'Progress, Pessimism, Critique', *Ephemera* 4(1): 40–9.

Foucault, Michel (1984 [1980]) 'Truth and Power', in *Power/Knowledge: Selected Interviews and Other Writings, 1972–1977*, edited by Colin Gordon, Brighton: Harvester; reprinted in Paul Rabinow (ed.) *The Foucault Reader: An Introduction to Foucault's Thought*, London: Penguin, 51–75.

Fox, Renée, C. (1995) 'Medical Humanitarianism and Human Rights: Reflections on Doctors Without Borders and Doctors of the World', *Social Science and Medicine* 41(12): 1607–16.

Fraser, Giles (2004) *Thought for the Day*, BBC Radio Four, 16 September. Transcript available online at www.bbc.co.uk/religion/programmes/thought/documents/t20040916.shtml (accessed 29 July 2005).

Geesey, Patricia (2000) 'Identity and Community in Autobiographies of Algerian Women in France', in Amal Amireh and Lisa Suhair Majaj (eds) *Going Global: The Transnational Reception of Third World Women Writers*, New York and London: Garland Publishing, 173–205.

Georgakopoulou, Alexandra (1997) 'Narrative', in Jef Verschueren, Jan-Ola Östman, Jan Blommaert and Chris Bulcaen (eds) *Handbook of Pragmatics 1997*, 1–19 (entries individually paginated).

Gergen, Kenneth J. and Mary M. Gergen (1997) 'Narratives of the Self', in Lewis P. Hinchman and Sandra K. Hinchman (eds) *Memory, Identity, Community: The Idea of Narrative in the Human Sciences*, Albany: State University of New York Press, 161–84.

Ghosh, Bishnupriya (2000) 'An Affair to Remember: Scripted Performances in the "Nasreen Affair"', in Amal Amireh and Lisa Suhair Majaj (eds) *Going Global: The Transnational Reception of Third World Women Writers*, New York and London: Garland Publishing, 39–83.

Goffman, Erving (1967 [1955]) 'On Face Work: An Analysis of Ritual Elements in Social Interaction', *Psychiatry: Journal for the Study of Interpersonal Processes* 18(3): 213–31; reprinted in Erving Goffman, *Interaction Ritual: Essays on Face-to-Face Behavior*, New York: Pantheon Books, 1967, 5–45.

Goffman, Erving (1981) *Forms of Talk*, Philadelphia: University of Pennsylvania Press.

Goffman, Erving (1986 [1974]) *Frame Analysis: An Essay on the Organization of Experience*, Boston: Northeastern University Press.

Good, Leslie (1989) 'Power, Hegemony, and Communication Theory', in Ian Angus and Sut Jhally (eds) *Cultural Politics in Contemporary America*, New York and London: Routledge, 51–64.

Goodwin, Charles (1994) 'Professional Vision', *American Anthropologist* 96(3): 606–33.

Gordon, Cynthia (2004) '"Al Gore's Our Guy": Linguistically Constructing a Family Political Identity', *Discourse and Society* 15(5): 607–31.

Greer, J. and K. Bruno (1996) *Greenwash: The Reality behind Corporate Environmentalism*, Penang and New York: Third World Network and The Apex Press.

Gumperz, John (1992) 'Contextualization and Understanding', in Alessandro Duranti and Charles Goodwin (eds) *Rethinking Context: Language as an Interactive Phenomenon*, Cambridge: Cambridge University Press, 229–53.

Gunn, Edward (1991) *Rewriting Chinese: Style and Innovation in Twentieth-Century Chinese Prose*, Stanford CA: Stanford University Press.

Hale, Sandra (1997) 'The Treatment of Register Variation in Court Interpreting', *The Translator* 3(1): 39–54.

Hall, John R., Mary Jo Neitz and Marshall Battani (2003) *Sociology on Culture*, London and New York: Routledge.

Hanna, Sameh F. (2005) '*Othello* in Egypt: Translation and the (Un)making of National Identity', in Juliane House, M. Rosario Martín Ruano and Nicole Baumgarten (eds) *Translation and the Construction of Identity. IATIS Yearbook 2005*, Seoul: IATIS, 109–28.

Harel, Amos (2005) 'IDF Reviving Psychological Warfare Unit', *Haaretz*, 25 January 2005. Available online at www.haaretzdaily.com/hasen/pages/ShArt.jhtml?itemNo=531712 (accessed 14 April).

Harris, Leah (2003) 'A Note on MEMRI & Translations', *Counterpunch*, 15 January. Available online at www.counterpunch.org/harris01152003.html (accessed 14 April 2005).

Harris, Paul (2005) 'Soldier Lifts Lid on Camp Delta', *The Observer*, 8 May. Available online at http://observer.guardian.co.uk/international/story/0,6903,1479040,00.html (accessed 24 July 2005).

Hart, Janet (1992) 'Cracking the Code: Narrative and Political Mobilization in the Greek Resistance', *Social Science History* 16(4): 631–68.

Harvey, Keith (1998) 'Translating Camp Talk: Gay Indentities and Cultural Transfer', in Lawrence Venuti (ed.) *Translation and Minority*, special issue of *The Translator* 4(2): 295–320.

Harvey, Keith (2003a) *Intercultural Movements: 'American Gay' in French Translation*, Manchester: St Jerome Publishing.

Harvey, Keith (2003b) '"Events" and "Horizons": Reading Ideology in the "Bindings" of Translations', in María Calzada Pérez (ed.) *Apropos of Ideology – Translation Studies on Ideology – Ideologies in Translation Studies*, Manchester: St Jerome Publishing, 43–69.

Hatim, Basil and Ian Mason (1990) *Discourse and the Translator*, London and New York: Longman.

Hauerwas, Stanley and David Burrell (1989) 'From System to Story: An Alternative Pattern for Rationality in Ethics', in S. Hauerwas and L. G. Jones (eds) *Why Narrative? Readings in Narrative Theology*, Grand Rapids MI: William B. Eerdmans Publishing, 158–90.

Herman, David, Manfred Jahn and Marie-Laure Ryan (eds) (2005) *Routledge Encyclopedia of Narrative Theory*, London and New York: Routledge.

Herman, Edward S. (2005) 'From Ingsoc and Newspeak to Amcap, Amerigood, and Marketspeak', in Abbott Gleason, Jack Goldsmith and Martha Nussbaum (eds) *On Nineteen Eighty-Four: Orwell and Our Future*, Princeton NJ: Princeton University Press, 112–23.

Hermans, Theo (1982) 'P. C. Hooft: The Sonnets and the Tragedy', *Dispositio: Revista Hispánica de Semiótica Literaria* 7(19–20): 95–110.

Hermans, Theo (2002) 'Paradoxes and Aporias in Translation and Translation Studies', in Alessandra Riccardi (ed.) *Translation Studies: Perspectives on an Emerging Discipline*, Cambridge: Cambridge University Press, 10–23.

Hersh, Seymour (2004) 'The Gray Zone', *The New Yorker*, 15 May. Available online at http://newyorker.com/fact/content/?040524fa_fact (accessed 11 July 2005).

Hinchman, Lewis P. and Sandra K. Hinchman (1997a) 'Introduction', in Lewis P. Hinchman and Sandra K. Hinchman (eds) *Memory, Identity, Community: The Idea of Narrative in the Human Sciences*, Albany: State University of New York Press, xiii–xxxii.

Hinchman, Lewis P. and Sandra K. Hinchman (eds) (1997b) *Memory, Identity, Community: The Idea of Narrative in the Human Sciences*, Albany: State University of New York Press.

Hovland, Carl and Walter Weiss (1951) 'The Influence of Source Credibility on Communication Effectiveness', *Public Opinion Quarterly* 15(4): 635–50.

Howe, Desson (2001) 'Shrek: A Funny, Fractured Fairy Tale', *The Washington Post*, 18 May. Available online at www.washingtonpost.com/wp-srv/entertainment/movies/reviews/shrekhowe.htm (accessed 18 April 2005).

Hugo, Victor (1833) *The Slave-King, from the Bug-Jargal of Victor Hugo*, trans. Leitch Ritchie [?], London: Smith, Elder & Co. Reprinted in 1837 and 1852 as *The Slave-King: An Historical Account of the Rebellion of the Negros in St. Domingo*.

Hugo, Victor (1844) *Bug-Jargal: or, A Tale of the Massacre in St. Domingo. 1791*, New York: James Mowatt & Co.

Hugo, Victor (2004) *Bug-Jargal*, trans. and ed. Chris Bongie, Peterborough ON: Broadview Press.

Huntington, Samuel (1993) 'The Clash of Civilizations', *Foreign Affairs* 72(3): 22–49.

Huntington, Samuel (1996) *The Clash of Civilizations and the Remaking of World Order*, New York: Touchstone.

Huntington, Samuel (2004) *Who Are We? The Challenges to America's National Identity*, New York: Simon & Schuster.

Hutcheon, Linda (1988) *A Poetics of Postmodernism: History, Theory, Fiction*, London and New York: Routledge.

Inghilleri, Moira (2003) 'Habitus, Field and Discourse: Interpreting as a Socially Situated Activity', *Target* 15(2): 243–68.

Inghilleri, Moira (2005) 'Mediating Zones of Uncertainty: Interpreter Agency, the Interpreting Habitus and Political Asylum Adjudication', *The Translator* 11(1): 69–85.

Ingram, Susan (1996) 'When Memory is Cross-Cultural Translation: Eva Hoffman's Schizophrenic Autobiography', *TTR: Traduction, Terminologie, Rédaction* 9(1): 259–76.

Jacquemet, Marco (2005) 'The Registration Interview: Restricting Refugees' Narrative Performance', in Mike Baynham and Anna De Fina (eds) *Dislocations/Relocations: Narratives of Displacement*, Manchester: St Jerome Publishing, 197–220.

Jacquemond, Richard (1992) 'Translation and Cultural Hegemony: The Case of French–Arabic Translation', in Lawrence Venuti (ed.) *Rethinking Translation*, London and New York: Routledge, 139–58.

Jones, Francis R. (2004) 'Ethics, Aesthetics and Décision: Literary Translating in the Wars of the Yugoslav Succession', *Meta* 49(4): 711–28.

Kahf, Mohja (2000) 'Packaging "Huda": Sha'rawi's Memoirs in the United States Reception Environment', in Amal Amireh and Lisa Suhair Majaj (eds) *Going Global: The Transnational Reception of Third World Women Writers*, New York and London: Garland Publishing, 148–72.

Keeble, Richard (2005) 'New Militarism, Massacrespeak and the Language of Silence', *Ethical Space: The International Journal of Communication Ethics* 2(1): 39–45.

Kellner, Hans (1989) *Language and Historical Representation: Getting the Story Crooked*, Madison: University of Wisconsin Press.

Kennedy, L. (2003) 'Remembering September 11: Photography as Cultural Diplomacy', *International Affairs* 79(2): 315–26.

Kinsella, Thomas (trans.) (1969) *The Táin*, London: Oxford University Press.

Kirkwood, William G. (1992) 'Narrative and the Rhetoric of Possibility', *Communication Monographs* 59: 30–47.

Klein, Naomi (2000) *No Logo*, London: Flamingo.

Kneale, Matthew (2000) *English Passengers*, London: Hamish Hamilton.

Knellwolf, Christa (2001) 'Women Translators, Gender and the Cultural Context of the Scientific Revolution', in Roger Ellis and Liz Oakley-Brown (eds) *Translation and Nation: Towards a Cultural Politics of Englishness*, Clevedon: Multilingual Matters, 85–119.

Kovala, Urpo (1996) 'Translations, Paratextual Mediation, and Ideological Closure', *Target* 8(1): 119–47.

Krog, Antje (1998) *Country of My Skull*, London: Vintage.

Krontiris, Tina (1992) *Oppositional Voices: Women as Writers and Translators of Literature in the English Renaissance*, London and New York: Routledge.

Kuhiwczak, Piotr (1990) 'Translation as Appropriation: The Case of Milan Kundera's *The Joke*', in Susan Bassnett and Andre Lefevere (eds) *Translation, History & Culture*, London and New York: Pinter Publishers, 118–30.

Kuhn, Thomas S. (1999) 'Remarks on Incommensurability and Translation', in Rema Rossini Favretti, Giorgio Sandri and Roberto Scazzieri (eds) *Incommensurability and Translation: Kuhnian Perspectives on Scientific Communication and Theory Change*, Northampton MA and Cheltenham: Edward Elgar, 33–7.

Labov, William (1972) *Language in the Inner City: Studies in the Black English Vernacular*, Philadelphia: University of Pennsylvania Press.

Lambertus, Sandra (2003) 'News Discourse of Aboriginal Resistance in Canada', in Lynn Thiesmeyer (ed.) *Discourse and Silencing: Representation and the Language of Displacement*, Amsterdam and Philadelphia PA: John Benjamins, 233–72.

Landau, Misia (1997) 'Human Evolution as Narrative', in Lewis P. Hinchman and Sandra K. Hinchman (eds) *Memory, Identity, Community: The Idea of Narrative in the Human Sciences*, Albany: State University of New York Press, 104–18.

Laughlin, Meg (2005) 'Lawyers at Al-Arian Trial Argue Over Translations, Meanings', *St. Petersburg Times Online*, 15 July. Available online at www.sptimes.com/2005/07/15/Hillsborough/Lawyers_at_Al_Arian_t.shtml (accessed 18 July 2005).

Liebovitz, Liel (2005) 'The Winter of His Discontent', 4 March. Available online at www.thejewishweek.com/news/newscontent.php3?artid=10599 (accessed 4 August 2005).

Lienhardt, Godfrey (1967 [1956]) 'Modes of Thought', in E. E. Evans-Pritchard (ed.) *The Institutions of Primitive Society: A Series of Broadcast Talks*, Oxford: Basil Blackwell, 95–107.

Liu, Yameng (1999) 'Justifying My Position in Your Terms: Cross-cultural Argumentation in a Globalized World', *Argumentation* 13(3): 297–315.

Livingstone, Ken (Mayor of London) (2005) *Why the Mayor of London will maintain dialogues with all of London's faiths and communities: A reply to the dossier against the Mayor's meeting with Dr Yusuf al-Qaradawi*, London: Greater London Authority.

Longinovic, Tomislav (2004) 'Balkan in Translation', *Eurozine*. Online journal, available at www.eurozine.com/articles/2004-01-16-longinovic-en.html (accessed 4 January 2006).

López, Marísa Fernández (2000) 'Translation Studies in Contemporary Children's Literature: A Comparison of Intercultural Ideological Factors', *Children's Literature Association Quarterly* 25(1): 29–37.

Lukes, Steven (1974) *Power: A Radical View*, Basingstoke and London: Macmillan Education.

MacIntyre, Alasdair (1981) *After Virtue*, London: Duckworth.

MacIntyre, Alasdair (1988) *Whose Justice? Which Rationality?*, Notre Dame IN: University of Notre Dame Press.

Manini, Luca (1996) 'Meaningful Literary Names. Their Forms and Functions, and their Translation', in Dirk Delabastita (ed.) *Wordplay & Translation*, special issue of *The Translator* 2(2): 161–78.

Manuel Jerez, Jesús de, Juan López Cortés and María Brander de la Iglesia (2004) 'Traducción e interpretación: Voluntariado y compromiso social' [Translation and Interpreting: Volunteer Work and Social Commitment], *Puentes* 4: 65–72. Available online at http://piit.beplaced.com/ECOSarticle.htm (accessed 7 April 2005).

Maryns, Katrijn (2005) 'Displacement in Asylum Seekers' Narratives', in Mike Baynham and Ana De Fina (eds) *Dislocations/Relocations: Narratives of Displacement*, Manchester: St Jerome Publishing, 174–96.

Masel, Ben (2004) 'A New Opium War', *Critical Montages*, 11 December. Available online at http://montages.blogspot.com/2004/12/new-opium-war.html (accessed 7 April 2005).

Mason, Ian and Adriana Şerban (2003) 'Deixis as an Interactive Feature in Literary Translations from Romanian into English', *Target* 15(2): 269–94.

May, Rachel (1994) *The Translator in the Text: On Reading Russian Literature in English*, Evanston IL: Northwestern University Press.

Mayoral Asensio, Roberto (2003) *Translating Official Documents*, Manchester: St Jerome Publishing.

McAdams, Dan P. (2004) 'Redemption and American Politics', *The Chronicle of Higher Education* 51(15): B14.

McCormick, Kay (2005) 'Working with Webs: Narrative Constructions of Forced Removal and Relocation', in Mike Baynham and Anna De Fina (eds) *Dislocations/Relocations: Narratives of Displacement*, Manchester: St Jerome Publishing, 144–69.

McGee, Michael Calvin and John S. Nelson (1985) 'Narrative Reason in Public Argument', *Journal of Communication* 35(4): 139–55.

McGreal, Chris (2005) 'Jewish Gunman was no Terrorist, Israel Rules', *The Guardian*, 1 September. Available online at www.guardian.co.uk/international/story/0,,1560147,00.html (accessed 25 September 2005).

McKie, Robin (2001) 'Journal Axes Gene Research on Jews and Palestinians', *The Observer*, 25 November. Available online at http://observer.guardian.co.uk/international/story/0,6903,605798,00.html (accessed 4 August 2005).

McMurran, Mary Helen (2000) 'Taking Liberties: Translation and the Development of the Eighteenth-Century Novel', *The Translator* 6(1): 87–108.

Mertz, Elizabeth (1996) 'Consensus and Dissent in U.S. Legal Opinions: Narrative Structure and Social Voices', in Charles L. Briggs (ed.) *Disorderly Discourse: Narrative, Conflict, & Inequality*, New York and Oxford: Oxford University Press, 135–57.

Miles, Hugh (2005) *Al-Jazeera: How Arab TV News Challenged the World*, London: Abacus.

Mishler, Elliot G. (1995) 'Models of Narrative Analysis: A Typology', *Journal of Narrative and Life History* 5(2): 87–123.

Morris, Ruth (1995) 'The Moral Dilemmas of Court Interpreting', *The Translator* 1(1): 25–46.

Morrison, Robert (1815) 'Miscellaneous Edicts Extracted from the Pekin Gazette', in *Translations from the Original Chinese: with Notes*, Canton, China: Printed by order of the Select Committee.

Moss, Stephen (2003) 'The Paper War', *The Guardian*, 6 March, 12–13.

Muhawi, Ibrahim (1999a) 'The Arabic Folktale as Gendered Genre'. Paper delivered at the *Gender and Translation* Conference, December 17–19, University of East Anglia, UK.

Muhawi, Ibrahim (1999b) 'On Translating Palestinian Folktales: Comparative Stylistics and the Semiotics of Genre', in Yasir Suleiman (ed.) *Arabic Grammar and Linguistics*, Richmond: Curzon Press, 222–45.

Muhawi, Ibrahim (in press) 'Towards a Folkloristic Theory of Translation', in Theo Hermans (ed.) *Translating Others*, Manchester: St Jerome Publishing.

Munday, Jeremy (2002) 'Systems in Translation: A Systemic Model for Descriptive Translation Studies', in Theo Hermans (ed.) *Crosscultural Transgressions: Research Models in Translation Studies II – Historical and Ideological Issues*, Manchester: St Jerome Publishing, 76–92.

Munday, Jeremy (2004) 'Advertising: Some Challenges to Translation Theory', in Beverly Adab and Cristina Valdés (eds) *Key Debates in the Translation of Advertising Material*, Special issue of *The Translator* 10(2): 199–219.

Naseem, Iftihar (2004) 'To Wear or not to Wear the Hijab?', translated from Urdu by Mohammed Jehangir, *Pakistan News*, 26 May. Available online at www.indypressny.org/article.php3?ArticleID=1467 (accessed 31 March 2005).

Naudé, Jacobus A. (2005) 'Translation and Cultural Transformation: The Case of the Afrikaans Bible Translations', in Eva Hung (ed.) *Translation and Cultural Change*, Amsterdam and Philadelphia PA: John Benjamins, 19–41.

Nelson, Daniel (2002) 'Language, Identity and War', *Journal of Language and Politics* 1(1): 3–22.

Nida, Eugene (1998) 'Bible Translation', in Mona Baker (ed.) *Routledge Encyclopedia of Translation Studies*, London and New York: Routledge, 22–8.

Niranjana, Tesjawini (1990) 'Translation, Colonialism and Rise of English', *Economic and Political Weekly*, 14 April, 773–79.

Niranjana, Tesjawini (1992) *Siting Translation: History, Poststructuralism, and the Colonial Context*, Berkeley: University of California Press.

Noakes, John (2000) 'Official Frames in Social Movement Theory: The FBI, HUAC, and the Communist Threat in Hollywood', *The Sociological Quarterly* 41(4): 657–80.

Nord, Christiane (1995) 'Text-Functions in Translation: Titles and Headings as a Case in Point', *Target* 7(2): 261–84.

Nossek, Hillel (1994) 'The Narrative Role of the Holocaust and the State of Israel in the Coverage of Salient Terrorist Events in the Israeli Press', *Journal of Narrative and Life History* 4(1–2): 119–34.

Novitz, David (1997) 'Art, Narrative, and Human Nature', in Lewis P. Hinchman and Sandra K. Hinchman (eds) *Memory, Identity, Community: The Idea of Narrative in the Human Sciences*, Albany: State University of New York Press, 143–60.

Ortiz, Emmanuel (2002) 'A Moment of Silence'. Available online at www.seeingblack.com/2003/x020403/poetry_feb.shtml#ortiz (accessed 25 July 2005).

Palmer, Jerry and Victoria Fontan (2006, in press) '"Our Ears and Our Eyes": Journalists and Fixers in Iraq', *Journalism*.

Patai, Raphael (1973) *The Arab Mind*, New York: Charles Scribner's Sons.

Patai, Raphael (1988) *Arab Folktales from Palestine and Israel*, Detroit, MI: Wayne State University Press.

Pérez González, Luis (in press) 'Interpreting Strategic Recontextualization Cues in the Courtroom: Corpus-based Insights into the Pragmatic Force of Non-Restrictive Relative Clauses', *Journal of Pragmatics*.

Pettersson, Bo (2001) 'The Finnish National Anthem in Translation: Deixis and National Sentiment', in Pirjo Kukkonen and Ritva Hartama-Heinonen (eds) *Mission, Vision, Strategies, and Values: A Celebration of Translator Training and Translation Studies in Kouvola*, Helsinki: Helsinki University Press, 187–94.

Philips, Susan U. (2001) 'Power', in Alessandro Duranti (ed.) *Key Terms in Language and Culture*, Oxford: Blackwell, 190–6.

Picchione, John (1999) 'Poetry, Science, and the Epistemological Debate', *TTR: Traduction, Terminologie, Rédaction* 12(1): 19–30.

Pilger, John (2005a) 'The G8 Summit: A Fraud and a Circus', *The New Statesman*, 22 June. Available online at http://pilger.carlton.com/print/133469 (accessed 27 July 2005).

Pilger, John (2005b) 'From Iraq to the G8: The Polite Crushing of Dissent and Truth', *The New Statesman*, 6 July. Available online at http://pilger.carlton.com/print/133471 (accessed 28 July 2005).

Polezzi, Loredana (1998) 'Rewriting Tibet: Italian Travellers in English Translation', *The Translator* 4(2): 321–42; special issue on *Translation and Minority*, guest-edited by Lawrence Venuti.

Polezzi, Loredana (2001) *Translating Travel: Contemporary Italian Travel Writing in English Translation*, Aldershot: Ashgate.

Polkinghorne, Donald E. (1995) 'Narrative Configuration in Qualitative Analysis', in J. Amos Hatch and Richard Wisniewski (eds) *Life History and Narrative*, London and Washington DC: The Falmer Press, 5–23.

Polletta, Francesca (1998) '"It Was like a Fever ..." Narrative and Identity in Social Protest', *Social Problems* 45(2): 137–59.

Pratt, Jeff (2003) *Class, Nation and Identity: The Anthropology of Political Movements*, London: Pluto Press.

Pratt, Mary Louise (1987) 'Linguistic Utopias', in A. Aldridge, A. Durant and C. McCabe (eds) *The Linguistics of Writing: Arguments between Language and Literature*, Manchester: Manchester University Press.

Pratt, Mary Louise (1994) 'Travel Narrative and Imperialist Vision', in James Phelan and Peter J. Rabinowitz (eds) *Understanding Narrative*, Columbus: Ohio State University Press, 199–221.

Rafael, Vicente L. (1984) *Contracting Christianity: Conversion and Translation in Early Tagalog Colonial Society*. PhD Dissertation, Cornell University, Ithaca NY.

Rafael, Vicente L. (1993 [1988]) *Contracting Colonialism: Translation and Christian Conversion in Tagalog Society Under Early Spanish Rule*, Durham NC and London: Duke University Press.

Reeves-Ellington, Barbara (1999) 'Responsibility with Loyalty: Oral History Texts in Translation', *Target* 11(1): 103–29.

Reynolds, Mike (2004) 'How Does Monsanto Do It? An Ethnographic Case Study of an Advertising Campaign', *Text* 24(3): 329–52.

Ricoeur, Paul (1981a [1979]) 'La Fonction narrative', *Etudes théologiques et religieuses* 54: 209–30; English translation by John B. Thompson, in *Paul Ricoeur: Hermeneutics and the Human Sciences. Essays on Language, Action and Interpretation*, Cambridge: Cambridge University Press, 1981, 274–305.

Ricoeur, Paul (1981b [1980]) 'Narrative Time', in W. J. T. Mitchell (ed.) *On Narrative*, Chicago and London: The University of Chicago Press, 165–86.

Rimmon-Kenan, S. (1983) *Narrative Fiction: Contemporary Poetics*, London: Methuen.

Robinson, Douglas (1995) 'Theorizing Translation in a Woman's Voice: Subverting the Rhetoric of Patronage, Courtly Love and Morality', *The Translator* 1(2): 153–75.

Saar, Erik and Viveka Novak (2005) *Inside the Wire: A Military Intelligence Soldier's Eyewitness Account of Life at Guantanamo*, New York: The Penguin Press.

Said, Edward (1994 [1990]) 'Embargoed Literature', *The Nation*, 17 September 1990; reprinted in Edward Said (1994) *The Politics of Dispossession: The Struggle for Palestinian Self-Determination, 1969–1994*, New York: Pantheon Books, 372–8.

Said, Edward (2001) 'The Clash of Ignorance', *The Nation*, 22 October 2001 issue. Available online at www.thenation.com/doc/20011022/said (accessed 4 January 2006).

Said, Edward (2005) 'The Public Role of Writers and Intellectuals', in Sandra Bermann and Michael Wood (eds) *Nation, Language, and the Ethics of Translation*, Princeton NJ and Oxford: Princeton University Press, 15–29.

Schäffner, Christina (2004) 'Political Discourse Analysis from the Point of View of Translation Studies', *Journal of Language and Politics* 3(1): 117–50.

Seely, Hart (2003a) 'The Poetry of Donald Rumsfeld: Recent Works by the Secretary of Defense', *Slate*. Available online at http://slate.msn.com/id/2081042 (accessed 25 April 2005).

Seely, Hart (2003b) *Pieces of Intelligence: The Existential Poetry of Donald H. Rumsfeld*, New York: Free Press.

Séguinot, Candace (1988) 'Translating the Ideology of Science: The Example of the Work of Alfred Tomatis', *TTR: Traduction, Terminologie, Rédaction* 1(1): 103–12.

Sha'rawi, Huda (1986 [1981]) *Harem Years: Memoirs of an Egyptian Feminist*, trans. Margot Badran, New York: The Feminist Press.

Shibamoto Smith, Janet S. (2005) 'Translating True Love: Japanese Romance Fiction, Harlequin-Style', in José Santaemilia (ed.) *Gender, Sex and Translation: The Manipulation of Identities*, Manchester: St Jerome Publishing, 97–116.

Shohat, Ella (2000) 'Coming to America: Reflections on Hair and Memory Loss', in Amal Amireh and Lisa Suhair Majaj (eds) *Going Global: The Transnational Reception of Third World Women Writers*, New York and London: Garland Publishing, 284–300.

Silver, Mark (2004) 'The Detective Novel's Novelty: Native and Foreign Narrative Forms in Kuroiwa Ruikō's *Kettō no hate*', *Japan Forum* 16(2): 191–205.

Silverstein, Michael (2003) *Talking Politics: The Substance of Style From Abe to "W"*, Chicago: Prickly Paradigm Press.

Smallman, Tom, Pat Yale and Steve Fallon (1998 [1994]) *Ireland*, Hawthorn, Australia: Lonely Planet Publications.

Smith, Dan (1997) 'Language and Discourse in Conflict and Conflict Resolution', *Current Issues in Language & Society* 4(3): 190–214.

Somers, Margaret (1992) 'Narrativity, Narrative Identity, and Social Action: Rethinking English Working-Class Formation', *Social Science History* 16(4): 591–630.

Somers, Margaret (1994) 'The Narrative Construction of Identity: A Relational and Network Approach', *Theory and Society* 23(5): 605–49.

Somers, Margaret (1997) 'Deconstructing and Reconstructing Class Formation Theory: Narrativity, Relational Analysis, and Social Theory', in John R. Hall (ed.) *Reworking Class*, Ithaca NY and London: Cornell University Press, 73–105.

Somers, Margaret R. and Gloria D. Gibson (1994) 'Reclaiming the Epistemological "Other": Narrative and the Social Constitution of Identity', in Craig Calhoun (ed.) *Social Theory and the Politics of Identity*, Oxford and Cambridge MA: Blackwell, 37–99.

Sotiropoulou, Marina (1996) *Διαδρομὲς του πολιτκού βιβλίον στην Ελλάδα 1967-1974* [The course of political books in Greece 1967–1974], Athens: Ethniko Kentro Vivliou.

Soueif, Ahdaf (2004) 'This Torture Started at the Very Top: A Profound Racism Infects the US and British Establishments', *The Guardian*, 5 May. Available online at www.veteransforpeace.org/This_torture_started_050404.htm (accessed 15 April 2005).

Spence, D. P. (1982) *Narrative Truth and Historical Truth. Meaning and Interpretation in Psychoanalysis*, New York: Norton.

St André, James (2004) '"But do they have a notion of Justice": Staunton's 1810 Translation of the Great Qing Code', *The Translator* 10(1): 1–31.

St André, James (forthcoming) '"Long Time No See, Coolie": Passing as Chinese through Translation', in *Discourses on Translation and the Future of History*, Ottawa: Univesity of Ottawa Press

Stecconi, Ubaldo and Maria Luisa Torres Reyes (1997) 'Transgression and Circumvention through Translation in the Philippines', in Mary Snell-Hornby, Zuzana Jettmarová and Klaus Kaindl (eds) *Translation as Intercultural Communication*, Amsterdam: John Benjamins, 67–78.

Sturge, Kate (2002) 'Censorship of Translated Fiction in Nazi Germany', *TTR: Traduction, Terminologie, Rédaction* 15(2): 153–69.

Sutton, Philip C. (1997) 'A Translator's Dilemma', in Karl Simms (ed.) *Translating Sensitive Texts: Linguistic Aspects*, Amsterdam: Rodopi, 67–75.

Tannen, Deborah and Cynthia Wallat (1993) 'Interactive Frames and Knowledge Schemas in Interaction: Examples from a Medical Examination/Interview', in Deborah Tannen (ed.) *Framing in Discourse*, New York: Oxford University Press, 57–76.

Taylor, Charles (1989) *Sources of the Self*, Cambridge MA: Harvard University Press.

Tekiner, Roselle (1990) 'Special Report: Israel's Two-Tiered Citizenship Law Bars Non-Jews from 93 Percent of Its Lands', *The Washington Report on Middle East Affairs*, January, p. 20.

Thicke, Lori (2003) 'The Humanitarian Face of Translation', *Multilingual Computing & Technology* 13(4).

Thompson, Paul (1988) *The Voice of the Past: Oral History*, Oxford: Oxford University Press.

Tymoczko, Maria (1999) *Translation in a Postcolonial Context: Early Irish Literature in English Translation*, Manchester: St Jerome Publishing.

Tymoczko, Maria (2000) 'Translation and Political Engagement: Activism, Social Change and the Role of Translation in Geopolitical Shifts', *The Translator* 6(1): 23–47.

Tymoczko, Maria (2003) 'Ideology and the Position of the Translator: In What Sense is a Translator "In Between"?', in María Calzada Perez (ed.) *Apropos of Ideology – Translation Studies on Ideology – Ideologies in Translation Studies*, Manchester: St Jerome Publishing, 181–201.

Wallbank, T. Walter, Alastair M. Taylor and Nels M. Bailkey (1976 [1960]) *Civilization Past & Present, Volume 1*, Dallas: Scott, Foresman & Co.

Warnick, Barbara (1987) 'The Narrative Paradigm: Another Story', *The Quarterly Journal of Speech* 73: 172–82.

Watts, Richard (2000) 'Translating Culture: Reading the Paratexts of Aimé Césaire's *Cahier d'un retour au pays natal*', *TTR: Traduction, Terminologie, Rédaction* 13(2): 29–46.

Whitaker, Brian (2004) 'Selective MEMRI', *The Guardian*, 12 August. Available online at www.guardian.co.uk/elsewhere/journalist/story/0,7792,773258,00.html (accessed 27 December 2005).

Whitaker, Brian (2004) 'Its Best Use Is as a Doorstop', *The Guardian*, 24 May.

White, Hayden (1987a [1980]) 'The Value of Narrativity in the Representation of Reality', *Critical Inquiry* 7(1); reproduced in Hayden White (1987) *The Content of the Form: Narrative Discourse and Historical Representation*, Baltimore MD and London: The Johns Hopkins University Press, 1–25.

White, Hayden (1987b) *The Content of the Form: Narrative Discourse and Historical Representation*, Baltimore MD and London: The Johns Hopkins University Press.

Whitebrook, Maureen (2001) *Identity, Narrative and Politics*, London and New York: Routledge.

Wickeri, Janice (1995) 'The Union Version of the Bible & the New Literature in China', *The Translator* 1(2): 129–52.

Williams, Patricia (1991) *The Alchemy of Race and Rights*, Cambridge, MA: Harvard University Press.

Wolf, Michaela (2000) 'The *Third Space* in Postcolonial Representation', in Sherry Simon and Paul St-Pierre (eds) *Changing the Terms: Translating in the Postcolonial Era*, Ottawa: University of Ottawa Press, 127–45.

Venuti, Lawrence (1998) *The Scandals of Translation: Towards an Ethics of Difference*, London and New York: Routledge.

Vermes, Albert Péter (2003) 'Proper Names in Translation: An Explanatory Attempt', *Across Languages and Cultures* 4(1): 89–109.

Young, Robert (2003) *Postcolonialism: A Very Short Introduction*, Oxford: Oxford University Press.

Zapatistas! Documents of the New Mexican Revolution (1994). Editorial Collective, New York: Autonomedia. Available online at http://lanic.utexas.edu/project/Zapatistas (accessed 18 July 2005).

Zhang, Longxi (2004) 'History and Fictionality: Insights and Limitations of a Literary Perspective', *Rethinking History* 8(3): 387–402.

Zureik, Elia (2001) 'Constructing Palestine through Surveillance Practices', *British Journal of Middle Eastern Studies* 28(2): 205–27.

Index

Related titles from Routledge

Translation and Globalization
Michael Cronin

Translation and Globalization is essential reading for anyone with an interest in translation, or a concern for the future of our world's languages and cultures. This is a critical exploration of the ways in which radical changes to the world economy have affected contemporary translation.

The Internet, new technology, machine translation and the emergence of a worldwide, multi-million-dollar translation industry have dramatically altered the complex relationship between translators, language and power. In this book, Michael Cronin looks at the changing geography of translation practice and offers new ways of understanding the role of the translator in globalized societies and economies. Drawing on examples and case-studies from Europe, Africa, Asia, and the Americas, the author argues that translation is central to debates about language and cultural identity, and shows why consideration of the role of translation and translators is a necessary part of safeguarding and promoting linguistic and cultural diversity.

ISBN10: 0-415-27064-2 (hbk)
ISBN10: 0-415-27065-0(pbk)

ISBN13: 978-0-415-27064-9 (hbk)
ISBN13: 978-0-415-27065-6 (pbk)

Available at all good bookshops
For ordering and further information please visit:
www.routledge.com

Related titles from Routledge

Analysing Political Discourse
Theory and Practice
Paul Chilton

'Paul Chilton, the godfather of political linguistics for decades, has
written another fascinating study of political discourse'
Teun A. van Dijk, *Universitat Pompeu Fabra, Spain*

Based on Aristotle's premise that we are all political animals, able to use language to
pursue our own ends, *Analysing Political Discourse* uses the theoretical framework of
linguistics to explore the ways in which we think and behave politically.

Domestic and global politics come under the linguistic microscope. What do politicians really do in a radio interview? What verbal games do they play in a parliamentary knock-about? What does the increasing use of religious imagery tell us about
the changing landscape of global political language post-September 11?

Written in a lively and engaging style, and using contemporary, high profile and
international case studies, *Analysing Political Discourse* offers a new theoretical
perspective on the study of language and politics, and provides an essential introduction to political discourse analysis.

ISBN10: 0-415-31471-2 (hbk)
ISBN10: 0-415-31472-0 (pbk)

ISBN13: 978-0-415-31471-8 (hbk)
ISBN13: 978-0-415-31472-5 (pbk)

Available at all good bookshops
For ordering and further information please visit:
www.routledge.com

Related titles from Routledge

The Translation Studies Reader

Second Edition

Edited by Lawrence Venuti

'This is bound to be the most authoritative anthology of theoretical reflection on translation currently available in English. The selection of primary documents is varied and imaginative, the editorial introductions lucid and informed.'
Theo Hermans, *University College London, UK*

This new and fully revised edition of *The Translation Studies Reader* provides a definitive survey of the most important and influential approaches to translation theory and research, with an emphasis on the developments of the last thirty years. With introductory essays prefacing each section, the book places a wide range of seminal and innovative readings within their thematic, cultural and historical contexts.

The new edition features nine new readings, by authors such as Jerome and Derrida. These provide an historical dimension as well as exploring the interdisciplinary nature of translation studies through readings in fields such as philosophy and film studies.

Contributors: Kwame Anthony Appiah, Walter Benjamin, Antoine Berman, Shoshana Blum-Kulka, Jorge Luis Borges, Annie Brisset, Lori Chamberlain, Jean Darbelnet, Jacques Derrida, John Dryden, Itamar Even-Zohar, Johann Wolfgang von Goethe, Keith Harvey, James S. Holmes, Roman Jakobson, Jerome, André Lefevere, Philip E. Lewis, Ian Mason, Vladimir Nabokov, Eugene Nida, Friedrich Nietzsche, Abé Mark Nornes, Nicolas Perrot D'Ablancourt, Ezra Pound, Katharina Reiss, Steven Rendall, Friedrich Schleiermacher, Gayatri Spivak, George Steiner, Gideon Toury, Hans J. Vermeer, Jean-Paul Vinay

ISBN10: 0-415-31919-6 (hbk)
ISBN10: 0-415-31920-X (pbk)

ISBN13: 978-0-415-31919-5 (hbk)
ISBN13: 978-0-415-31920-1 (pbk)

Available at all good bookshops
For ordering and further information please visit:
www.routledge.com